Alan S. (Alan Summerly) Cole

Cantor lectures of the Art of Lace-Making

Alan S. (Alan Summerly) Cole

Cantor lectures of the Art of Lace-Making

ISBN/EAN: 9783741178566

Manufactured in Europe, USA, Canada, Australia, Japa

Cover: Foto ©Thomas Meinert / pixelio.de

Manufactured and distributed by brebook publishing software
(www.brebook.com)

Alan S. (Alan Summerly) Cole

Cantor lectures of the Art of Lace-Making

SOCIETY FOR THE ENCOURAGEMENT

OF

ARTS, MANUFACTURES, AND COMMERCE.

CANTOR LECTURES

ON THE

ART OF LACE-MAKING,

BY

ALAN S. COLE.

DELIVERED BEFORE THE SOCIETY OF ARTS, APRIL AND MAY, 1881.

The right of reproduction is reserved.

LONDON:

PRINTED BY WILLIAM TROUNCE, 10, GOUGH SQUARE, FLEET STREET, E.C.

1881.

Price One Shilling.

THE ART OF LACE-MAKING.

LECTURE I.—Delivered Monday, April 4, 1881.

Introduction. Early forms of twisted, plaited, and looped threads. Ornamental borders of costumes. Sumptuary laws. Venetian books of patterns for embroidery and lace. Flanders a centre of linen trade of Europe. Spanish and French importations of early lace. Effect of production of machine-made lace upon production of hand-made lace.

I. In undertaking to deliver a course of Cantor lectures upon "The Art of Lace-making," in compliance with a gratifying invitation from the Council of the Society of Arts, I am sensible of the responsibility I incur. I cannot, however, hesitate to claim your indulgence, since the position of lecturer is new to me. An experienced and able lecturer knows at once how to engage the sympathy of his audience. He leads them over difficult ground, making the difficulties interesting, just as a good guide does, who shows you the way up a mountain, through forest and rocky lands, across crevasses, and over snow fields. The tracing of a history of lace-making is not, however, likely to be beset with many difficulties. It covers a considerable space of time—over three hundred years—and involves the consideration, as all history does, of a number of circumstances. A tolerably straight course must, if possible, be adhered to, so that we may not stray off into tempting by-paths. Many works have been written and published upon lace-making, and I can hardly hope to bring to light many facts or reflections which have not been previously placed before the public. If I am successful in adding anything which may assist a true view of the development of lace-making I shall be fortunate.

II. Every one present, I presume, knows what lace is, in the ordinary and modern sense of the word. The shop-windows of linendrapers are filled with it. It is universally worn. About twice a week we may read in our newspapers that the lace trade is full of activity at Nottingham, in Belgium, in France, and elsewhere. If we go abroad, we see lace much like that we have left at home. Sometimes the lace trade is reported to be less vigorous than it was, sometimes it is more. A fair demand is maintained for Coraline and Vermicelli laces, whilst Bobbin, Bretonne, and Mechlin sell pretty well at "late" prices. The market, however, is dull on the whole, and there is no business in Valenciennes. This sort of intelligence usually comes to us at breakfast time, but it is not of the exciting character of some news which spoils our meal. After breakfast, if we happen to have absorbed the intelligence about the lace market, in the shops. Not at all, however. A constant supply of cheap laces is to be purchased.

III. Now, I think that it would take some of us by surprise were an announcement to be made that Parliament had passed a Bill ordering that no lace wider than two inches was henceforth to be worn. What a disturbance this would create amongst lace workers and lace wearers! It would be almost more exciting than many recent points of domestic news. Judging from past events in similar circumstances, the ingenuity of people would be sharpened into all sorts of evasions of the law, both numerous and humorous.

IV. In the 14th, 15th, and 16th centuries, laws regulating costume were in force, and a result of them has been a number of entertaining anecdotes about evasions of them—smuggling, and so forth. An incident in the history of these laws was the imperturbability with which fashion displayed itself to be stronger than the laws. In spite of regulations and edicts, which one might suppose would have prevented people from teaching one another their fashions, and from interchanging their national productions and manufactures, this teaching and interchanging went on generally in an overt way, but still persistently forming and virtually ruling what is called fashion. At the outset of lace-making, difficulties like those just mentioned were imposed upon its development. Nevertheless, fashion has stimulated lace-making, and has raised lace work to an eminence in public favour, the hold upon which modern machinery is certainly striving to perpetuate, by widely disseminating lace of a special class.

V. The plan which I have adopted for my lectures is, roughly, as follows:—First, I propose to make a few observations upon the ability to twist, plait, and loop threads together, upon the invention of patterns, upon the result which ensued when the twisting and plaiting were rendered subject to the pattern, and upon incidents connected with the development of this subjection of handicraft to design. Secondly, I propose to describe the features of specimens in the two chief divisions of hand-made lace; and thirdly, to touch upon the present condition of lace-making by hand, and the history of lace-making by machinery.

VI. When one wishes to make the acquaintance of a person, one generally desires to see her or him face to face, and to interchange ideas by conversation, and so forth. Probably what others have said has given us this wish. This was my case as regards lace. I heard a good deal about lace when I had the honour of serving on a committee which was formed to promote an Exhibition of Ancient Lace for the International Exhibition at South Kensington, in 1874. But when I came to be presented to some of the most splendid productions of the art, I found that hearsay did not give me much assistance in making myself really acquainted with these works. It was necessary to do more than express satisfaction at a beautiful piece of work, or to allow oneself to be carried away with enthusiasm over the interesting fact that some Venetian Dogeress had actually made a certain length of vandykes. Throughout the collection shown at the Exhibition there was an immense variety of pattern and of workmanship. It seemed to me that I should be more likely to understand this if I applied myself to a careful examination of a few of the important specimens. Accordingly, a pocket magnifying-glass became a necessity, and through its help I began to arrive at some sort of classification of laces by stitches. As soon as I had satisfied myself as to the marked difference between needle-made and pillow-made lace, I began to study the catalogue and the descriptions printed in it. I confess to having been surprised, and inclined to doubt my eyesight, at the frequency with which my opinion clashed with the descriptions. It seemed as though tradition was more often than not exactly the reverse of personal experience. Some of the best traditions were only credible, subject to important "if's;" others, however, seemed to gain in historic value as they harmonised themselves with results of actual observations. A sense of gratitude to the spirit which moved me to closely examine specimens, and not to rely too much upon traditions and so-called authentic records, required me to give you this little account of my experience in studying lace.

VII. From examining lace-work, with all the minute twistings, plaitings, and loopings of fine thread, and with all the variety of patterns so rendered, one is naturally led to think of the workwoman or man, under whose skilful fingers such extraordinary works have grown. What were the materials and implements used? and to what purposes has the work been put?

VIII. A first element in lace-making is the human ability to twist, plait, and loop thread together. In restricting my remarks to this human ability, I think one should not assign an absolute originality to man in his craft of making elaborate patterns in delicate materials. The amazing domiciles and structures—homes without hands, as the Rev.

J. G. Wood calls them in his admirable book on the subject—made by many kinds of creatures, like moles, foxes, squirrels, birds, crabs, snails, beetles, ants, spiders, and bees, at once suggest varied forms of patterns, some of which are produced by plaitings and twistings. The marvellous, mathematical regularity of the hexagons in the bees' honeycomb, the radiations within polygonal shapes of the spider's web, the beautiful patterns of snow crystals, are all evidences of occult powers to design what we may call ornament; and the mere mention of them opens up an inexhaustible field of study, which would carry us far from lace-making. Even human skill in stitching—so notable a feature in some sorts of lace-making—has a prototype in the sewing done by tailor birds. I cannot resist the temptation of quoting a passage from Dr. Wood's book, which tells us how the tailor bird makes its hanging nest:—

"The bird chooses a convenient leaf, generally one which hangs at the end of a slender twig; it pierces a row of holes along the edge, using its beak in the same manner that a shoemaker uses his awl, the two instruments being very similar to each other in shape, though not in material. These holes are not at all regular, and in some cases there are so many of them that the bird seems to have found some special gratification in making them just as a boy who has a new knife makes havoc on every piece of wood he can obtain. When the holes are completed, the bird next procures its thread, which is a long fibre from some plant, generally much longer than is needed for the task which it performs. Having found its thread, the feathered tailor begins to pass it through the holes, drawing the sides of the leaf towards each other, so as to form a kind of hollow cone, the point downwards. Sometimes a single leaf is used for this purpose, but whenever the bird cannot find one that is sufficiently large, it sews two together, or even fetches another leaf and fastens it with the fibre."

IX. You will, I hope, pardon me for this digression from the point we were considering, namely, man's ability in twisting and plaiting threads. I think we may take it that this ability is hardly a sort of spontaneous invention. It appears to be the development of certain natural functions of the fingers. Therefore, where there are hands and fingers, and a governing intelligence, the ability to plait, twist, and loop threads can display itself. One might not expect to find that the ability is restricted to one nation, or to one period of the world's history. Still, certain conditions, no doubt, especially favour the exhibition of this twisting and plaiting ability, and perhaps chief amongst such conditions is the existence in marked quantities of articles like flax or silk, and fibres of all kinds.

X. The Egyptian sculptures of Beni Hassan, as described by Sir Gardner Wilkinson, furnish us with a record, perhaps 2,500 years before Christ, of all sorts of employment, of customs social and domestic, in Egypt. Upon these Beni Hassan sculptures we have pictorial descriptions of how flax was beaten, the striking of flax after it is made into yarn, twisting the yarn into rope, weaving the yarn into a cloth by a loom, and hundreds of similar interesting details in the practice of arts by dexterous handicraftsmen. At the British Museum is an Egyptian chair with a seat of plaited cords.

Fine threads of twine are stretched in parallel lines at about half an inch from each other, from back to front of the frame of the seat. Similar threads are also stretched from side to side. Thus a simple square meshed foundation is made. Upon it are intertwisted—diagonally across the meshes—rows of some eight or twelve strings or cords, and so the seat, not unlike our modern cane seats, is constructed. This sort of plaiting and intertwisting, however, cannot be said to have decorative pretence, and is not so germane to ornamental work we call lace, as are fringed borders of the robes sculptured upon Assyrian monoliths, of the time of Assur-nazir-Pal, about 800 B.C. (See Fig. 1.) The lines forming a trellis pattern in

FIG. 1.

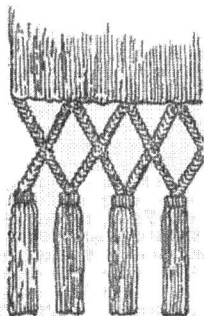

Assyrian border, 800 B.C.

the upper part of these borders appear to consist of round, plaited cords, very similar in their plaiting to that which we see upon fringed borders of Persian carpets now in the market, or to plaited leather whip thongs. On the mantle of the king, the trellis pattern is rather more elaborate than those on the dresses of the attendants. The design is, however, quite primitive.

XI. In our English Bible lace is frequently mentioned, but its meaning must be qualified by the reserve due to the use of such a word in James I.'s time. It is pretty evident that the translators used it to indicate a small cord, since lace for decoration would be more commonly known at that time as "purls," "points," or "cut works."

XII. Of lace amongst the Greeks we seem to have no evidence. Upon the well-known red and black vases are all kinds of figures, clad in costumes which are bordered with ornamental patterns, but these were painted upon, woven into, or embroidered upon the fabric. They were not lace. Many centuries elapsed before a marked and elaborately ornamental character infused itself into twisted, plaited, or looped thread work. During such a period the fashion of ornamenting borders of costume and hangings existed and underwent a few phases: as, for instance, in the Elgin marbles, where crimped edges appear along the loose flowing Grecian dresses.

XIII. It is recorded that our "general parents" in the Garden of Eden, wore aprons of leaves,

overlapping one another, an arrangement subsequently modified for their scale armour by Greeks and Romans. The scales of the armour

FIG. 2.

Overlapping leaves of armour.

were of leaf (see fig. 2) and billet (see fig. 3) forms, as were the edges of the under skirt and

FIG. 3.

Overlapping scales of armour of billet forms.

sleeves. If you want to see an attractive example of this method of varying the line of the edge, the costume of Mr. Irving, as Synorix, in Mr. Tennyson's drama of "The Cup," presents you with one. Along the borders of Mediæval costume, this custom of indenting the border was perpetuated. (See Fig. 4.) The French word, "dentelle," is

FIG. 4.

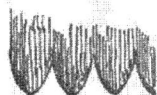

Cut, scalloped edge.

evidently derived from the tooth-shape of such scallops.

XIV. To continue, however, our rapid glimpse of fashion in patterns for bordering costumes and in decorative accessories to dress, which seems to have led up to lace. Mosaics, dating from the 6th century after Christ, preserved in churches at Ravenna, give us representations of early Christian saints, Cecilia, Crispina, Lucia, and others, attached to whose white head-dresses are fringes. Besides these, there are resplendent mosaics of the Empress Theodora and her ladies in waiting, all arrayed in sumptuous apparel, some of which is ornamented with dentations, and others with wavy and undulating borders. In 1078, Benedetto Antelami, recording the fashion of his time, wrought a patterned edging to the robe of the Virgin, who appears in a composition he carved in stone for an altar or panel at Parma. A border, consisting of a series of holes, no doubt cut and worked upon

6

the vestments of figures sculptured by Nicolo Pisano, brings us to the year 1260, and seems to lead us a little nearer to ornamental open work which might be considered to be lace. Somewhat later, we have a repetition of this sort of border treatment in figures sculptured by Tino da Camiano. At Florence, in Or San Michele, Orcagna has decorated the costumes of figures carved in his splendid shrine. Fifty years later, Ghiberti indulged his decorative fancy in a similar way, as is shown in the panels of figure subjects which adorn his doors of the Florence Baptistery. In 1447, various art workmen engaged in sculpturing the temple erected at Rimini, to the glorification of the Malatesta family, decorated the borders of the robes of the figures. But in mentioning these Italian instances of the fashion in borders of dresses, it must not be supposed that similar fashions had not also penetrated to other European countries.

XV. In Edward IV.'s time, in England,

"Cut werke was greate in Court and towns,
Both in men's hoddes and also in their gowns."

but this "cut werke" is not cut work embroidery as we know it. It was the cutting out into shapes, the dentation or scalloping of the borders of stuff "hoddes" and gowns, as we find it with the Romans. (See Fig. 4.) This kind of ornamentation undoubtedly influenced the shapes in which most of the first laces were to be inserted, and we trace such shapes in "points" of the 16th century, an example of which I will show you (Fig. 5). Chaucer, too, in his Parson's tale,

FIG. 5.

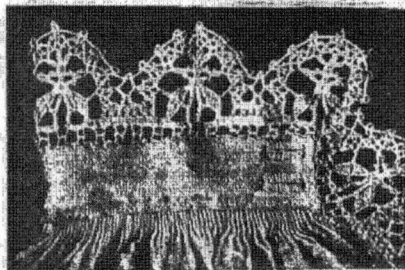

Cuff trimmed with lace-work in "points," or Vandykes. Late 16th century.

gives us an insight into fashions of dress, when he deprecates "the superfluitee of clothing, which maketh it so dere to the harme of peple, not only the cost of embrouding, the disguising, endenting or barring, ounding, palming, winding or bending, and semblable wast of cloth in vanitee," but also of much else that need not, perhaps, be quoted. Both Flemish and Italian painters, the Van Eycks, the Bellinis, and Carpaccios, supply us with rich representations of gold thread and jewelled fringings worn by the wealthy. Besides these we find that the small linen collars and cuffs of the period were ornamented with some simple and delicate embroidery in black and red silks. Borders of small plaited loops or "purls" were frequently fastened along the edges of these linen collars and

cuffs, but as late as the end of the 15th century there is no marked display of ornamental open work done in white threads.

XVI. We may now glance at the use of white thread materials like linen, &c., about this time. Northern countries of Central Europe were foremost in the cultivation and employment of flax. Flanders was especially notable in this respect. Holland gave its name to the flax cloth woven in the Middle Ages, and much used in Europe. The town of Cambray gave its name to cambric; and from "d'Ypres" we are supposed to derive diaper, just as damask comes from Damascus, sarcenet from the Saracens, and baudekin from Bagdad. In the 14th and 16th centuries the Venetian Republic was in the glory of the commercial relations with all European countries; she was virtually one of the most prosperous and artistic of European centres. Her "argosies" and "Flanders galleys" were well-known above all other trading vessels on the coast line of Western and Northern Europe. The name "Flanders galleys" marks in a way the considerable commerce Venice had with Flanders. These galleys used to lie along the quays of the delightful old town of Bruges, and there discharge their cargoes. However much during four hundred years the mercantile prestige of Bruges may have declined, there are now signs that the use of the old town as a Belgian Liverpool is being considered. But during all this Northern trafficking four hundred years ago, much trade with Oriental countries was carried on. The wealth and taste of Venice attracted riches and luxuries of costumes, silks, gold and silver clothes, velvets, and much else from the East. An extravagant indulgence of wealthy Venetians in their use of these costly materials stirred the Council of the Republic to pass sumptuary laws from time to time, prohibiting or limiting the use of such things. Venice, however, must not be understood to have been singular in this respect, for similar laws were in force in other countries. These laws, principally aimed at vanity, were, in the circumstances of the times, not without influence in educing artistic ingenuity. And I think that in regard especially to lace-making at Venice, they have an important bearing. A writer of the 17th century, describing Venice, speaks of a pre-eminence that Venetian ladies, among Italian women, enjoyed for the whiteness and fineness of their linen, as well as for their skill in sewing and embroidering. An old Venetian proverb runs, "La camicia preme assai piu del giubbone," or "The shirt before the coat." Now, since the rich coloured decorations used by Venetians in their costumes were, to a considerable extent, placed under the ban of sumptuary edicts, the idea of elaborating ornamentation for their far-famed white linen seems to have arisen. The seeming modesty and economy of such white thread-work, to be adopted as a successor to the gorgeous gold fringes and fine coloured embroideries was, I think, an ingenious but perfectly logical recommendation which helped to give life to this new fancy of fashion. Besides giving the regular embroiderers in Venice a new diversion for their talents, this white thread-work commended itself to the peasant spinners of thread wherever they might be, whether in Italian hills or lower lying lands of Flanders. Spinning from off the distaff has always been a favourite occupation with women in many countries of Europe. The making of simple twisted and plaited white thread edgings to collars and cuffs could be readily taken up by the thread spinners. A new occupation was thus provided, which could be followed by peasants in their homes and out of doors, or by sailors in their leisure time on boardship. In convents, too, where a gentle art like embroidering has always found favour, the taste for white thread and linen ornamentation infused itself. Embroidering linen became so fashionable that designers compiled and published books of patterns, which, as a rule, were dedicated in high-flown, courteous language of the time to "le belle donne," who were addressed by the various compilers in their dissertations on the subject as their gentle, delicate, and magnanimous, and most beautiful readers.

XVII. Two or three antiquaries have paid close attention to the history of these pattern-books. Some claim the honour of first publication for France, others for Italy, and others for Germany. The fashion of pattern-books came to England as well. On looking over many of these rare books (of which, by the way, Signor Oncagnia, of Venice, has recently published some admirable reproductions in fac-simile), I find that with none of them are practical directions supplied of how the different sorts of works, for which there are patterns, are to be executed. It is agreed, I think, that of the pattern-books that by Alessandro Pagannino, dated Venice, 1527, is one of the earliest. It is entitled a "First Book of Embroidery," as well as for instructing "oneself in diverse methods, uses, and ways of embroidery never before attempted or published, the which methods the willing reader may teach himself." Putting aside the author's ascription to himself of the credit of having published the "first" book on the subject, it is not unlikely that the embroidering of shirts, socks, cuffs, and gloves was in vogue before the book appeared. Be this as it may, neither patterns nor titles indicate lace work. In a book by Taglicnte, published in 1531, we find an enumeration of stitches, such as "punto a filo" (perhaps a darning stitch), "punto sopra punto" (cross-stitch, perhaps), "punto ciprioto" (Cyprus stitch), "punto croceato" (perhaps a stitch done with a hooked needle, like crochet), "punto in aere" (which might be "punto in aria," or needle-point lace) "punto fa su la rete" (which would be work done upon a species of canvas), "punto disfilato" (or drawn thread-work), and others. The title "punto in aere," or point in the air, should interest us particularly. But the pattern entitled "punto in aere" is not specially distinguished as a lace pattern; with the exception of this doubtful "punto in aere," all the embroidery indicated is intended, as you have seen, to be done upon a foundation of stuff. The materials named to be used are silks of various colours, gold and silver threads, and other sorts of threads; whilst amongst the implements depicted are compasses, pens, pencils, scissors, a pad for pouncing pricked designs, hanks of threads, but there are no bobbins, pins, cushions. The designs are to be worked for costumes and hangings, and besides those I have shown, consist of scrolls, arabesques, birds, animals, flowers, foliage, herbs, and grasses; in fact, so far as lace would be concerned, involve the execution of work as none but practised lace

makers would be able to overcome. Twenty years later we have special geometric patterns workable by lace makers, who were at the threshold, so to speak, of the **practice** of their art. (See Fig. 6.)

FIG. 6.

Part of a border of needle-point lace, geometric design. About 1550

At this time, about 1550, the "punto gropposi" (knotted work) is named. The designs, too, of the same time, for "punto in aria," are clearly geometric lace designs.

XVIII. Monsieur Aubry, member of the jury appointed to make awards of prizes to lace manufacturers, who exhibited specimens at the Great Exhibition in 1851, is one of the first of modern writers on the art of lace-making. For the groundwork of her "History of Lace," I find that the late Mrs. Bury Palliser, as all students of this subject must be, is indebted to him. M. Aubry says that Italy and Belgium dispute the honour of the invention of lace-making. Without attempting to settle the dispute, he says that we can easily imagine that the fabrication of lace in each of these countries was quite different, and thus having drawn upon our imagination, Mons. Aubry is assured enough to say that if Venice is the cradle of needle-point laces, at Brussels it is certain that the first pillow and bobbin-made laces were produced. After examining the evidence, which he brings forward to support his statement, as well as considering remarks made by Mons. Seguin in his "History of Lace," I have formed the opinion that so distinctive a method of using threads as that involved in ornamental lace-making has not a contemporary double origin; and in a later lecture I hope to show you a series of specimens which appear to indicate how elaboration of plaiting, twisting, and looping white threads developed according to the demands made upon workmen's ingenuity by the designers of patterns. The workmen's ingenuity developed two distinct classes of work, the one needle-point lace, the other pillow-made lace. The former is, undoubtedly, an offspring of embroidery, just as the latter is of fringes or twisted cords. Both, however, in respect of artistic pretence, are traceable to the pattern-books. We have noticed the appearance of "punto in aria" or needle-point lace, and that of "punto gropposi" or knotted work. A modification of the "punto gropposi" is the "merletti a piombini." (See Fig. 7, p. 8.) In this specimen you would see that plaiting is used. There are no knottings, and few simple twistings. The first patterns for both plaiting and needle-point work then appear to have been made in

Venice in the 16th century, say about 1560, and thus M. Aubry's supposed double origin of lace vanishes, that is, if my statement be correct.

FIG. 7.

Plaited and twisted thread-work known as "Merletti a Piombini." About 1560.

XIX. No sooner, however, are novelties produced, than imitations quickly follow. The twisted and plaited thread-work was by some more easily done than needle-point work by others; and the Flemish, the chief spinners and weavers of thread, very naturally I think, were the first imitators of Venetian patterns of this sort of work, which was plaited on cushions. We have already seen that commercial relations long existed between Venice and Flanders. It had been chiefly carried on by ships, and this, of course, in respect of heavier merchandise, but in the 15th and 16th centuries an overland route *via* Augsburg, Cologne, and Bruges, was also used, probably for lighter wares. Copies of pattern-books, and dentated and scalloped trimmings, were no doubt included amongst these lighter wares. It is not, therefore, surprising to find pattern-books, evident imitations of Venetian books, springing into publication along the route overland. At Augsburg and Cologne, and as far north as Antwerp, we know such books were issued. At this last-named city, possibly about 1540, one of the first of the foreign imitations of Venetian books of patterns was produced. It is called "A New Treatise; as concerning the excellency of Needlework, Spanish Stitch, Weaving in the Frame, very necessary to all who desire perfect knowledge of Seamstry, Quilting, and Broidering work, containing 138 plates."

XX. The mention of "Spanish stitch" makes one almost expect to find Spanish books on needle-work. But, curiously enough, no such books corresponding to the Italian, German, Flemish, French, and English pattern-books have been found or known to have been published in Spain. Spanish stitch is now supposed to have been a black silk embroidery upon linen, and its use is assigned to the early 17th century. This is not a lace, however. Of the supposed manufacture of artistic lace in Spain, it may be convenient for me now to speak. It will, no doubt, be a matter of surprise to many, who are so accustomed to hear of and see what they are told in "Spanish point," if I say that Spain cannot be identified with the making of ornamental and fine white thread lace, as are Italy, Flanders, and France. Señor Riaño, an authority in these matters, writes that, "The most important ordinances relating to Spanish industries are those published at Toledo and Seville in the 15th and 16th centuries, and at Granada in the 16th and 17th centuries, and in none of them do we find

lace even alluded to." A Friar, Marcos Antonio de Campos, 1592, preaches, "I will not be silent and fail to mention the time lost these last years in the manufacture of 'cadenetas,' a work of thread, combined with silver; this extravagance and excess reached such a point, that hundreds and thousands of ducats were spent in this work, which, besides destroying the eyesight, wasting away the lives, and rendering consumptive the women who worked it, and preventing them from spending their time with more advantage to their souls, a few ounces of thread and years of time were wasted with so unsatisfactory a result." Señor Riaño seems to argue from this that the Friar adopted "cadenetas" as a term meaning lace-work. But, further on, he says "cadenetas" is chain stitch. Bearing in mind that the fashion of the 16th century directed itself towards "points," and "dentelles," and bands of insertion of lace-work, it might seem perhaps more likely that the Friar would have consumed such adornments with the fire of his wrath —naming them by their proper names—like "puntas," "randa," and "entredos." The Friar may, no doubt, have been inveighing against a sinful extravagance in the use of some sort of embroidery; I do not think, however, that we can safely rely upon what would be a misapplied term, as proof that Spain made lace; that she embroidered is well-known. Whilst the female portion of his family embroidered, Cervantes, it is said, wrote much of his "Don Quixote."

XXI. Ornaments made of plaited and twisted gold and silver threads, much in the way that some lace was made, were produced in Spain during the 17th century. Mention of those is to be found in the ordinances of that time. Towards the end of the century, Narciso Felin, author of a work published in Barcelona, quoted by M. Aubry, writes, that "edgings of all sorts of gold, silver, silk, thread, and aloe fibres are made at Barcelona with greater perfection than in Flanders." In the 16th century Flanders was part of the Spanish dominions. She is then always spoken of as Spanish Flanders. To her, Spain was indebted for a quantity of manufactured and artistic goods, linen and lace included, I conclude, therefore, that the Barcelona lace-making was more or less an imitation of that which had pre-existed in Spanish Flanders. Apart from this, the gold and silver lace of Cyprus, Venice, Lucca, and Genoa, preceded that from Flanders. It appears to me that Spain was later in the field of artistic lace-making than Italy, Flanders, and France. As a great commercial and wealthy power, Spain, I think, in the 16th and 17th centuries, imported the greater portion of the fantastic and fashionable luxuries she required. Even the celebrity of the gold "Point d'Espagne" is due, I fancy, more to the use of gold lace, by Spanish grandees, than to the production in Spain of a gold lace, better in design, in workmanship, and quality, than that from Italy and France. The manufactories at Paris and Lyons were in full force, supplying the fashionable world with gold lace in the 17th century. The name "Point d'Espagne" was, I think, a commercial name given to gold lace by French makers. It is interesting to note that Beckmann in his "History of Inventions," says that it was a fashion to give the name of Spanish to all kinds of novelties, such as Spanish flies, Spanish wax, Spanish green, Spanish grass, Spanish seed, and others. This in a measure establishes the value set upon the qualification or title "Spanish," and, at least, indicates that the custom of Spaniards was much courted by other nations. In concluding these observations as to claims that Spain may have for being considered an early maker of artistic lace, I may quote the following passage from Señor Riaño, which greatly affects the value of what would otherwise be a fact of importance contained in Mrs. Palliser's "History of Lace":—

"Notwithstanding the opinion of so competent an authority as Mrs. Palliser, I doubt the statement, finding no evidence to support it, that thread lace of a very fine or artistic kind was ever made in Spain or exported as an article of commerce during early times. The lace alb, which Mrs. Palliser mentions to prove this, as existing at Granada, a gift of Ferdinand and Isabella in the 15th century, is of Flemish lace of the 17th century."

XXII. Of France and her connection with early lace-making, there is not much at present to be said. It is evident that a great deal of foreign lace, chiefly from Flanders and Venice, were imported into France, and that all sorts of prohibitions were issued to prevent the expenditure of the French upon foreign goods, and so, if possible, to encourage the manufacturers to make articles for home consumption; but the importations went on, and France was at this time unable to make laces to compete with those from Italy and Flanders. The compilers of commercial dictionaries and encyclopædias, Diderot, Savary, Roland de la Platiere, and others, writing in the 18th century, give the names of insignificant little primitive twistings and plaitings like "gueuse" "mignonette," and "campane." These bear about as much relation to fine artistic laces as a flint instrument does to a Cellini's sword-handle. Taste in manufacturing lace in France was not evoked until Frederic Vinciolo came to Paris about the end of the 16th century, and supplied the Court of Henry IV. with varieties of white thread work, including the geometric points of Venice. But even Vinciolo's influence was limited, and only laid the seeds of a condition of taste in France, which enabled Colbert forty years later to induce Venetian lace designers and workmen to come over to France and to help in the establishment of a number of places where lace should be regularly made. Many of the towns nearest to Flanders were judiciously chosen for these new lace establishments. But the chief of the French towns subsequently most famous of all for its lace was Alençon in Normandy. Of the influence of Alençon we shall hear more in the course of our investigations of needle-point lace making.

XXIII. Of incidents concerning workpeople engaged in the manufacture of lace, we have little precise information. History is almost silent in respect of guilds, or bodies of lacemakers (if there were such) in the 16th century. Venetian archives might be expected to reveal some light upon this; but at present the search has not been very fruitful. Documents exist to show that a noble lady Bianca Capello, was able to monopolise the making of certain laces for her own use, in 1578; and that in 1582 Juan Isepo worked a splendid collar, very likely of Reticella work, for Maria Morosoni di Francesco. A note is given in

a pamphlet by Signor G. M. de Gheltof, of the foundation of a school of 120 lacemakers at Venice, by Morosina Morosini, in the 17th century.

XXIV. Valuable State records, from which some information might probably have been obtained about the Flemish lace trade, were burnt in a fire at Brussels in the year 1731. Private papers of nunneries in Italy and Flanders would probably be an interesting source to examine. Evidence, such as it is, points to lace-making having been at first an occupation of individual peasants, rather than of organised bodies of persons. Nuns in convents no doubt produced a good deal of lace, as well as children in schools; and by Italian trimming makers and French guilds of "passementiers," probably much lace of a primitive kind was made. Lace of later periods, that is, from the middle of the 17th century onwards, can generally be identified with centres of manufacture, like Valenciennes, Mechlin, Brussels, Alençon, Honiton, &c. But of the earlier laces, excepting those done according to Venetian patterns, we have not much to rely upon for guidance.

XXV. The 16th century Italian patterns are sometimes named "punto Fiamenghi," "punto Genovese," and "punto Francesco;" but there is little variety in the style of the patterns, so that the names, even if they meant more than the celebrated "Point d'Espagne," do not give us new clues as to other centres of manufacture if they existed. These names were apparently pattern-makers' names for styles, intended to catch the fancy of the different people to whom they were dedicated, and may have been made in various towns in Italy, such as Rome, Venice, Genoa, Milan, Piacenza, and elsewhere. I am afraid, therefore, that much of the classification of early lace has to be somewhat vague.

XXVI. An elaborate design, for instance, is hardly likely to have been worked out by humbly trained peasant hands; it is more likely to have emanated from some place where workmen and women were employed for the purpose of lace-making, and where they had access to good patterns, plenty of materials, and so forth. Such conditions existed probably also in Italian and Flemish convents. On the other hand, simple patterns would, from the ease with which they could be executed, recommend themselves to makers of the less important laces, whose operations would have a tendency to become restricted to the repetition or modification of such simple designs, the sale of which would no doubt take place amongst the villagers, or else be promoted by some *Autolycus*, and such hawkers of wares, at fairs and markets.

XXVII. The excellence of much of the early lace is perhaps due in a great degree to the good taste of the wealthy, who bought and wore the work. Demand ruled supply, whereas now-a-days, supply seems to rule demand so far as beauty of design and quality of workmanship goes. There are few Mæcenases now. The recommendation of the salesman is a chief moulder of public taste. The salesmen in turn regulate the style and quality of the goods to be made, according to their opinion of public taste and fashion. Such relations do not seem to have existed when the great Alençon factories were established. For the wealthy lace wearers, then, at that time, the number of lace workers was insignificant as compared with the number now. One might say that lace wearers could be counted by the thousand, whilst those not wearing laces were the millions. This is now almost reversed. The millions now wear lace, or something like it. Louis XIV. and Colbert determined that French taste in lace should be good, and virtually took into their own hands the supply of lace to the country. From Alençon were sent out admirable patterns and exquisite workmanship, which were readily accepted by lace fanciers. Brussels unquestionably adopted styles of Alençon designs for her pillow laces, which in time superseded French needle-point laces. Our English pillow-lace workers adopted some of the Brussels patterns and some of the Mechlin; but English taste was easily gratified by less skilfully arranged patterns, and found sufficient pleasure in the peasant laces of Buckinghamshire and Devonshire. It is these patterns that a good deal of the machine-made lace imitates, though within the last three or four years there has been a marked phase of other more ambitious imitation in the machine-lace trade. Something akin to the rich patterns of ancient hand-made lace is now made by the machine, and to the majority this substitution of machine-made for hand-made goods is satisfactory. As a rule the difference between machine and hand-made lace is not detected by the many. If there is a difference, to some it is that machine-made lace, from some points of view, is the more wonderful and more to be prized of the two sorts of work. Setting aside any prejudices one may have, and reviewing the variety of forms wrought years ago, we may consider some of the circumstances of the production of laces. Sometimes laces were made in dim and dank cellars, so that the soft fragile threads should retain their elasticity, and not become brittle. A ray of light alone was allowed to fall

upon the workwoman's cushion. What an expense of eyesight and health must then have taken place. Compare truly costly works produced in such circumstances, with the low-priced repetitions done in taut wiry cotton threads which grow with precise monotony of pattern in the bustle and clatter of machinery, at the expense of iron and steam, and one is perhaps inclined to be glad at the release of human labour from penalties like those which formerly accompanied lace-making. I do not think anyone can well say what may succeed to the mechanically devised and produced materials now called lace? They seem to satisfy present demand and to reflect the taste and ability of the age. Is it vain to hope for a revival of hand-made works? Is the time to arrive when machinery shall have exhausted itself in its endeavours to infuse into its productions the quality of hand-work—or has a period commenced when people shall be contented with mechanical instead of manual art? and so from this possibly pass on to a condition of indifference to fine artistic works of handicraft, which not many years since were reported to have been pronounced by a philosopher and leader of opinion to be but the rubbish of human labour.

XXVIII. In my next lecture I hope to deal with the various needle-point laces, and besides the examples shown on the screen there will be a few fine specimens of lace, and some photographs. I must not conclude my remarks this evening without acknowledging the advantage I think both you and I have received from Sir Philip Cunliffe-Owen, director of the South Kensington Museum, who kindly caused many of the transparencies of lace to be made, as well as from Sir William Drake and Mr. Edmund Dresden, who lent specimens, some of which have been exhibited, and others photographed, by Sergeant Jackson, R.E., the able assistant of my friend, Captain Abney, R.E., F.R.S.

LECTURE II.—Delivered Monday, April 11, 1881.

Needlework upon a material. Needlework upon separate threads. Venetian needle-point lace. Needle-point and tape lace. French needle-point lace-making centres. English and Flemish needle-point lace.

I. In my previous lecture I tried to show when the art of lace-making arose, and by whom it was first practised. This evening I propose to deal with one of the principal methods of lace-making, and the designs worked in this method. Lace, as an ornamental and open arrangement of threads, has been and is still produced in various sorts of threads. We have laces of gold and silver threads, of white, black, and coloured silks, and of white threads, which latter may be of linen or cotton. The white linen thread lace is that in the production of which most notable artistic designs have been used. Accordingly, with this particular class of lace, I propose mainly to deal. Broadly speaking, hand-made white thread lace is a textile fabric perfectly distinct in character from a woven textile fabric. As a rule, a woven material is close, and patterns are wrought in it by varying the interweavings of the threads, and by using variously-coloured threads.

II. Now, hand-made lace is produced by looping, or plaiting, or twisting threads together. The looping is done with a sewing needle, and the thread, by means of the needle, is constantly at work, being twisted and looped around and between certain fixed threads, which form the backbone of the pattern to be wrought. Plaiting and twisting is done by using several free and loose threads one after another, so that single threads are by turn brought into operation. This latter method comes under the heading pillow and bobbin-made lace, and with this we shall deal in the next lecture.

Fig. 1.

Valenciennes pillow lace.

For the present, we are to consider the looped and twisted thread work done with a needle, and hence called needle-point lace. Needle-point and pillow-laces are the two chief divisions of the hand-made laces. Without some acquaintanceship with the methods of their productions, it would be difficult to detect certain of their salient characteristics. To the sight, the difference between these two classes of lace (pillow and needle-point) is often quite marked. For instance, one may compare a piece of Valenciennes pillow-lace with a piece of Venetian needle-point lace. The Valenciennes pillow lace is quite flat and thin in appearance, whilst the Venetian needle-point lace is marked by portions in relief and a sort of modelled appearance. (Figs. 1 and 2.) A similar difference would

Fig. 2.

Venetian needle-point lace.

not be apparent if we compared the same piece of Valenciennes with a very delicate Venetian needle-point lace, called "point de Venise à réseau." The variety of pattern which we should find in three such specimens could not even be taken as a guide to class of work, as respects needle-point and pillow-lace, since, in the halcyon days of lace-making, the same pattern might be worked by the needle and on the pillow.

III. Attention to the characteristics of workmanship in laces has often been too slightly paid by those who have otherwise shown themselves to be connoisseurs in the matter. The late Mrs. Bury Palliser, whose name is closely associated with the history of lace, not unfrequently had failed to acquaint herself with such characteristics. She described some needle-point lace as pillow-made lace and *vice versâ*. It would be ungrateful on my part if I allowed you to infer from these remarks that I was not sensible of my indebtedness to Mrs. Palliser's "History of Lace." Her patient research was almost exclusively devoted to the exhumation and laborious accumulation of records about lace. In this respect chiefly her history of lace is a valuable volume of reference. I must repeat, however, that records and writings hardly seem to be a first source from which materials for forming an acquaintanceship with lace-making are to be drawn. The abundance of existing specimens of all sorts of lace invites our attention, and enables us to trace developments and phases of the art in its productions. When methods of workmanship and styles of design have impressed themselves upon us, then we may have recourse to records and writings, and fit together in as complete a way as we can, the evidences we have thus obtained. I will not say more on this matter, but proceed now to ask you to consider with me features of workmanship in needle-point laces.

IV. Without referring to any particular class of needle-point lace, it will be seen that a beginning must be made somewhere. The pattern governs this beginning. Say then we want to make a little square in lace. We first draw the form on a piece of paper or parchment. Parchment being less destructive is the best. Then lay upon the lines a thread which is fastened here and there to the parchment by stitches. Having completed this thread skeleton pattern, we begin to build a compact covering of white threads upon it, which we do in ordinary button-hole stitch, the result of which is that the skeleton outline becomes a well-marked figure. This is the very simplest form of needle - point lace. If we want to go a little further, and place, say, a pattern in the centre of the square, we should draw one pattern, and then outline it with thread, taking care to attach the lines of this addition to the main lines of the square, and then we proceed with one over-casting of button-hole stitches. There remains now the question how the pattern is to be taken off the parchment. This is easily done, by neatly cutting the stitches at the back of the parchment, which stitches you will remember were those which held the first skeleton outline down. The lace is thus released from the parchment, and the pattern is ready for use for another piece of lace. However, all that we have done is to produce a sort of geometric form of even lines, and this is virtually all that was done at the commencement of needle-point lace-making. Much depends, as you readily perceive, upon nice thread and careful patient working; the least scamping or putting a loop out of its order, takes away from the compactness of the work; and irregularity and loosely made lace condemns itself.

V. Before leaving the early and geometric stage of lace, as we have seen it, which, by the way, was called "punto in aria" (see Fig. 3), a term you will recollect from my first lecture, I think we may find it useful to glance at a few of the classes of white thread embroidery which existed before, and contemporary with "punto in aria." We have seen that the beginning of lace

is separate threads. This is quite reverse of embroidery, which requires a stuff as a foundation.

FIG. 3.

"Punto in aria."—Geometric design, with an edging of plaited and twisted threads.

VI. When the fashion of ornamenting white linen garments was getting up to its zenith, people devised methods of decoration other than that of merely loading the surface of a stuff with embroidery. A lightness was obtained by cutting out bits of the stuff, or by punching a series of little holes, like the tailor bird. One of the more elaborated forms of this cutting-out work was 16th century Venetian "reticella," which is also called sometimes "tagliato," or cut work. The designs for this sort of work, difficult to distinguish from much "punto in aria" done from similar patterns, are also geometric. The principal lines are rectilineal; and this arises from the fact that the cuttings-out from the stuff generally followed the woof or warp of the linen. These rectilineal lines consist of either very narrow strips of linen, or three or four of the uncut threads, worked over with button - hole stitches, just as our skeleton outline in "punto in aria" was secured. Between these lines may be circular and radiating forms, which were worked like "punto in aria;" and it is curious to notice that, although the embroiderers of linen soon devised methods of inserting into places cut into linen such open ornamented work as done in Fig. 4,

FIG. 4.

Enlarged diagram of stitching in close portions of needle-work lace.

yet they seem to have been some little time before they were able to work this sort of ornament, so as to form a band or trimming, independently of linen as a foundation.

VII. Another cut or "tagliato" work done with linen was of a very obviously cut character, as you see from the specimen here shown. This vandyked scroll is cut out of a strip of linen, and is picked out with fine gold wire, fastened along its edges. (Fig. 5.) The name "tagliato a foliami," or cut work with leaves, was given to a very rich kind of lace, and this has led to some confusion; as the term "cut" indicates a process

FIG. 5.

Vandyke of cut linen work.

having nothing to do with the making of lace like that of Fig. 2, which was, nevertheless, called "tagliato a foliami." Much as it may look like cut linen, with little reliefs and ornaments embroidered upon it, it is a fine specimen of very elaborate lace-work, produced entirely by needle and thread upon a parchment pattern, so that cutting has nothing to do with the shaping or ornamentation of the pattern.

VIII. Continuing with the white embroideries upon stuff, we may look at a specimen of drawn thread-work. Here we have another sort of work, differing from either of the cut works. The withdrawal of the threads regulated the pattern to be produced. A well-curved scroll had to be content with being approximately rendered in small squares. The back ground to such work appeared to consist of a net of square meshes. This effect was obtained by whipping fine thread around the undrawn threads of the stuff. Just the reverse of this work is the very well-known darning upon net, of which there are many machine-made imitations now. For this sort of work, Frederic Vinciolo made many patterns, some of the earliest of which date from about 1570. The Italian name for the work was "punto a maglia," and the French "lassis" or "lacis." The Italians, or rather Venetians, preceded the French in this sort of work, though the French carried it to a degree of admirable perfection. I remember that in the South Kensington Exhibition of 1874, there was a most complete specimen of this darned work, a large linen curtain, or altar cloth, set with squares of darning upon a net ground, in which were represented figures of the zodiac and of the seasons. All of them were after designs by Vinciolo, as may be seen in such well preserved copies of his works as those belonging to Mr. Alfred Huth, who kindly allowed me to consult his copies of them. It was particularly interesting in this church hanging to notice the final squares, in one of which were the words, most carefully darned,

Louant Dieu j'ai fini mon ouvrage, "praising God I have finished my work," and in the other the name of the worker, "Suzanne Lescallez, 1595." The cloth, after the Exhibition, went back to France, and I don't know where it is, but it is so complete a specimen, that if by chance any one happens to meet with it, I hope they will make a careful note of its whereabouts. On a far smaller scale, and of altogether less artistic importance, are the few squares of "lacis" or darning, introduced into this cloth. (See Fig. 6.) These appear to be reproductions of some

FIG. 6.

Corner of an embroidered linen with squares of "lacis" and "Reticella" inserted, and edged with twisted and plaited threads.

of the smaller designs by Vinciolo. This Vinciolo is an important personage in the history of lace. Besides the darning work, or "lacis," which is not lace, he popularised the taste in France for "points coupés," the French name for "reticella" and cut-work, and also for "punto in aria." He seems to have borrowed much from different sources, and it is interesting to compare his patterns with those done by C. Vecellio, a notable and rather later designer and writer about costume towards the end of the 16th century, and some relation to the great Titian, and with those done by a much-esteemed woman, named Isabetta Catanea Parasole, whose patterns were published in Rome about 1590 and early in the 17th century. No doubt Vinciolo owed much of his success to the patronage which Henry III. and Henry IV. of France and the ladies of the French Court accorded him, though, at the same time, we must not forget that he was a man of energy and refinement, as his books show. He is almost the only early pattern maker who attempts a description of how the patterns are to be worked. His descriptions, however, are more enthusiastic than instructive. They are given by him in verse, in what he calls a discourse upon "Lacis." His divine *chef d'œuvre* is not a matter of chance; it has been well considered and planned by number and measure. Before leaving the "lacis" or darning on net, I would observe that the name given to the net was "résuil," and this name must be noted, since we find it, later on, applied to ground-works of meshes used in laces. You, all of you, know what netting is, and how simple an operation it is to

FIG. 7.

make one mesh. I will show you a few meshes done with the needle (see Fig. 7), and you will then see the far greater complication of this work, as compared with netting, and yet the name "réseau" in France applies to both.

IX. We have now examined different sorts of embroidery on linen. (1) Work done by cutting holes into a linen foundation; (2) work done by cutting linen into shapes; (3) work done by drawing out threads, and so leaving a linen pattern; and (4) work done by darning a pattern into network. We have also seen specimens of the early geometric laces—the "punto in aria," or button-hole stitch work done upon a thread skeleton; and now I should like to show you a piece of mixed work, in which a little more than mere geometric form is displayed. (See Fig. 8.) The

Fig. 8.

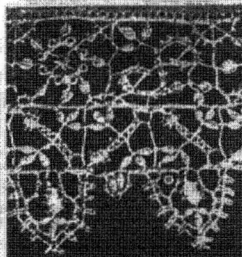

Vandyked border of mixed work, the upper part of needle-point, the lower and dentated part of plaited and twisted threads.

upper part is all of needle-point work, whilst the lower is of plaited work. Some of this plaiting may, no doubt, have been done with a hooked needle. However this may be, I thought it useful to show this specimen, in order that you might not fancy that the whole of a single piece of early work was done in one method only. Patterns for lace like this are to be found, especially in Vecellio's books, about 1590 or 1600.

X. We will now look at a few specimens, from which I think we shall trace a freer sort of design, and, consequently, an increased display of ingenuity in workmanship. We have hitherto seen ornaments, more or less dependent in their construction upon squares and their diagonals. But the pattern-

Fig. 9.

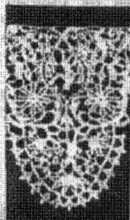

Italian needle-point vandyke.

books of the end of the 16th century give us designs for scrolls, with the introduction of all kinds of odd figures to be worked in lace. The specimen of this class (see Fig. 9.) dates, probably, from about 1580. I want you to notice how the different details in the design touch one another at different points of contact. There are very few little tyes. Considerable parts are of flat-looking work, work which in this photograph looks like linen. It is composed of a series of closely-drawn loops worked very much as shown in Fig. 4.

XI. In the specimen in Fig. 10, I want

Fig. 10.

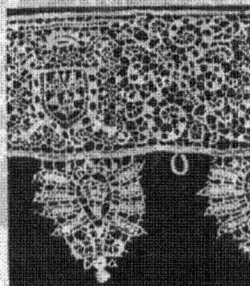

Needle-point lace, showing use of tyes or "brides."

you to notice the numerous little tyes which are used to hold the pattern together. These tyes are called "brides." The design too of this piece is more vivacious than the simple rosettes and radiations. In the centre we have a shield surmounted by a crown. Curves slope from each side of it, to meet beneath a sort of fan pattern, from the top of which grow a little *fleur de lys.* The vandykes which hang beneath, are repetitions of this fan device, and are terminated with little balls. Between the vandykes are small loops, which suggest loops for buttons, but I cannot say for what particular use this specimen was intended. From the character of the design I think the specimen dates from about 1680 to 1690, and is Italian. It might, of course, be a French or other imitation of Italian work.

XII. Very important work of this flat character was made, and amongst the white threads gold threads were introduced. I believe that Sir William Drake possesses as fine specimens as ever were wrought of this white and gold thread needle-point lace. They are, I think, of early 17th century design and workmanship. Originally they came from Messina, to which place they may have been taken by some wealthy person at the time when that city was a centre of considerable importance, notable for its independent and aristocratic prosperity.

XIII. In the succeeding examples, you will notice a development of flowering stems and scrolls. A change of design had thus begun to take place at the end of the 16th and beginning of the 17th centuries. Here (in Fig. 11) you will see too a greater use of the "brides" than any we have previously noticed. Along the borders of the stems or scrolls is a little raised line. This is called the "cordonnet," a feature not observable in the fine gold and white flounce of Sir William Drake's. Parts of the pattern are diversified by changes of stitch. Instead of compact work everywhere we should see little open works. In the centre of some of the little blossoms there are wheels and

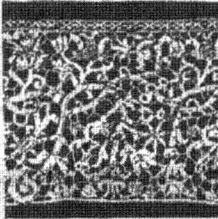

Fig. 11.

Venetian needle-point lace.

radiating lines. These details are worthy of our attention, and are called fillings-in, or "modes." They are specimens of the first forms of elaboration in lace, which in their further matured state became important features, giving delicate grace in appearance to laces of the best period.

XIV. It may have been about this time, namely, the commencement of the 17th century, that lace workers pressed tape into their service. Instead of patiently composing their scrolls and flowers in button-holed stitched fabrics, they found tape could, for comparatively rough and ready general effect, answer their purpose. Here we have two

Fig. 12.

Tape lace, with needle-point work and an edging of plaited and twisted threads.

examples of tape lace combined with needlework. Workers in pillow lace also used tape in a similar way. This little strip (see Fig. 12) may be Italian,

Fig. 13.

Tape lace worked with the needle.

but tape lace was not only produced in Italy. This specimen (see Fig. 13) may not unlikely be of Flemish workmanship. My reason for thinking it Flemish is the style of the flowers along the

borders, which appears in a lace (see Fig. 14) much liked by the Flemish in the first half of the 17th century. The points of resemblance lie in the

Fig. 14.

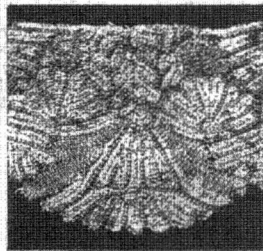

Flemish lace of the 17th century.

arrangement of the petals of the blossoms, which takes a fan shape.

XV. Before leaving the question of tape laces, it may be well to state that the weaving of tape seems to have been begun in Flanders, about the end of the 16th century, or the beginning of the 17th. Tape, so far as I have been able to ascertain, did not come to be made in England until the 18th century, when, according to a note I have had from Messrs. Phillips, the well-known tape manufacturers at Manchester, their predecessors brought over, in the year 1747, two Dutchmen, of the name of Lanfort. Under the tuition of these Dutchmen, the people in the village where Messrs. Phillips have mills at the present time, learned how to weave tape in the loom. The start in England was up-hill work, because of Dutch competition. There were at least 1,000 looms at work in Holland before there was one in England. However, in about thirty years, the trade greatly developed, and, in the course of a half century later, several other tape looms were started. This was about 1820. Since then the manufacture has increased. Before 1822, tape was made in cottages; but, in or about 1822, the idea of getting the workers and their looms under one roof had taken root, and mills were built. Then came steam power and water power for driving the looms, instead of human power. Effective work has been done with tape, in connection with the method of pillow-lace making. Work of this sort is sometimes called guipure. But guipure is a class of work totally distinct from this, and about guipure we shall hear something in the next lecture.

XVI. However, we must now return to needle-point laces. Up to the present we have arrived at scroll designs more or less flatly worked, held together by ties or "brides," enriched with little varieties of "fillings in" or "modes," and emphasised with small raised lines or "cordonnets." All this sort of work was done upon a thread skeleton pattern just as the first needle-point laces were made. Fancy in design and workmanship, however, was now becoming quite vigorous. We enter a period, soon after the commencement of the 17th century, when lace workers produced beautiful solid looking work, which is almost like fine 14th century Gothic tracery, carved in ivory. Its exquisitely worked relief carried recent admirers of it far away from the time when it was first produced. They tried to identify it with a needlework which an Italian poet, Firenzuola, a hundred of years before the existence of this relief-lace, described as "sculptured in relief." As the size of the altar-cloth, flounce, border, or collar seemed to demand, so did the lace-workers vary the size of their designs and work. For instance, a collar would be designed and worked as this one. (See Fig. 15.) The

Fig. 15.

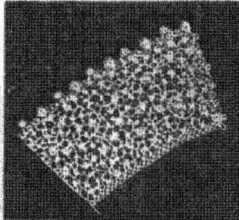

Part of a collar of minute Venetian needle-point lace.

figure is not quite distinct, in showing the amazing delicacy of the relief work and its enrichment. Each of these little blossoms, actually about the size of sixpence or threepence, is a bouquet in itself of hundreds of the most finished lilliputian loops, finely worked in button-hole stitches. Again, for a border or an ornament to hang beneath the chin, we have specimens such as this (see Fig. 16),

Fig. 16.

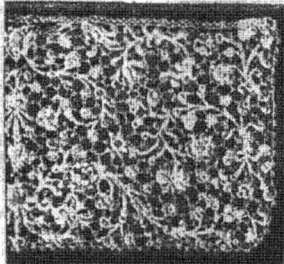

Venetian needle-point lace.

and in this specimen the decorations worked upon the little tyes should be noted ; while, for a sort of collar, the ends of which spread flatly over the breast of some courtier or minister, say like Colbert, we have samples as shown in Fig. 2. In all these specimens is a rich expression of stately scroll design—varied fillings - in or "modes," "galleries," or successions of minute loops "picots" placed one above the other. This was the kind of splendid needle-point lace, exclusively originating, I think, from Venice in the 17th century, which the nobility and wealthy personages of the time wore, and of which vestments and altar-cloths were made for churches.

XVII. A contrast to this galaxy of wonderful lace is to be found in the needle-point lace of England during the 17th century. A photograph lies on the table, in which is shown various scallops on vandykes of English needle-point lace of the 17th century. Remarkable amongst them are the two larger vandykes, which you will see contain— the one, a figure of a man—the other, a figure of a woman, depicted in the costume of the period. The way in which this work was done is precisely similar to 17th century flat Venetian needle-point lace. Here is a specimen of the English work. (See Fig. 17.)

Fig. 17.

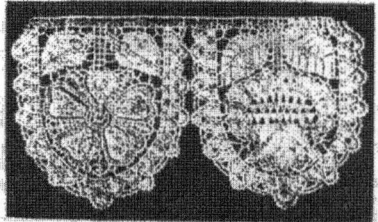

English needle-point lace.

XVIII. Scallops of "punto in aria," insertions of "reticella," and of similar design, may also be seen in Westminster Abbey carved upon the tombs of the

Fig. 18.

English sampler with needle-point stitches.

infant daughters of James I., which are dated 1606 and 1607. Who may have made these, who can say? In the English sampler of lace stitches (see Fig. 18), we have, luckily, the maker's name and date. "Margreet May, 1654" wrought this sampler, and in it you will see cut-work, drawn linen work, "reticella" work, and "punt in aria," or true needle-point stitches. It is a most valuable little epitome of English lace work in the Puritanical times, when school children like "Margreet May" were trained to have an interest and to take a pride in their own labour. Such as she were, evidently, not to be extinguished by a mere registration number, or lost in the midst of numerical grades in some "standard."

XIX. I must now ask you to put yourselves twenty years or so back before this 1654, and to consider the position up to which we seem to have traced needle-point lace making and design.

XX. The little tyes holding the patterns together have hitherto been but arbitrarily arranged. We have seen that at first they were plain little lines, as in Figs. 10 and 11; we have noted the decoration of them by means of the addition to them of little loops or "picots," as in Fig. 16. We now come to a period when the designers arranged them into an orderly pattern, similar to the honeycomb of the bee. Messrs. Hayward have kindly lent a very remarkable flounce, in which this character of honeycomb ground is seen, and Fig. 19, is taken from smaller specimen, which was

FIG. 19

Venetian needle-point lace.

used as the veil to a chalice. The little tyes ornamented with small loops form a background of hexagons. The style of design is no longer the flowing and dignified scroll, but consist of a balanced arrangement of fragmentary details, in the ornamentation of which clusters of picots is noticeable. A similar style in using disconnected ornaments is observable in Messrs. Hayward's flounce.

XXI. But before quitting the long flowery scrolls, I want you to observe the varieties of fillings-in, the growth of which we had begun to notice in Fig. 11, and I again refer you to the collar of raised scroll work. (See Fig. 2.) At the same time that new effects were being tried by designers and workers, the best forms which had preceded these attempts were also preserved in use. Hence you will see that, although in time styles of design supplanted one another,

there were lingerings of old styles contemporaneously worked with new styles. And it is the consideration of incidents like this which I think must always puzzle connoisseurs of styles of ornaments in their attempt to give a very precise date to a certain pattern. We may know that such and such a pattern may have been worked at a certain date, but we cannot fix with precision its first introduction, or its final appearance, neither can we be confident that a repetition of it may not be of very later date.

XXII. With the style of balanced arrangements of detached ornaments which is closely connected with the style known as Louis XIV., we find the first indications in lace of a groundwork of meshes made with a needle. (See Fig. 20). This

FIG. 20.

Needle-point lace with ground of fine meshes.

figure is rather indistinct, and does not show the ground of meshes clearly. Perhaps, however, the indications of it are sufficient to let me ask you to take my word for it that the ground is composed of meshes, which are in the main similar to those of Fig. 7.

XXIII. You will hence note how that we are getting into a period when grounds of meshes were being used. The daintiest of all Venetian needle-point laces, with fine grounds, is the "Point de Venise à réseau." This most delicate work was contemporary with soft pillow-made laces, which no doubt were intended to be its rival. In its production were combined the highest elaboration of design and workmanship, together with a thinness and beautiful softness of texture. It is one of the rarest of all laces. It marks a transition from preceding heavy to succeeding light laces. It followed the change which articles of costume, like collars and cuffs and trimmings, underwent from the 16th to 17th centuries.

XXIV. High-standing ruffs, like those worn by Queen Elizabeth, had been trimmed with "reticella" and geometric "punto in aria." But the vandykes expanded in size, and instead of shooting off from borders of the ruffs, became unmanageable for such

B

use, and so began to lay down, falling over the shoulders, instead of starting from them. The size of lace-trimmings grew too. Instead of vandykes or "dentelles" pendent from the knee or along the edge of a skirt, whole flounces offering greater field for display of more ambitious designs were produced. The Dauphin of Louis XIV., when christened, is pourtrayed as having worn a mantle with a deep bordering of handsome scrolls of raised Venetian point similar to that in Figs. 2 and 16. Tabliers and aprons of ladies' dresses were similarly composed of such lace. As patterns and work became less cumbersome, ladies adopted expansive sleeves of delicate lace, which well became their soft arms. A degree of softness thus asserted itself, and a climax of this softness is to be found in the remarkable "Point de Venice a réseau." The old vandykes had, in fact, disappeared, though their name, "dentelles," was retained for their successors, from which the dentated character was almost entirely extinguished.

XXV. We have now arrived at about 1660 to 1680, and this is an important date to remember in connection with the history of lace.

XXVI. A view of the situation might be stated to be, Venetians, at the end of their famous hundred and twenty years of work, to bring lace to a perfection, and other countries doing their utmost to acquire the art from them; some, like the Flemish, progressing slowly and naturally, following Venetian patterns upon the pillow; others, like the French, bent upon stepping by any means to a front rank.

XXVII. The desire of the French to be able to make fine lace was undoubtedly most strongly expressed in an edict dated 1665. Louis XIV.'s minister—Colbert—was the prime mover. He had taken stock of the increasing love of the French people for Venetian and Flemish laces. His love for the fine arts in all their branches, and his great energy, were principal elements in the framing and issue of this celebrated edict. Through it lace-making establishments were founded at Alençon, Quesnoy, Arras, Rheims, Sedan, Chateau Thierry, Loudun, and elsewhere. The State made a contribution of 36,000 francs in aid of the formation of a company to carry out the work. Instructions were included in the edict that the lacemakers should produce all sorts of thread-work—as much those done with the needle as those worked on a pillow or cushion, in the style of the points which were made at Venice, Genoa, and Ragusa, and other foreign countries. These French imitations were to be called "Points de France;" and although attempts have been made to identify certain laces as "points de France," I think, considering the variety of laces which were to be imitated, and the classification of them under the one name, that such attempts at identification of "points de France" cannot be very successful. As we know well, clever handicraftsmen can succeed in producing counterfeits which defy detection from originals. The local origin of a good deal of lace, made, perhaps, in France, in the middle of the 17th century, cannot, therefore, be determined. I mention this, since Monsieur Seguin has made up his mind that certain Venetian "rose point" laces are French. They are essentially Italian in style of pattern and work. To the extent of their being possibly worked by French hands, they may be

French. A French work, re-printed in England, might analogously be called an English book.

XXVIII. An excellent article in the *Edinburgh Review* of January, 1872, contains some interesting particulars about the establishment of the lace factories in France. The writer was furnished by the well-known antiquary, Mr. Rawdon Brown, of Venice, with extracts from Venetian State papers. A most important incident connected with the starting of these French lace-centres, was the employment in them of Venetian lace-workers. Intrigue and diplomacy were put into action to secure the services of Venetian workers. The Italian Ambassador at Paris in 1671 writes:—"Gallantly is the Minister Colbert on his way to bring the 'lavori d'aria' to perfection;" and six years later, Domenigo Contarini, jealous of the ill-effects which were evidently ensuing, to the prejudice of lace-making in Venice, alludes to the "punto in aria," "which the French can now do to admiration." Thus, from 1665 to 1677, we have a period when French labour, under State protection, was being systematically trained, by imported Venetian instructors, in the art of lace-making.

XXIX. The style of design adopted by the French was certainly much more floral than the Venetian. It was lighter, and more in accord with that lightness of texture which lace was developing for itself. Great attention was paid by the French to ground-works, which, in respect of the honeycomb "brides" (see Fig. 19), and meshed grounds (see Fig. 20), they distinctly copied from their Venetian masters. Mrs. Bury Palliser considered that French lace-makers could not be taught to imitate the true Venetian stitches, and that designs for points d'Alençon were planned accordingly to meet this deficiency, but I think the study of a few specimens here before us will be sufficient to show us that, however fresh a departure may have been taken by the French in the matter of design, their cunning in doing delicate needle-point stitches became as great as that of their instructors, the Venetians. It is surprising, I think, how confused people become if they have not fixed in their minds the difference between design and workmanship. The best ability in representing the worst design generally runs a risk of being condemned. It is the pattern, and not the workmanship, that should be condemned; and very often precisely the reverse of such cases occurs, when a well-drawn pattern, in spite of bad or inferior workmanship, asserts itself, and is then held up as a good piece of work.

XXX. To return, however, to French ground-works, and their particular connection with early distinctive French needle-point laces, you will remember the regular hexagonal grounds of Venetian laces (see Fig. 19). This feature, done generally on a smaller scale, is the distinguishing mark of what was called Point d'Argentan. I am afraid I shall make too great a demand upon your patience if I go into the question why Point d'Argentan and Point d'Alençon are virtually one and the same class of lace; frequently in style of design, and always in character of work. If you want to see my views upon this question, I must ask you to let me refer to my book on ancient lace, which the Arundel Society published for me in 1875. I will now show you a piece of lace in which the special ground work of Point d'Argentan and that of Point d'Alençon appears. (Fig. 21.) The clearly defined honeycomb ground in the centre of the figure is Argentan (so called), and the cloudy ground, composed of fine meshes, is the Alençon ground. Judging from the pattern of this lappet, I think it is likely to be of the latter end of the 17th century.

Fig. 21.

French needle-point lace.

XXXI. The variety of groundworks and fillings-in the Alençon laces is very remarkable. Large flounces, like one which belongs to Mrs. Alfred Morrison, are rich in all sorts of fantastic devices, of design, and of work. The underlying principle of the stitchery is the button-hole stitch, worked upon skeleton patterns of fine thread, and sometimes of horsehair. Here is another specimen of Alençon lace. The groundwork is composed of what is termed "réseau rosacé." This "réseau rosacé" consists of little solid flat hexagons of button-hole stitched work set in frames of hexagons. A special characteristic of the Point d'Alençon laces is the button-hole stitched "cordonnet." In the Venetian "Point à réseau" the outlines are of a thread. You will notice this if you examine the actual specimens here shown. To thoroughly enter into minutiæ like these of fine lacework would, I am afraid, take us into considerations almost never-ending. I hope I have been able to present to you this evening a sort of connected chain of phases of needle-point lace-making. I might extend it further, and speak of the Brussels needle-point laces. It is, however, more or less evident that the Flemish or Belgian, in the matter of needle-point lace, imitated their neighbours the French, though no doubt they had imbibed a large amount of knowledge in the course of their far earlier relations with the Venetians.

XXXII. I would conclude my remarks this evening by saying that the basis of all needle-point lace is the button-hole stitch, and that the features of work which you have to detect in judging a needle-point lace from a pillow-made lace are those of this button-hole stitch.

LECTURE III.—Delivered Monday, May 2, 1881.

Pillow-made lace. Fibres and threads twisted and plaited to make rope, cord, twine, and braids. Fringes Grecian fillets. Twisted thread-work in England in the 15th century. Plaited and twisted thread-work. Purls. Merletti a Piombini. Simple work done on a pillow. Manufacture of pins, guipure, tape lace. Pillow laces of scroll design. Grounds of meshes and other characteristics of pillow laces. Italian, Flemish, German, French, and English pillow lace.

I. This evening we are to consider the second division of hand-made lace, namely, pillow-made lace. The outgrowth of needle-point lace from embroidery done upon a foundation of stuff, then upon a web or net of some sort, and at length upon a skeleton pattern of threads, was, I hope, established when we last met. The workmanship of our present subject is quite different. Pillow-made lace is built upon no substructure. It is a representation of a pattern obtained by twisting and plaiting threads. In the midst of the endless combinations of forms inspired by the sight of objects of all sorts, men, animals, flowers, leaves, fruits, as well as historic treatments in depicting such forms, that which in primeval times claimed respect as being a pattern, now seems to relegate itself to a position, which, if not considered to be contemptible, is at least so humble as to pass into insignificance. Nevertheless, students of the history of ornament find much that is admirable and instructive in the simplest juxta-posings of lines and curves. And in glancing at the use of patterns wrought in twisted and plaited threads we must not, of course, omit to note patterns of primitive character.

II. The ancestry of laces made on the pillow may be found in examples of primitive twistings and plaitings of fibres and threads. In my first lecture I alluded to a few such examples, and I hope you will excuse me if I again briefly remind you of them. They must be dissociated from works of the loom. They come into the class of rope, cord, and twine making. They are also nearly related to smaller cords, such as corset laces, sleeve laces, boot laces, and to another branch of the same family, namely, narrow braids and tapes. Rope making was known by the Egyptians in early times, and it appears probable, if not certain, that this manufacture was at a similar early date practised by Oriental people living much further west, as in the Hindoo Peninsula, and the immense Mongolian Continent. Amongst the peoples living there, the use of ropes and cords for purely utilitarian purposes was apparently followed by the manufacture of finer plaited and twisted cords and threads made of finer materials than rough fibres, such as coloured silks and metallic threads, wires, or delicate metal strips for decorative purposes. These came "in response to the first spiritual want of barbarous man," which, as Carlyle says, is decoration. At what date fringes were used it is perhaps impossible to say. Besides fringes, there seem to be coeval fine twisted threads

upon which to string pearls, precious stones, and beads for personal adornment. As well as these we should not forget girdles or cinctures, which come to us from impenetrable epochs of religious myths. Nets of plaited, golden, and silken threads were worn by Grecian women. Fillets for binding their hair and foreheads were often narrow braids made with silken and metallic threads. Müller specifies the *diadema*, or fillet, which was placed among the hair, and was of equal breadth all round the head. The *tænia* was usually a broader fillet with two narrower ones at each end. Hercules and athletes are represented as wearing fillets composed of several *tæniæ* twisted together.

III. We saw an example of the art of plaiting and twisting cords together for borders, 800 years before Christ in Assyria. But the design of this was quite primitive. This primitiveness of design in twisting and plaiting threads appears to have continued for a long time. A different treatment of borders occurs upon the costume of certain Dacians who are depicted in the famous column, coming before the Emperor Trajan. (Fig. 1.) This is some 900 years later than the Assyrians,

Fig. 1.

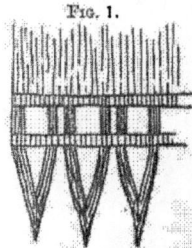

Border from Dacian costumes, sculptures on Trajan's column (2nd century).

IV. Evidences of similar minor details of costume from the 2nd to the 12th century are scattered, and rather difficult to obtain. Something, however, can be gleaned from early Christian sculptures, frescos, and Mosaics, and from Byzantine works of art.

V. As I mentioned above, the term lace has long been applied to braids and such like. Gold braid especially, or as it is called, gold lace, is of ancient origin. Scandinavians and Danes apparently made such gold lace, remnants of which have been discovered buried in England.

VI. Before stockings came to be knitted, Romans and Barbarians used to encase their legs in strips of coarse, plaited, and woven material. These braids, as they might be called, were neatly plaited round the leg, from the knee to the ankle, as may be seen in the leg coverings on an early sculpture, probably of the 2nd century, if not earlier, of the "Good Shepherd."

VII. But I must not detain you with these instances of antique plaitings and twistings. We have to arrive at the use of finer twistings and plaitings as they may occur in decorating edges of costume. Refined and graceful little ornaments, consisting very much of small golden and silken threads plaited to form flattened cords, appear to have been common in the early 15th century. These little ornaments are frequently indicated along the borders of dresses and robes, such as those painted by Gentile da Fabriano, Fra Angelico (Figs. 2, 3,

FIG. 2.

A sketch, with indications of ornament along neck and cuffs. From a painting of Fra Angelico da Fiesole (14th and 15th century).

and 4), and Carlo Crivelli. These names particularly occur to me as I have noted examples of the ornamented work we are considering, in pictures by them.

FIG. 3.

Sketch of gold thread ornament, taken from a robe painted by C. Crivelli (15th century).

VIII. About the time of these artists, that is from 1387 to 1493, the wearing of linen garments develops. While women wore linen wound round

FIG. 4.

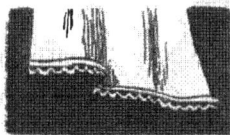

Sketch of veil, with border of open loops, taken from a painting by Botticelli (15th century).

their heads and necks, the ends falling over their shoulders, men wore scarcely anything which we should now recognise as a collar. A minute indication of an under-linen shirt appeared above the low out jacket, plaited, or hanging loosely from the neck.

IX. In Holbein's time, which carries us into the middle of the 16th century, the linen collar had come into fashion, as may be seen from his various portraits. Along these early collars, and also upon the first ruffs, a series of small loops, made of plaited threads, was fastened. This sort of trimming was called "purling," and is similar to the series of loops shown upon the edge of a cloth in Fig. 4. The purse of the carpenter, in the Canterbury tales, is "purled with latoun." Latoun appears to have been a sort of metal-twisted thread. The purling, in its application to collars and ruffs, then, was just the reverse of those Italian thread ornaments depicted by Crivelli and others, which were fastened on to the stuff of the dress, as in Figs. 2 and 3. The purl was open thread work, attached to the edge of a border, and was in use in the 15th century.

X. An interesting inventory of articles belonging to the Sforza family in 1493 contains mention of a pointed border made with "doii fuxi" two bobbins perhaps, or else knitting or hooked needles. And this pointed border has been much relied upon by different writers as being early pillow lace. I think, however, we might correctly surmise that it was a "purling." And if we may call "purling" lace, then plaited and twisted lace work belongs to the 15th century. It is, however, almost as much a lace as the bolder Assyrian and Roman fringings.

XI. We need not perhaps here dive into etymological depths for the origin of the word lace. The meaning attaching to it has like that of many other words undergone change. Long before plaiting and twisting had been applied to produce rich and varied designs, the word lace had described the plaited threads used in the manners above mentioned. And of this we have a remarkable instance in an Harleian MS. of the time of Henry VI. and Edward IV., about 1471. Directions are given in it for the making of lace Bascon, lace indented, lace bordered, lace covert, a brode lace, a round lace, a thynne lace, an open lace, lace for Hattys, and such like. The MS. opens with an illuminated capital letter, in which is the figure of a woman making these articles. But her implements are not those with which lace of ornamental quality from the middle of the 16th century and onwards has been made. A clear description is given how threads in combinations of two, threes, fours, fives to tens and fifteens were twisted and plaited together. Instead of the well-known pillow, bobbins, and pins with which pillow lace is now made, the hand was used. Each finger of a hand had the function assigned to it of serving as a peg. The writer of the MS. says that it shall be understood that the first finger next the thumb shall be called A, the next B, and so on. According to the sort of twisted cord or braid which had to be made, so each of the four fingers, A, B, C, D, might be called upon to act like a reel, and to hold a "bowys," or bow, or a little ball of thread. Each ball might be of different colour from the other. A "thynne lace" might be made, with three threads, and then only fingers A, B, C would be required. A "round lace" stouter than the "thynne" lace might require the service of four or more fingers. By occasionally dropping the use of the thread from certain fingers, a sort of indented lace or braid might be made. But when a lace of more importance had to be made, such as broad lace for "Hattys," the hands of an assistant were required. In the quaint language of the period, the MS. tells us how we should take a fellow and set him on our right or left hand. Thus the worker would have an additional ten fingers or pegs in the two hands of his assistant. For still more important work, two assistants—one standing on each side of the worker—would be required, and so twenty pegs or reels would come into use. A process like this, involving the employment of so many people to produce an insignificant article of luxury, leads us to reflect upon the immense change which has been effected in four hundred years, not only in respect of the improved allotment of labour to willing hands, but also as regards the increased demand and consumption of trivial articles. The very idea of employing fingers as pegs, sounds ludicrous. The unfortunate men or women who passed their time in holding up their ten fingers, cannot have had as much enjoyment out of their work as that which a confirmed player at cat's cradle derives from his strings. Indeed, according to Adam Smith's opinion upon the division of labour, they "must have lost habits of exertion, and become as stupid and ignorant as it is possible for human creatures to become." Fortunately, however, in the little domain of lace-making, conditions like this were not to last long.

XII. The ingenuity of labour in producing ornaments in plaited and twisted cords, or laces, and of curling them in open loops, and such like, along linen collars and cuffs, was not lost upon designers of patterns. For soon after the publication of designs in "reticella" and "punto in aria," we find designs for "merletti a piombini" (Fig. 5). "Merletti" is the Italian for lace work, and

FIG. 5.

Part of the neck of a shirt, trimmed with "Merletti a Piombini." Italian. Late 16th century.

" piombini" means leaden bobbins. To work a design like that in Fig. 5, it is apparent that implements other than fingers, or even a series of pegs, were necessary. And since traditional practice indicates an origin of implements used, we are more or less forced into an inquiry as to the first employment of the pillow, of bobbins, and of pins, all of which must have been somewhat used for the Venetian patterns of "merletti a piombini" in the latter part of the 16th century. A cushion or pad, on which were fixed stuffs to be embroidered by the needle, was possibly as early in use as the open frame, and this latter was well known in mediæval times and even before then. But an essential of pillow - lace making is the

means of holding in fixed places the little threads as they are being plaited and intercrossed according to the patterns required. This, I think, implies the necessity of pins of some sort. Now, before metal pins were in common use, we had rather the reverse of this process. Instead of the balls of thread being pendent, free to be thrown over the other, and thereby to twist and plait threads into patterns, we saw that balls or " bowys " of thread were, in the 15th century, placed upon fingers, and thus were kept in fixed position, the loose threads coming from them were plaited and twisted. But in pillow - lace making the loose threads from the bobbins are fastened on to the pillow, and the bobbins, with their balls of threads, are constantly thrown about.

XIII. The process of making lace on the pillow is very roughly and briefly, as follows:— A pattern is first drawn upon a piece of paper or parchment. It is then fastened to the pillow. The pillow or cushion may vary in shape. Some lace-makers use a circular flattened pad, backed with a flat, circular board, in order that it may be placed upon a table. Other lace-makers use a well-stuffed round pillow or short bolster flattened at the ends, so that they may hold it between the knees. On the upper part of the pattern are fastened the ends of the threads from the bobbins. The bobbins thus hang over the pattern. The lace worker must be versed in the knowledge of where her fixed points are to be. These fixed points rule the way in which the plaiting and twisting shall follow the pattern. Into these points she puts her pins, as she comes up to them in the course of her work. They are, in lace of simple pattern even, so close together that a dense forest of them is soon massed into a very small compass. Without attempting to convey an idea to you of the growth of such

FIG. 6.

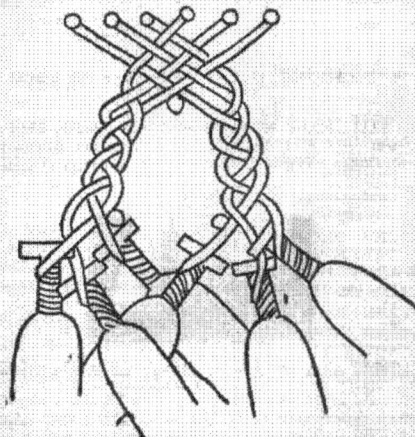

Diagram showing six bobbins in use.

a forest, I will merely take a simple form, and endeavour to show you how, say a triangle, might be worked in pillow lace. These fixed points are mainly necessary for this—one at each angle. Around these points the lace worker would have to work her plaitings. Fig. 6 is intended to indicate this.

XIV. When you look into the minute devices, in which there are forms more complicated than a triangle, you may realise the extraordinary labour involved in pillow-lace making. This, at least, I think, is pretty clear, namely, that the method of making this kind of lace is totally different from that of needle-point lace. Yet often do we so slightly acquaint ourselves with the characteristics of our possessions, that we placidly call a piece of pillow-made lace needle-point lace, and vice versa. Anyone who owns a piece of lace ought to know something of how it was made. A realisation of the pains and troubles expended and caused in producing it should increase our appreciation of it. We may regret the tremendous amount of labour. Still, whether we regret it or not, a piece of lace is a record—proper or improper, but, nevertheless, a record—of labour and time expended. And expenditure of labour and time, devoted either to the production of an ironclad or a bit of lace, seems, I think, worth that recognition which a knowledge of it forces upon us.

XV. You will have remembered the "purled" edges of plaited thread and silk, and the "merletti a piombini," in making which pins became necessary. Almost coincidently with the development of the "merletti a piombini," the rapid manufacture and use of metal pins seems to arise. A few years ago, the Commissioners of Patents published some abridgments of specifications of patents. And as regards pins, some interesting facts are stated, which are worth quoting:—"Pins formed of wire seem to have been unknown in England until about the middle of the 15th century, before which time they were larger than the present pins, and were made of boxwood, ivory, bone, and some few of metal." In Richard III.'s time, about 1483, there was a prohibitory statute against the importation of pins. Queen Catherine Howard is said to have imported them into England about fifty years later, and at this time Henry VIII. sanctioned an Act to regulate the "true making of pynnes." They were to be well pointed, with heads firmly soldered on to the stems. The price of them was not to be more than 6s. 8d. (or say, about 80s. of our money) per 1,000. Though used as dress fasteners, it is evident, from their then value, that pins cannot have been at all plentiful. The manufacture of them seems to have been of foreign origin, and when once started, it developed fairly rapidly. On the Continent, in Italy, Germany, Spain, and France, perhaps, pins became almost sufficiently numerous for common use about the latter part of the 16th century. And it is at this period when I think we find that pillow-lace making commenced.

XVI. Of the history of bobbins there is not so much to be said. Little bits of wood, bone or lead, would without much special ingenuity be converted into winders for thread. The shape given to bobbins was a result of convenience in throwing the winders full of thread one over the other. An elongated shape is obviously more suited to such a purpose than a reel. An oft-quoted evidence of

pillow-lace making is an engraving by a Flemish artist of the 16th century—Martin de Vos. He drew a series of plates illustrative of occupations throughout the seven ages. One of them is a girl seated with a square cushion upon her lap, apparently plaiting threads. The drawing is scarcely detailed enough to show the process of the girl's work. A pattern seems to be fixed to her cushion, and six pear-shaped weights or bobbins depend from it. It cannot, I think, be decided that these weights are bobbins. If they are bobbins they are clearly not numerous enough to work such a lace design as that which the size of the roll upon the cushion would warrant one to believe was contemplated. I rather hold to the opinion that the supposed bobbins are weights. In any case, however, assuming that Martin de Vos has drawn a pillow-lace maker at work, his drawing is not so conclusive on the matter as are certain designs by Parasole, published at the end of the 16th century. On these is a statement of the numbers of leaden bobbins to be used for different patterns. Some require 18, others as many as 68 bobbins. Fig. 5 supplies us with a specimen of the sort of plaited and twisted thread-work of the time we are considering.

XVII. Judging from some slightly earlier specimens of nearly similar work, I think that many of the plaited lines in it were plaited separately, in lengths. When a sufficient supply had been worked, then the lengths of these plaitings might be wound round a sort of bobbin. Supplemented by a few other bobbins containing perhaps single threads, a number like 12 or 16 bobbins so charged would probably suffice for working out designs without a multitude of small metal pins. This conjecture is to some extent corroborated by specimens in which we can trace a use of plaited fine cords. The question, however, is somewhat involved, and without wishing to press my idea as to such a method of work, I would merely observe that four or five plaited fine cords used in combination would be but a development of the "purling," which was done with one or two fine cords interplaited.

XVIII. Before entering into the territory of white thread laces of maturer designs, I should like to make one or two remarks upon a work done with stiffened cords or wires, which in some respects allies itself with wire filagree work. This ornamentation in stiffened cords, seems to be earlier, quâ importance of design, than the plaited and twisted thread-work. It was known under the name of "guipure," and was made with gimp. Gimp is a small cord made by closely whipping fine threads of silk or flax, and sometimes little metal strips, round a narrow strip of parchment, or a small bundle of threads, or a wire. It appears to have been in existence in the 15th and 16th centuries in Italy, and France, and Spain. It is an entirely different work from either needle-point, or pillow-lace making. Patterns were made by laying gimps side by side, or singly, bending them to the shape required, and then holding them together by means of little loops of thread. The stiffness of the gimp also served to retain the pattern into which the gimp might be twisted. In spite of this distinctiveness, Venetian needle-point lace, and many laces in which brides or tyes predominate, have been called "guipure." Some gold laces are reasonably called "guipures," perhaps, though the greater portion of the gold laces extant are made after the manner of 17th century pillow-lace making, and are not therefore, as the true "guipure" is, dependent upon the ductile characteristic of gimp or wire for retaining their patterns.

XIX. Returning to pillow-laces proper, I wish to call your attention to the way in which compactly plaited white thread lines developed into flatter lines. An early instance of this we shall see in this specimen (Fig. 7), which dates

FIG. 7.

Plaited and twisted thread-work known as " Merletti a Piombini." About 1580.

from the end of the 16th century. Another development of these flat portions of plaited work may be seen in this specimen (Fig. 8). So flat and

FIG. 8.

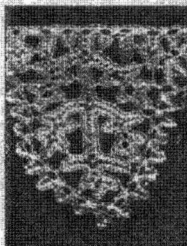

Vandyke or "Dentelle" of pillow-made lace. Late 16th or early 17th century.

close is the work here that it looks almost as though a piece of linen had been used, and from it had been cut out the various forms. However, all this is plaited and twisted thread-work done upon a pillow. Somewhat similar to this in respect of work are the *passements au fuseau* used in France in the early 17th century.

XX. You will, in the two recent specimens, have observed that the flat portions resemble narrow braids or tapes. Here is another specimen in which what might be called a tape treatment is quite apparent (Fig. 9). We have, therefore, soon come to a period in early twisted and plaited thread lace-making, when means had been devised for rendering broad and narrow forms, fine and heavy lines. In my last lecture I referred to the employment of tape for making ornamental work like lace. A specimen of tape lace, with a ground of meshes, lies on the table.

XXI. The art of pillow-lace making was not so strictly confined to geometrical patterns as

was that of needle-point lace-making. Curved forms, almost at the outset of pillow-lace making, seemed to have been found as easy of execu-

FIG. 9.

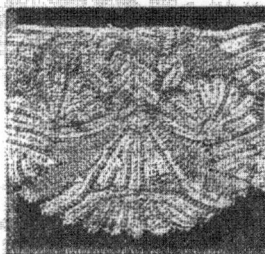

[Flemish pillow lace. 17th century.

tion. One reason for this, no doubt, is] that the twisted and plaited work was, as we have seen, not constrained by a foundation of any kind. The plaitings and twistings gave the workers a greater freedom in reproducing designs. They could be intertwisted between the fixed points of the pattern with comparative facility, whereas, as we remember, the first needle-point lace workers began their lace with a framework of rectilineal lines. Still the pillow-lace worker did not in the matter of pattern proceed altogether faster than the lace worker with a needle. They virtually kept an even pace side by side. If anything, the pillow workers seem to owe more to the designers of patterns for needle-point lace, than otherwise.

XXII. About the early 17th century, important designs for plaited and twisted thread-work were produced. Of such I have a specimen to show you. It is a bed-cover, about 4 ft. 5 in. square. Fig. 10 shows a quarter of the design. The

FIG. 10.

Corner of a bed cover of pillow-made work. 17th century. Flemish.

design is chiefly composed of double-headed German eagles, surmounted by a Germanesque crown, and of insignia of the order of the Golden

Fleece. In the South Kensington Museum it is described as being made of "tape guipure." But this clearly is a misnomer. There is no gimp in it; neither is there tape in the accepted sense of the word. Although no doubt made in separate portions, afterwards fitted and fastened together, the whole was plaited on the pillow. A revised edition of the catalogue of the lace collections at South Kensington will, I hope, shortly correct the errors I have pointed out. But there is another question of interest attaching to the existing description of this fine bed-cover. It was bought by the Kensington Museum from Mr. J. C. Robinson, who had acquired it in Spain. Its proprietor, a member of a noble family, had a history that it was of Spanish workmanship, and had belonged to Philip IV. of Spain. Decorated bed-covers were in the time of that king much affected by wealthy Spaniards. But this fact, and the legend, have not convinced me that it is of Spanish workmanship. Because Frenchmen like Stilton cheese, and because we can buy good Stiltons at Chevet's, in the Palais Royal, we don't decide that Stiltons are made in France. In my first lecture I quoted incidents strongly tending to show that Spain had never been a country of importance in the making of lace—at least, at so early a date as that of this bed-cover. Spain published no lace pattern books. Her archives are replete with records of imported laces. She appears to me to have been as a great political and commercial power, unlike artistic and industrious Italy and Flanders. She may have been more like France, though perhaps less artistic; and France, even in the early 17th century, had little prestige in making laces. France later on acquired a renown, when she, or rather her King and Minister, established lace-making centres. I have not yet found out that Spain took analogous steps towards promoting the art of lace-making. Indeed, as times went on, her political and commercial power declined with apparently no immediate compensating resurrection of artistic industry. Now, Flanders and Spain, during the 16th and part of the 17th centuries, were under one Government. From Flanders, or as they are called Spanish Flanders, Spain imported most of the laces she wanted. Looking to the excellent completeness of this bed-cover, it seems to me to have internal evidence of being the work of Flemish lace-makers. Had it been of Spanish workmanship we should surely have had other specimens more peculiarly Spanish. And we might have expected to have heard of distinct Spanish laces, just as we have Points d'Alençon from France, Valenciennes, Mechlin, and Brussels laces from Flanders, and Honiton from England.

XXIII. For reasons slightly like these I have given in respect of Spain, not having been a lace-making country of importance, I am disinclined to believe in the well-known record, that a native of Nuremberg, Barbara Uttmann, invented in 1561, pillow-lace making. Her tomb in the church-yard at Annaberg, is a construction apparently of the present century. The people who erected it have inscribed upon it, "Here lies Barbara Uttmann, died 14th January, 1575, whose invention of lace in the year 1561 made her the benefactress of the Hartz Mountains." The sort of work which she is said to have made and taught to

the people was a species of knitting. She was assisted in this by certain refugees from Flanders. It is quite possible that she may have made some sort of purling or even little borderings and insertions like the "merletti a piombini" of the Venetians. But since the Venetians directly influenced the Flemish, Barbara Uttmann's adoption of Flemish work can, I think, hardly be called an invention. I mention this point in connection with German laces, which by the way have not acquired any artistic reputation, since an idea seems to have got about that Barbara Uttmann was an original inventress. Early Flemish edgings are similar to the Venetian "merletti a piombini."

XXIV. We need perhaps trace the development of "brides" or tyes and other details in pillow-lace making. The history of them would be similar to that I gave in respect of needle-point work.

XXV. As I have before remarked, design in pillow lace very much followed that in needle-point; and this we may see by comparing these two specimens (Fig. 11 and 12). In both speci-

FIG. 11.

Venetian needle-point lace.

mens we have the scrolls held together by tyes. The tyes are ornamented with little "picots," or loops, and fillings-in, or "modes," are noticeable in both. In the pillow lace (Fig. 12), however,

FIG. 12.

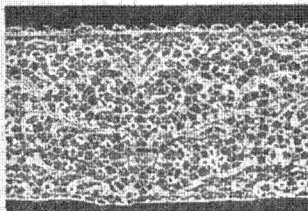

Pillow-made lace. 17th century.

there are no such raised masses as those of compact button-hole stitched work which we saw in the needle-point specimen. The general appearance of this specimen is quite according to a piece of Venetian scroll pattern, although it is flatly worked. Much of this scroll work, sometimes with tyes and sometimes with grounds of meshes, was done on the pillow, both in Italy and Flanders. The last specimen I showed you may, perhaps, be Italian. Here, however, is a specimen (Fig. 13) presumed to be Flemish. A great deal of this sort of lace

FIG. 13.

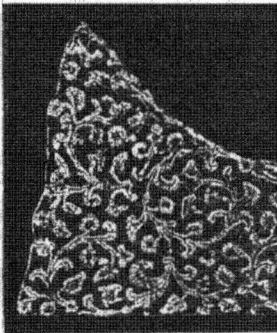

Pillow-made lace, "à brides." Flemish. 17th century. Sometimes called "Point d'Angleterre."

was imported into England in the middle of the 17th century, and went under the name of "Point d'Angleterre."

XXVI. The real English lace of this time was commonly known as "bone lace," and was apparently so-called because it was made with bone bobbins. It was a lineal descendant of the "purling" of Chaucer's time, and the plaited and twisted thread trimming to Queen Elizabeth's ruff. We may see border lace, probably bone lace, sculptured on the tomb of Lady Doddridge, at Exeter, and upon other monuments of the 17th century elsewhere. Such lace was allied in style of make and design to the Venetian "merletti a piombini." Bone lace was the name by which most English pillow lace made during the 17th century was known. In Charles II.'s time its manufacture was of sufficient importance to demand Parliamentary attention. We had been influenced by Flemish pillow laces, and were, no doubt, doing our best to imitate them. But our English imitations were not fine and artistic enough to please noble and wealthy people, who accordingly, as in other countries, obtained their supplies of lace from abroad, and chiefly from Flanders. Still it was thought wise to stimulate our bone-lace manufacture by stringently prohibiting importations of Flemish lace. To evade these stringent prohibitions, and to enable English lace dealers to supply the country with the esteemed Flemish laces, or as they had been called, "Points d'Angleterre," our manufacturers obtained the services of Flemish lace-makers, and induced some to settle in England. This took place about 1662, a date which closely corresponds with the time when France, by the help of Venetian employés, was thinking of establishing her lace-making centres. France, however, more under paternal government than constitutional Parliamentary England, seems to have been the more successful of the two countries in obtaining celebrity for her newly adopted industry. "Points d'Alençon," I am afraid, have always been more prized than Honiton

pillow lace. Bishop Berkeley in the early 18th century makes a remark upon the relative values set upon English, French, and Flemish laces. "How," he asks, "could France and Flanders have drawn so much money from other countries for figured silks, lace, and tapestry, if they had not had their Academies of Design." England has, however, now gone beyond France in the number of her Schools of Art, and through a solid progress of imperial and local co-operation she may soon be able to boast of a larger number of provincial museums, which in an important sense may become academies of design for the benefit of our manufactures.

XXVII. But we must return to our inquiries as to the development of pillow-lace making. We were particularly discussing pillow-made scroll designs held together by brides. Turning to pillow laces with grounds of small meshes, I have here a specimen of such work, and one in which a floral and more naturalistic treatment is noticeable (Fig. 14). Of about the same period—that is, I

FIG. 14.

Pillow-made lace, "à réseau." Flemish. 17th century.

think, near 1660—we have pillow laces in which other ornaments, such as heraldic devices and figures, were introduced. This (Fig. 15) is, perhaps, an Italian pillow lace of this period.

FIG. 15.

Pillow lace, with ground of meshes. Italian or Flemish. 17th century.

XXVIII. On the table are examples of Italian pillow lace, with a scroll pattern of conventional drawing, done with a ground of meshes. I am afraid that time will not allow me to trace the development of the various plaitings used at different lace-making centres for the meshed grounds or réseaux. Generally speaking, I do not think that these réseaux came to be made before the

17th century. The Flemish makers appear to have excelled in producing them; and there are three important classes of them which I will now proceed to show you. We may take the Mechlin first. Mechlin, as a lace-making centre, dates from early in the 17th century, at least. Here are two specimens of characteristic Mechlin laces; the one with a close design, in which appear boys blowing horns, and carrying bows and arrows, is in the style of Louis Quatorze ornament, while the other, with a ground sprinkled with little roses, is some 70 or 80 years later. A feature in Mechlin lace is the thread or *cordonnet* which outlines the pattern; and another is the particular plaiting of the threads forming the meshes (see Fig. 16). When a

Fig. 16.

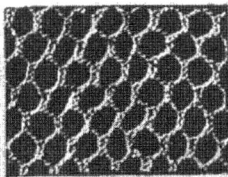

Enlargement of meshes in Mechlin lace grounds, showing the two plaited and four-twisted sides in each hexagonal mesh.

cordonnet and this sort of mesh appear in a pillow-made lace, it is safe to consider the lace to be of Mechlin manufacture.

XXIX. The second of the important pillow laces is the Valenciennes. I will show you the meshes first of all. You here observe that the threads composing the sides of the mesh are plaited (see Fig. 17). No sides, as in the Mechlin

Fig. 17.

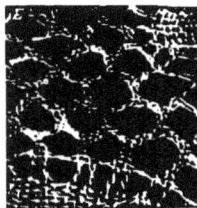

Enlargement of meshes in Valenciennes laces, showing the plaiting for all sides of the mesh.

meshes, are merely of twisted threads. No outlining thread or *cordonnet* is used in Valenciennes lace. The pattern is flat, as you see it in this specimen of late 17th century. (Fig. 18.) This Fig. 19*a* is a specimen of later date, after the middle of the 18th century, when the patterns for lace consisted of flowers and buds sprinkled upon the ground, as we saw it, not only in the Mechlin lace, but also, during our last lecture, in designs for Point d'Alençon. The second specimen 19*b* might be

called a piece of "Fausse Valenciennes." The work is less regular, and the meshes are differently plaited. The third specimen, 19*c*, is a piece of present century Valenciennes lace, made probably at Ypres, and is a much more wiry and less soft-looking

Fig. 18.

Valenciennes pillow lace.

lace than the old "Vraie Valenciennes" of the 18th century. An interesting example of a French lace, done in the style of Valenciennes, with ill-drawn

Fig. 19.

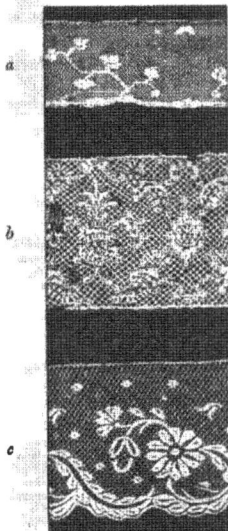

Pillow lace.
"Vrai Valenciennes."
Late 18th century.
French.

Pillow lace.
Valenciennes.
Early 18th century.
French.

Pillow lace.
Valenciennes.
Made at Ypres.
Flemish.

Scripture figures and legends, lies on the table. There are indications that the date of its production was about the first ten years of the 18th century. XXX. Now a third important pillow-made lace is the Brussels. In Brussels laces we find many sorts of designs. Some are placed on a groundwork of brides, others upon meshes. The plaiting of the meshes of Brussels lace is different from that of either Mechlin or Valenciennes (see Fig. 20). The plaited side of a Brussels mesh is longer than that of a Mechlin mesh, otherwise these two latter

FIG. 20.

Enlargement of mesh of Brussels ground, showing the four-twisted and two-plaited sides in each mesh.

sorts of meshes are much alike. But a further distinctive mark of Brussels pillow lace is the raised plaited *cordonnet* or edging which marks

FIG. 21.

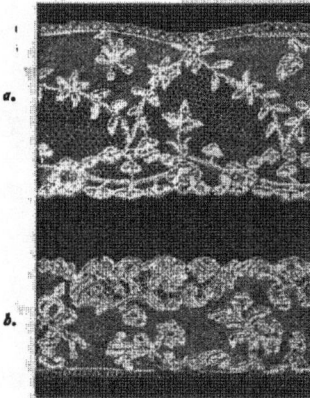

a.   Pillow lace. Brussels. 18th century.

b.   Needlepoint and pillow lace. Brussels, 18th century

the patterns. This you might notice in this specimen (Fig. 21a). This piece dates from about

the commencement of the 18th century, and the pattern is remarkable as being a pillow-lace rendering of an Alençon design. The second specimen (Fig. 21b) is of the same period. It is a mixture of needle-point and pillow lace. The floral details are worked with a needle and the ground is pillow made. The two specimens shown in Fig. 22 are portions of lappets. Fig. 22a is again an example of an adaptation of a Point d'Alençon pattern rendered in pillow lace. The rough indications of the variety of devices introduced into this lappet do poor justice to the extremely elegant manner in which the threads themselves have been plaited to represent the forms of flowers, birds, variegated

FIG. 22b.   FIG. 22a.

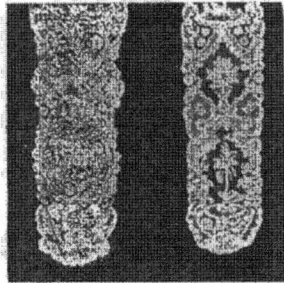

Lappets of pillow-made lace. Brussels, 18th century.

"modes," &c., actually shown in the original lace. The second lappet (Fig. 22b) is of close floral design, and this close arrangement of flowers and leaves, broken by small interspersed mesh grounds, has been considered to be a mark of early Devonshire lace. But the workmanship is precisely like the Brussels lace, and I am inclined to assign to such piece a Brussels rather than a Devonshire origin.

XXXI. Of the various methods used by Brussels lace-workers in executing portions separately, of bringing them and fixing them together to form a whole piece, as well as of the many combinations of needle-point and pillow-lace making, I am sorry not to be able now to speak. Such details would, if justly treated, supply matter enough for a separate lecture. The specimens upon the table are a small index of the variety of patterns worked by the Mechlin, Valenciennes, and Brussels pillow-lace makers, and some of them are, as you will see, of beautiful finish in workmanship, as well as of intricate design.

XXXII. My object this evening has been to place before you a summary of incidents respecting lace made on the pillow, and I hope I have to some extent shown you that it is a branch of the art of lace-making originating from a source different from that of needle-point lace-making, and yet, in the progress of its design and pattern growth, becoming much allied with that of needle-point lace.

LECTURE IV.—Delivered Monday, May 9, 1881.

Résumé as to styles of design in hand-made lace. Traditional patterns. Modern hand-laces at Burano, Bruges, Honiton, &c. Sketch of the development of inventions for knitting and weaving threads to imitate lace. Differences between machine and hand-made laces.

I. This evening, in my concluding lecture, I propose to take a passing survey of a few of the principal topics in the history of the art of lace-making, to which I have called attention.

II. In tracing the history of the two great divisions of lace-making by hand, needle-point and pillow, I have sought to establish a gradual development of the art, rather than to insulate it by itself, and to regard it as some freak of handicraft of unaccountable spontaneous birth.

III. Needle-point lace-making is distinctly a child of embroidery ; pillow lace-making, a lineal descendant of plaited thread-work and fringes. Both chiefly owe such fame as they have acquired to the beauty and variety of form imported to their productions by the genius of designers of patterns. When artists considered free threads (looped, plaited and twisted) as a fitting vehicle for representation of patterns, a higher career for the employment of looping, plaiting, and twisting commenced. This career shows first signs of development in Venice early in the 16th century. From Venice, fancy, fashion, imitation, and other such ever lively influences, spread the newly-developed white thread-work to other countries. In each country where the art happened to become implanted, the special circumstances of the various people gave it some sort of character, either in a strong or a weak degree.

IV. Thus, the laces of Flanders, in their first stages of growth linking themselves to those of Italy and Venice, later on are entirely different in appearance from their ancestors. This is particularly so as regards the Valenciennes, Mechlin, and Brussels pillow lace. French needle-point laces, again, have, as we have seen in the Point d'Alençon, a specialty in appearance which, without the gradual steps by which we have traced them from the "Punt in aria," might be said to have no likeness to their antecedent Venetian parents. English laces, on the other hand, are not so markedly detached from the general family. On the whole, they closely resemble Brussels, Mechlin, and Valenciennes laces, though at the same time Honiton lace, with its prettinesses of floral devices, may claim to stand by itself. In respect of other countries, the methods of making lace are similar to those involved in one or other of the categories above specified. The designs of such laces are either direct imitations of older laces, or else are of so unmarked and general a character as to lose themselves in the primitiveness of design, which may be said to be the common property of all form-depicting countries.

V. I have prepared a diagram to show, in a general manner, the periods of different styles of patterns in lace-making (Fig. 1, p. 30). These extend from 1540 to the present time; and I have roughly divided them into seven epochs, some of them overlapping, preceding, and succeeding ones. Upon the diagram you will observe black bands of varying size. The first one is intended to indicate the growth and progress of needle-point lace-making ; the second, that of pillow-lace making ; and the third, that of machine-made lace.

VI. In respect of hand-work, I think needle-point lace developed itself sooner than pillow-made lace. But the difference in date is possibly so slight as not to be worth close inquiry. Needle-point, at starting, took the stronger growth of the two perhaps. It seems to have reached a climax from between 1650 to 1720. Then it declined, and from 1790 to the present time it seems to have preserved an even life. It is now not of such strong life as that of either pillow-made or machine-made lace. As regards pillow lace, it appears to have expanded in vigour, as needle-point declined, so that its period of supremacy might be placed at from 1680 to 1780. From 1790 to about 1850 the annual quantity of pillow-made lace became smaller perhaps than formerly, but soon it revived, and now seems to be larger. As to machine lace, that may be said to have begun its life with the machine-making of nets about 1770, and in a hundred years to have become probably more than a hundred times as important in quantity as needle-point and pillow lace combined.

VII. We have discussed, principally in their respective classes, those laces which have celebrity for beauty of pattern, as well as for fineness of workmanship. And we have seen that these come from Venice, Alençon, Valenciennes, Mechlin, Brussels, and I think it would be unpatriotic if we did not add Honiton. But, now, we should give a share of attention to other less celebrated laces, and I will therefore show you a few specimens of them. Of German provincial laces—evolutions, as we may take them to be of Barbara Uttmann's 16th century work—there are two pieces, both from the district of the Erzgebirge (Fig. 2, p. 31). Although made recently, the patterns displayed in these laces might almost be of any date. They are, evidently, traditional patterns, handed down through generations of lacemakers, without much modification since the time when they were first made, which was, probably, in the 17th century. The upper specimen, with its large circular device and quaint plant form, is similar to some lace made in

Holland. The lower is what would be called a sort of "torchon" lace. The principles of design in this are simple, the pattern consisting of various lozenge shapes. It is not unlike that used by the peasants of Dalecarlia, in Sweden, who, for some hundred and fifty years, have made this sort of lace, only in coarser thread than that used by the Germans.

VIII. Patterns, somewhat similar, have been used by the inhabitants of the Island of Crete. There is a large collection of Cretan laces at the South Kensington Museum. Little, if anything, is known

Fig. 1.

	I.	II.	III.	IV.	V.	VI.	VII.
DATE	1540 to 1590.	1590 to 1650.	1620 to 1650.	1650 to 1720.	1720 to 1780.	1790 to 1851.	1851 to 1861.
STYLE OR PATTERN	Geometrical forms as worked in Reticella and Punt in aria. No "toilé" or meshed ground used.	Introduction of floral and human forms and slender scrolls, held together by "brides" or "ties."	Development of scrolls, and elaboration of details in scroll patterns. Commencement of "toilé" or meshed grounds.	Arrangements of detached ornamental details. More naturalistic imitation of flowers and pictorial representation of figures and portraits, and considerable use of ground of small meshes.	Designs composed of small details sprinkled over meshed grounds, and perpetuation of the patterns of 1690 to 1720. Use of machine made net commenced about 1770.	Perpetuation of some few traditional patterns, and conventional reproduction in machine laces. Revival of patterns. Repetition of old motives. Loss of freshness in design.	Production of designs, especially those used in regard to their reproduction in machine laces. Mixture of all preceding styles.

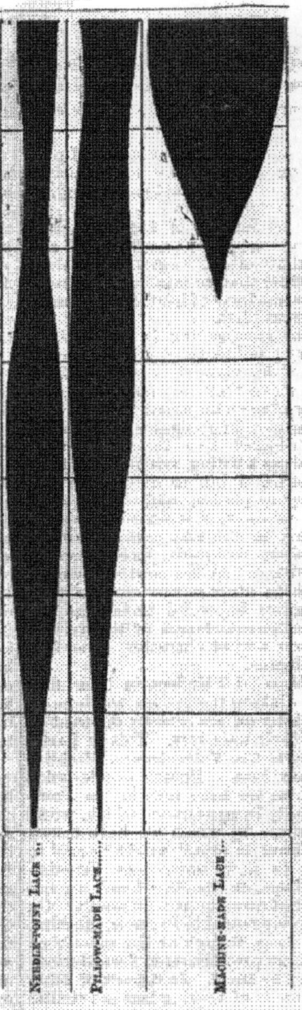

NEEDLE-POINT LACE — PILLOW-MADE LACE — MACHINE-MADE LACE

of the origin of lace-making there. It has a likeness in many respects to the quaint pillow laces of South Italy. Crete has been intimately connected with Venice, and very probably Cretans learnt the art of lace-making from Venetians and other Italians. The workmanship displayed in these Cretan laces is remarkable. The ability to plait and twist threads is almost as good as that of artistic lace-makers at Brussels and Mechlin. The Cretan laces are chiefly of silk. The patterns in the majority of the samples at the South Kensington Museum are outlined with one, two, or three bright coloured silken threads, which form the *cordonnet* of the lace. As a rule, the motives of the Cretan lace patterns are traceable to orderly arrangement and balance of simple symmetrical

FIG. 2.

German pillow-made laces. 18th century.

and geometrical details, such as diamonds, triangles, and odd polygonal figures. Sometimes the patterns owe their origin to untutored imitation of a blossom or leaf. Here are two specimens of the Cretan lace (Fig 3, *a b*). I have specially selected one of the more ambitious of the Cretan design, that

FIG. 3.

Pillow-made laces from South Italy (16th century), and from Crete. Early 18th century.

in which we have a line of stately figures, holding hands, strongly suggestive of those delightful persons which are cut out of paper for infantile delectation. The specimen beneath is of silk. Lace, I believe, is no longer made in Crete. The specimen in which two birds appear, together with forms, the meaning of which I cannot elucidate, is of South Italian lace (Fig 3 *c*).

IX. From Italy we may cross Bohemia, and place ourselves in Central Russia. Pillow lace has been made there for over a hundred years, by peasants of different districts. Following in the wake of fashion of Western Europe, Russia, under Peter the Great, towards the end of the 17th century, took up with lace-making. A silk lace factory was then established, but no cultivated artistic spirit ever raised the productions of this factory to special distinction. The patterns now used by Russian lace-makers bear all the stamp of traditional provincial patterns used by different European peasantries. Lace is made in Russia in the districts of Belev, Vologda, Riazan, and Mzensk. This scalloped border (Fig 4 *a*) is made in the Belev district. Its

FIG. 4.

Russian pillow laces. 19th century.

big meshed ground is plaited similarly to Italian and Valenciennes grounds. The border (Fig 4 *b*) with small vandyked edge reminds us of the style of German and Swedish "torchon" lace. It is also suggestive of a lace made a few years ago at Ripon, in Yorkshire.

X. Thus, over a great area in Europe, we may judge how lace-making of nearly uniform style of design has spread itself. It is a humble and rather precarious means of support for peasants, and in this condition it cannot be expected to rise to any status of artistic importance. Sometimes a little stimulus is given to the efforts of one set of peasants, sometimes to another, as for instance, at the present time, when fanciers of hand-made lace purchase in fairly considerable quantities trimmings and borders of Russian lace.

XI. From specimens, the origin of which is identified with various countries, we may pass to lace-makers themselves, their training to the practice of the art, and a few of the circumstances of their practice.

XII. The name manufacture seems at once to call into view smoky towns with lofty many-storeyed buildings, high chimneys, roaring furnaces, belching steam-engines, and crowds of busy workmen. In such places we may, in a single great house, pass from masses of raw material, and, traversing a series of rooms, note in each, perhaps, some phase in the metamorphosis of, say, clods of damp clay into stores of hard clear-glazed vases, cups, saucers, and such like, or of pigs of iron into workmen's utensils and complicated machinery.

XIII. Now, as regards lace made by machinery, the process of converting the raw material into a length of lace is not so complete as either of the two instances above referred to. Threads used for lace are made in a manufactory distinct from the lace manufactory. A like arrangement exists in respect of hand-made laces, that is to say, that the lace-worker is not also her own spinner of thread, though three hundred years ago, the spinner of threads, with her distaff and wheel, would sit in the same room with the needle worker; but this association of two separate employments in time was broken up, and division of labour, a subject full of interest, and intimately connected with the development of organisation in respect of manufactures, arose.

XIV. The present position of lace-workers does not appear to differ very materially from what it always has been, and some interesting facts concerning it have been kindly supplied by Mrs. Percy Smith, in regard to Belgian pillow-lace workers at Bruges. Lace there is made by children and by adults. The children begin work in convent schools, when they are as young as five or six. They first make a small "torchon" lace, smaller and less elaborate than specimen in Fig. 4b (p. 801), but of that character of work, in which you will not observe any subtleties of "modes" or fillings-in, like those we saw in the fine specimens of Brussels lace exhibited last Monday. Many of the Belgian generation of artisan children are thus, early in life, grounded in the art of lace-making. This grounding takes up a principal part of their school-time, for whilst two hours a day are given to reading, writing, and arithmetic, the remainder of the day is devoted to lace-making. In a few parish schools, which are distinct from convent schools, lace-making is taught, but in a lesser degree than in the convent schools.

XV. As regards the class of lace-making women, the work by them is done in their cottages in the town. In summer you may look down long and wide back streets of the town, and see hundreds of women in groups of three, four, and five outside their cottages plying their bobbins most industriously. In winter if you walked down such streets you would find the women at work, sitting by the windows indoors. It is estimated that there are over 4,000 lace-makers at Bruges, and of these many, doubtless, help to sustain Bruges in her mediæval reputation for pretty faces. Lace-makers have to be careful of their hands, as roughness in the skin is liable to make the lace yellow-looking and dirty, a factor which considerably depreciates its value, hence lace-makers should not also follow agricultural pursuits. The picture of these lace workers at Bruges very much resembles that given by Bishop Berkeley in the 18th century. When he speaks of English labourers in the South, he says, " on a summer's evening, they sit along the streets of the town or village, each at his own door, with a cushion before him, making bone lace, and earning more in an evening's pastime than an Irish family would in a whole day."

XVI. To return, however, to Belgians of the present day, the laces made are collected for the merchants, whose agents, on market day, sit in little boxes, like ticket offices, in the market place. To these the makers bring their laces, which are received and paid for by the agent. At the same time, the agent gives to the worker fresh orders, and serves out the pattern to be done. Every pattern, after it has been worked, has to be brought back to the agent, under penalty of a heavy Government fine, which thus is a protection of designs.

XVII. Now, as regards the design, you may remember how much a good rendering of pattern depends upon the skill of the pricker, who determines where the pins are to be placed as the twisting and plaiting proceed. In convents, the instructors usually undertake to prick the patterns; but for the other body of lace-makers, the pricking is done (at least, in Bruges) almost entirely by one woman, whose renown as a pattern pricker is such, that, at the present time, she has commissions which will take her eighteen months to execute.

XVIII. Coming now to thread used by the workers, it is a curious fact that, although the flax is grown in Belgium, the twisting it by machinery into fine threads is done in England. The thread, when made, however, is not found to be a pure flax thread, for there is a slight admixture of cotton with it; and this imparts a measure of hardness to the lace, a detrimental quality which earlier laces, made with hand-spun thread, do not, fortunately, possess. When lace-makers have to use hand-spun thread, they obtain it from the town of Alost, where Belgian spinners make the thread. This purer and softer thread is used for the better qualities of Belgian needle-point lace, specimens of which lie on the table. Work of such sort is done to special order; and its price, £12 to £15 per yard for widths of four or five inches, renders it scarce.

XIX. I now wish to offer you a few remarks upon styles of patterns used in the United Kingdom. The laces of Buckinghamshire and Devonshire stand first perhaps amongst English laces. Here is a figure (5, p. 33), showing three sorts of Buckinghamshire lace. In the first one (a) we may notice a variety of fillings in. This variety gives the name of Trolly lace to such specimens. It is of 19th century work, but an adaptation of Mechlin " Trolle Kant," or sampler lace, sent round to dealers and purchasers to show the variety of patterns which the lace-makers happened to [be engaged upon. The other two specimens (b, c) are also of Buckinghamshire workmanship, and like the first, are clearly indebted for patterns and general style to Flanders.

XX. Lace made in Devonshire, at Exeter, Honiton, and elsewhere, is very much in the style of Brussels laces. The little separate sprays of flowers worked on the pillow, and then used in application to net, &c., have to some extent become celebrated. A naturalistic treatment in the drawing of the flowers, and leaves, and insects, which appear in so-called Honiton guipure, or pillow lace with ties, is a distinguishing characteristic of this class of English lace. Sometimes a costly specimen of Honiton lace is made for a special purpose, and

Fig. 5.

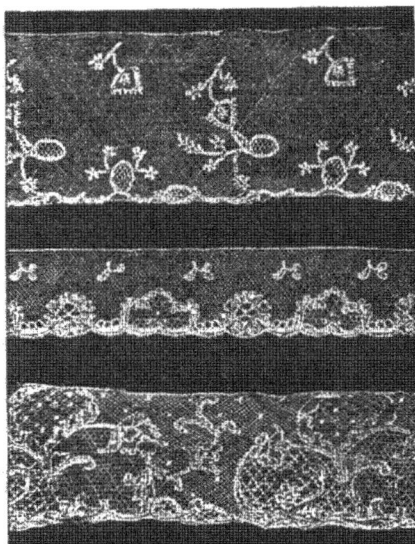

English pillowlaces.   18th century.

then, according to the requirements of the person who may have ordered the work, the lace is made with better care than usual. Of such works we have two important specimens, lent by Messrs. Hayward and by Messrs. Howell and James.

XXI. Although private enterprise and courtly patronage have essayed, and to an extent succeeded, to implant the art of lace-making in the United Kingdom, and although from time to time direct foreign influences have been infused into it, as by refugee Flemings in the 17th century, a practice of the higher ornamental phases of the art has never fairly and successfully rooted itself here. Before artistic lace-making had fairly developed in the later years of the 16th century, England had been gradually slipping away from Papal supremacy. Convents and monasteries, in which those branches of fine art have ever been fostered, almost disappeared from England, and no institutions so strict for artistic and disciplinarian purposes succeeded to them. To a cause like this we might assign the failure of England to become a leading producer of lace. A Frenchman, who wrote in 1852 upon lace-making, gives, however, a different cause, which is amusing. Granting that if the product of all products, requiring grace in its development, be lace, how, he asks, is it possible to find grace in England? Do you want proof of this, writes this Frenchman? Look,

then, at an Englishman walking; look at him when he makes a bow; look at him as he takes a seat, as he enters a room, as he hands a cup to anyone, and so forth. The conclusion clearly is that the Frenchman was right—we were awkward, we had no grace, and so were incapable of making good lace. But now, remembering that such observations were made thirty years ago, when England, "perfidious Albion," was in her final stage of perfidy towards France, it will not surprise us much to find a vast and admitted improvement in regard to much of our lace-work. In the matter of machine lace, a subject we shall shortly touch upon, we may boast of as good quality of design and workmanship as exists anywhere; while for our hand-made laces, the specimens of Honiton pillow lace and Irish needle-point lace are surely re-assuring to anyone who is doubtful of British powers in this art. At the same time, in speaking of this Irish needle-point lace, called "lacet," I must tell you that the greater part, if not the whole of it, is produced in Irish convents. Of other Irish laces I may say that there are about eight so-called different sorts. But Limerick lace is a tambour embroidery, I think; Carrickmacross lace is a sort of cut muslin work; pearl tatting, or "Frivolite," is clearly neither genuine pillow nor needle-point lace, and the varieties of crotchet imitations do not of course belong to either of the two important branches of the art.

XXII. Some thirty odd years ago, Parliament voted money for the encouragement of normal schools for lace-making in Ireland. From causes which do not require discussion, the Governmental encouragement was withdrawn, after having existed for some ten years, and the schools are now closed.

XXIII. Lace is made by Irish peasants in their cottages and cabins. They work chiefly from traditional patterns. No inspection for instructive purposes, or for suggestion of new patterns is provided, save such as may be derived from the relations between lace-dealer and lace-maker. The peasants are left somewhat to their own devices, and so one does not look for much artistic work from them. The better Irish lace—lace which may rank with lace of the finer classes altogether—comes from the convents, where fine old patterns and well selected new designs can be re-produced.

XXIV. Returning once more to the Continent, we shall find, in France, Austria, and Italy, a considerable life in the making of lace by hand. It is a popular fancy to suppose that the art is dead. The patronage which the wealthy can and do accord to the art, stimulates the production of new works, and while such patronage is intelligently and discriminately extended, the art lives.

XXV. From Vienna come occasional specimens of needle-point lace-work. The extraordinarily fine collar of needle-point lace, a modern version of raised Venetian Point of the 17th century, lent by Mrs. Alfred Morrison, was, I believe, made under the direction of a Viennese lace merchant, who employs Bohemian lace-makers. Putting aside the question of design, which in this over-elaborated collar has not the dignity of an Italian 17th century raised scroll point, you will see here an astounding combination of almost incredible minutiæ, executed with a perfection of

C

finish which rivals that displayed in earlier work. Needle-point lace is also made in France, exceptionally, perhaps, but still sufficiently to show that what has been done can be done again.

XXVI. In Italy a new departure has been taken in the making of hand-made laces, at the Island of Burano, near Venice. "This island, in the 16th and 17th centuries, was one of the principal seats of the celebrated lace manufacture of the Venetian provinces. The formation of the school recently established there, and the revival of the art of lace-making in Burano, arose out of the great distress which, in 1872, overtook its inhabitants. The extraordinary severity of the winter of that year rendered it impossible for the poor fishermen, who form the population of the island, to follow their calling. So great was the distress at that time, that the fishermen and their families were reduced to a state bordering on starvation, and for their relief contributions were made by all classes in Italy, including the Pope and the King. This charitable movement resulted in the collection of a fund of money, which sufficed to relieve the immediate distress and leave a surplus applicable to the establishment of a local industry, which seems to be not unlikely to permanently increase the resources of the Burano population.

"Unfortunately, the industry at first fixed upon, namely, that of the making of fishermen's nets, gave no practical result, the fishermen being too poor to purchase the nets. It was then that a suggestion was made by Signor Fambris that an effort should be made to revive the ancient industry of lace-making. Princess Chigi-Giovanelli and Countess Andriana Marcello were asked to interest themselves in and to patronise a school for this purpose. To this application these ladies yielded a ready assent, and at a later period Queen Marguerite graciously consented to become (as her Majesty still is), the president of the institution.

"When Countess Marcello (who from that time has been the life and soul of the undertaking) began to occupy herself with the foundation of the school, she found an old woman in Burano, Cencia Scarpanile, who preserved the traditions of the art of lace-making, and continued, despite her seventy years and upwards, to make "Burano Point." As she, however, did not understand the method of teaching, the assistance was secured of Madame Anne Bellorio d'Este, a very skilful and intelligent woman, for some time mistress of the girls' school at Burano, who in her leisure hours took lessons in lace-making of Cencia Scarpanile, and imparted her knowledge to eight pupils, who, in consideration of a small payment, were induced to learn to make lace.

"As the number of scholars increased, Madame Bellorio occupied herself exclusively in teaching lace-making, which she has continued to do with surprising results. Under Madame Bellorio's tuition, the school, which in 1872 consisted of the eight pupils (who received a daily payment to induce them to attend), now numbers 320 workers, paid, not by the day, but according to the work each performs. In this way they are equitably dealt with, their gains depending on their individual skill and industry.

"In Burano everything is extremely cheap, and a humble abode capable of accommodating a small family may be had for from 600 to 1,000 Italian lire. It is not a rare occurrence to find a young girl saving her earnings in the lace school, in order to purchase her little dwelling, that she may take it as a dower to her husband. Nearly all the young men of Burano seek their wives from among the lacewomen, and the parish priest reported last year facts which showed conclusively that the moral condition of the island, consequent on the establishment of the lace school, has improved in a very striking degree.

"The lace made in this school is no longer exclusively confined, as in the origin it was, to Burano Point, but laces of almost any design or model are now undertaken.

"In order the better to carry out the character of the different laces, the more apt and intelligent of those pupils whose task it is to trace out in thread the design to be worked, have the advantage of being educated by means of drawing lessons from professional artists.

"The 320 workwomen now employed are divided into seven sections, in order that each may continue in the same sort of work, and as far as possible, in the same class of lace. By this method each one becomes thoroughly proficient in her own special department, executes it with greater facility, earns consequently more, and the school on its part gets the work done better and cheaper (although of course cheapness must always be very relative)."

XXVII. Besides specimens of lace now made at Burano, on the table before us, I can show you two slides of the lace. The first (Fig. 6) is a needle-

FIG. 6.

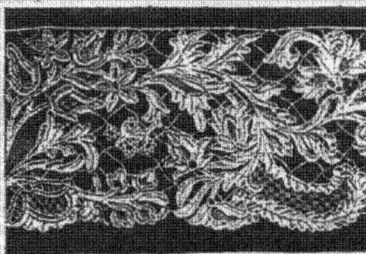

Needle-point lace. Burano. 19th century (1879).

point lace, "à brides," with a marked *cordonnet*. It is rather in the style of so-called Argentan designs. The second (Fig. 7) is more in the style

FIG. 7.

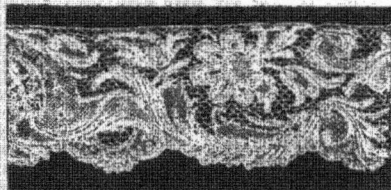

Needle-point lace. Burano. 19th century (1879).

of 17th century Venetian needle-point lace, with a ground of hexagonal "brides" with "picots." We have now to consider machine-made lace. And in approaching this section of my lecture, I must tell you beforehand that it is difficult to attempt to give a short description of the process. Of course, if we had had to discuss the mechanism of man, why and how his mechanism permits the manufacture of lace, in the same way that we may discuss the lace-making machine, the human machine would be the more wonderful of the two. Still, whereas I have devoted two lectures to processes of making lace by hand, and now propose merely to give a portion of a lecture to lace-making by machinery, you will not suppose that this determines the relative importance between the two branches of lace-making by hand and by machinery.

Mr. William Felkin has written a considerable work upon the lace machine. He shows that it is very much from the art of knitting that we trace the origin of the machine for making lace. Knitted caps and hose date in England from the end of the 15th century at least; as various Acts of Parliament testify. Knitted stockings, however, possibly from the difficulty of forming the heels and feet, seem to have been later, for Henry VIII. is said to have had, for ordinary wear, cloth stockings, "except there came from Spain by chance a pair of silk stockings." Even as late as 1610, "so unfashionable were young gentlemen commoners," that George Radcliffe, writing from University College, Oxford, to his mother, asks for a green baize table-cloth, "of which, if too little for my table, I will make a pair of warm stockings." But some 27 years previously to this, the town of Sheffield can claim the credit of having given from its trust funds 13s. 3d. to "William Lee, a poore scholler of Sheffield, towards the settynge him to the University of Chambridge and buyinge him bookes and furniture." This William Lee, who became a clergyman, was for some reasons expelled from his college (St. John's), where he held a fellowship. He appears to have married an innkeeper's daughter, and after the loss of his fellowship soon fell into extreme poverty. In his distress to find a source of income, his inventive faculties were called into play. The only support for his wife and child appears to have been derived from the sale of hand-knitted stockings. Sitting constantly with his wife, the scholar often fixed his attention on her dexterous management of the needles. In course of time he invented a mechanical contrivance, by which stockings might be more quickly knitted than by the hands. This is generally accepted as the first stocking-loom. The news of this invention, which was at once recognised as a formidable rival to hand-work, soon spread, but the antipathy to it prevented its becoming successful in England. Queen Elizabeth regarded with contempt a man's invention of a mechanical weaver of stockings, and the Rev. William Lee's petition to her Majesty for Royal patronage passed unnoticed. From James I., Lee gained as little encouragement. He accordingly went to France. Henry IV. and his minister Sully warmly espoused his cause, and matters went prosperously with Lee until his death. It might from this be supposed that France remained in solitary possession of this valuable invention, but Mr. Felkin tells us that Mr. James Lee, son of Rev. William Lee, soon after his father's death, determined to transplant the manufacture of knitted stockings by machines to England. He accordingly brought frames and experienced workmen to London, and started operations in Old-street-square. Upon this becoming known, a spirit of imitation seized different people. Stocking-knitting frames were set up in Nottingham. Venice, the old home of artistic lace-making, was almost foremost in striving to establish stocking-knitting factories, but her attempts in this direction, through lack of skilled workmen, who should replace plant as it was worn out, soon collapsed. England, however, rapidly developed the number of her stocking looms, and between 1670 and 1695, upwards of 400 such machines were exported to France, Flanders, Spain, Italy, and Sicily. The English Legislature about this time placed its veto upon such exportation. The manufacture in this country continued in great force. Charters were granted incorporating companies for the working of stocking machines, and Parliament was called upon to consider petitions on the matter from the various manufacturing centres. In 1758, Mr. Jedediah Strutt introduced a method of ribbing stockings as they were made, and the machine for so doing was called the Derby rib machine. Other modifications of the stocking machine followed. It was about this time that taste for lace ruled that meshed grounds lightly sprinkled with small ornaments should be the most fashionable laces. Hence fine meshed fabrics like net and tulle seem to have arisen. Manufacturers in London and Nottingham applied themselves to make lace net upon stocking frames, about 1770, and so far as plain nets were concerned, they were successful in producing looped net fabrics of perfect regularity. Early in the present century, Mr. Heathcoat, of Nottingham, invented a machine for making bobbin net. After him came Mr. John Leaver, whose lace-making machines and modifications and improvements of them, to which have been applied the apparatus of the celebrated Jacquard loom, are in use at the present time.

XXX. Broadly speaking, lace-making by machinery is more nearly like the pillow-lace making process than that of needle-point. The machine contrives to twist any desired threads around one another. In pillow-lace making, besides twisting, we have plaiting. This plaiting has not been reproduced by the majority of lace machines. Quite recently, however, a French machine, called the "Dentellière" has been invented to do plaiting. Time will not allow me to refer in detail to the "Dentellière," of which a description has been published in a journal, entitled La Nature, dated 3rd March, 1881. Whilst, as we shall see, the ordinary lace-making machine belongs to the family of weaving machines, the "Dentellière" more nearly resembles the pillow of a lace worker, with the threads arranged over the pillow. In general appearance it looks something like a large semi-circular framework of iron, with thousands of threads from the outer semi-circle converging to the centre, representing the table or pillow. Over this central table is the apparatus which holds the end threads side by side, and which regulates the plaiting of them. The cost of producing lace in this manner is said to be greater at present than by hand, and the mechanism is under revision.

XXXI. In respect now of the lace machine which is in common use, I would ask you to reflect, that the mechanism to obtain and regulate the motions of each thread is intricate, and represents the sum total of much scientific thought, and its application to guide practice over a long course of years. Of the number of threads worked by a Leaver's machine, like that described in the *Journal of the Society of Arts* (18th and 25th Sept., 1874), it may be sufficient to say that there may be some 8,880. Of course the pattern to be worked into lace governs the number of threads. To produce the pattern shown in the *Journal* above-mentioned, 48 bobbin or shuttle threads, and 100 beam or warp threads were employed for each piece of lace. Sixty pieces of lace were simultaneously wrought, and thus sixty times 148 threads were brought into operation. This gives a total of 8,880 threads. Now, each of these 8,880 threads had its own particular duty to perform, and I hope to be able to convey to you some slight notion of these duties.

XXXII. The threads in a Leaver's lace machine then, may be divided, as they are in the loom, into two sets, the one which we may call the warp or beam

FIG. 8.   FIG. 9.

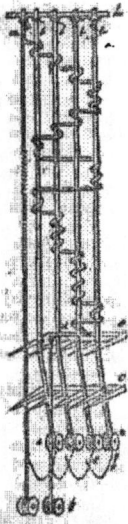

Diagram showing action of a slack weft thread in connection with taut warp threads.

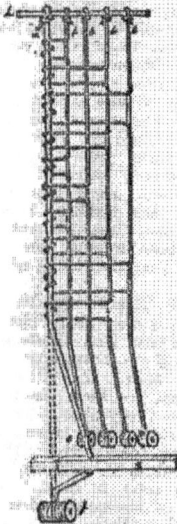

Diagram showing action of taut weft thread in connection with slack warp threads.

threads, and the other the weft or shuttle threads. The ends of both sets of threads are fixed on a cylinder or lace beam, which corresponds in its use with the first row of pins on the pillow, in pillow-lace making. The supply of the threads, warp and weft, is held by reels or bobbins. The reels of the warp threads are different from those

of the weft threads. The warp thread reels are arranged in trays or frames beneath the stage, above which, and between it and the cylinder, the twisting of the weft with the warp threads takes place. The supplies of the weft threads are contained in flattened reels or bobbins, which are of a shape as to be conveniently passed between the stretched warp threads. Each bobbin for the weft thread can contain about 120 yards of thread. By most ingenious mechanism, varying degrees of tension can be imparted to the warp or weft threads. The bobbins of the weft threads, as they

FIG. 10.

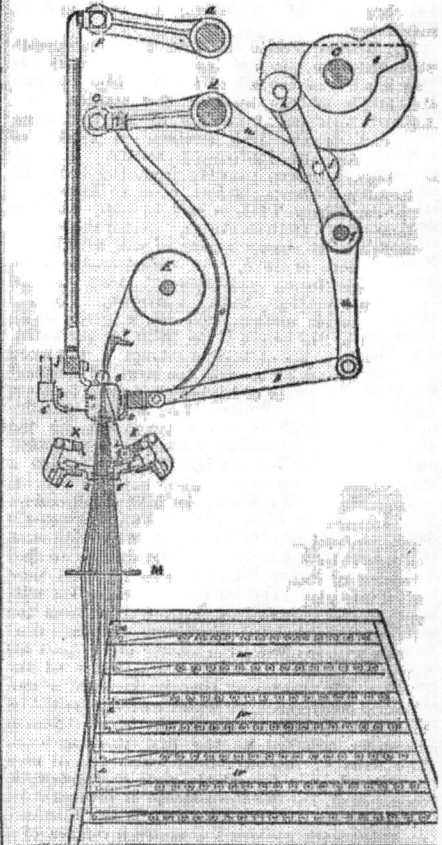

Diagram of principal details in a lace-making machine.

pass like pendulums between the warp threads, are made to oscillate, and through this oscillation the threads twist themselves, or become twisted with the warp threads. As the twistings take place, combs passing through both warp and weft threads compress the twistings. Thus the ordinary machine-made lace may generally be detected by its compressed twisted threads. In it will not be seen any plaiting, such as we find in pillow-lace, or lace made by the "Dentellière" machine. We cannot, moreover, trace in machine lace any simulacrum of button-hole-stitch work, as we have it in needle-point work.

FIG. 11.

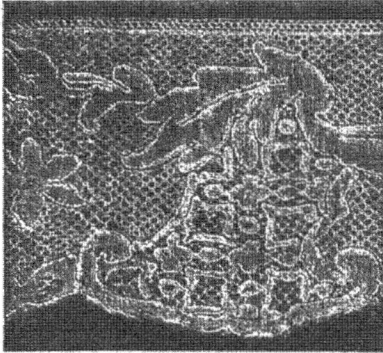

Pillow-made lace. Mechlin. Early 18th century.

XXXIII. The diagrams (Figs. 8, 9, p. 806) are intended to show the effects obtained by varying the tensions of weft and warp threads. For instance, if the weft threads, (b b b b,) in Fig. 8, be taut, and the warp thread (a) be slack, the warp thread will be twisted on to the weft threads. But if the warp thread (a) be taut, and the weft threads (b b b b in Fig. 9) slack, then the weft threads will be twisted on to the warp

FIG. 12.

Machine-made imitation of Mechlin pillow lace.

thread. At the same time we should remember that the twisting in both these cases arises from a conjunction of the movements of the two sets of threads in this matter, namely, the movement from side to side of the beam or warp threads,

and the swinging or pendulum-like oscillations of the bobbin or weft threads between the warp threads.

FIG. 13.

Pillow-made lace. Mechlin. 18th century.

XXXIV. The diagram (Fig. 10, p. 806) represents a section of part of a lace machine, showing E, the

FIG. 14.

Machine-made imitation of Mechlin pillow lace.

cylinder or lace beam, upon which the ends of both warp and weft threads are fixed at starting. Beneath is w w w, a series of trays or beams, one above the other, containing the reels of the supplies of warp threads; c c represents the slide bars, for the passage of the bobbin b, with its thread, from K to K, the landing bars one on each side of the rank of warp threads, s t, are the combs which take it in turns to press together the twistings as they are made. The combs are so regulated that they come away clear from the threads as soon as they have pressed them together, and fall into positions ready to perform their pressing operations again. This by no means exhausts the story of all that the lace machine does. The contrivances for giving each thread a particular tension and movement, at a certain time, are most subtle. They are closely related to the Jacquard system of pierced cards. The machine lace pattern-drafter has to know more of this mathematical calculation than of drawing lines and curves. His work consists, principally, of calculating how many holes shall be punched in a card, and of settling where each hole is to be punched. Each hole regulates the movement of a thread

XXXV. We may now look at a series of specimens of machine-made laces. The first specimen (Fig. 11) is that of a Flemish pillow-lace design of the early 18th century. In it you will notice the variegated appearance of the meshes of the ground. A thread, you see, outlines the pattern, which has a fine linen appearance. Now the manufacturer (see Fig. 12) has merely attempted to reproduce the pattern. His meshes are regular. No outlining thread marks the pattern, which, instead of being filmy, like linen or cambric, is ribbed. This specimen, recently made at Calais with a Leaver machine, which is worked upon the principles I have above mentioned. The cost of this machine lace is 1s. 2d. a yard, and the value of the original is £1 5s. per yard. The next specimen (Fig. 13, p. 37) is that of a piece of Mechlin pillow lace of the late 18th century. In this you will again observe the comparatively slack manner in which the threads in the ornament are twisted and intercrossed. Here is the mechanical counterfeit of this piece (Fig. 14). The ground is similar to wire netting, while the threads to imitate those slack twistings of the original are rigid and much more regular. This, too, was made at Calais. The value per yard of the hand-made lace is £1 10s., whilst that of the machine is 2s. 9d.

XXXVI. I have now a better example of machine imitation of Mechlin lace. Here is the original lace. The appearance of the thread, forming blossoms, which seem to be a kind of sunflower, a series of petals around a dark central disc, is similar in their looseness to those in the preceding specimen. Now, in the imitation produced by the machine, we have an ingenious twisting given to the threads of the ground, whereby, in lieu of the simple twisted ground-net of the previous example of machine, we have two sides of each mesh thickened to represent the two plaited sides of a hand-made Mechlin mesh. In obtaining this effect, however, the machine has to forego a looseness in twisting the other four sides of each mesh, which, consequently, have a tighter and harder appearance than that given to the corresponding sides of meshes, shown in the original pillow Mechlin and in the Calais imitation. This, however, is a very small matter, compared with the fidelity in general appearance,

which the Nottingham imitation before us possesses. This invention is considered to be the best of its kind. The cost of the hand-made lace, of which this is an imitation, is £1 10s. a yard. It was made last year at Louvain, and is a copy of a pattern introduced towards the end of the 18th century. The machine imitation wrought this year at Nottingham by a Leaver's machine costs 1s. 3d. a yard. The whole of the work is done by the machine, including, of course, the outlining thread. Machine lace, made with such outlining threads, has to be trimmed, so that these outlining threads which run from pattern to pattern, may be disunited, and left only around the required portion of the pattern.

XXVII. Here, however, we have an imitation lace, the cordonnets in which is worked in by hand. This specimen was made this year at Lyons. Hitherto we have seen machine-made imitations of the Mechlin class of pillow lace, i.e., laces with a thread outline to the pattern. Now, however, we will look at imitations of Valenciennes lace. First of all, we may remind ourselves of the appearance of hand-made Valenciennes.

XXXVIII. Here, now, in Fig. 15, is a good

FIG. 15.

Machine-made imitation of Valenciennes pillow lace.

quality of machine-made Valenciennes. It is made at Calais, by machines similar to those used at Nottingham. Another specimen is more elaborate in design, and woven with finer thread. It is considered to be as good as the machine can make.

XXXIX. The last illustration I have to show is a copy made at Nottingham last year of a specimen of that fine filmy needle-point lace made in the 17th century at Venice, and still made with great skill at Burano. This (Fig. 16, p. 39) is a specimen of the original lace, valued at about £5 5s. a yard. You will observe the flat and even appearance in the close portions of the pattern, the slight outline of thread, as well as the delicate tracery work, reminding one almost of a distant view of some fine Gothic rose window.

Fig. 16.

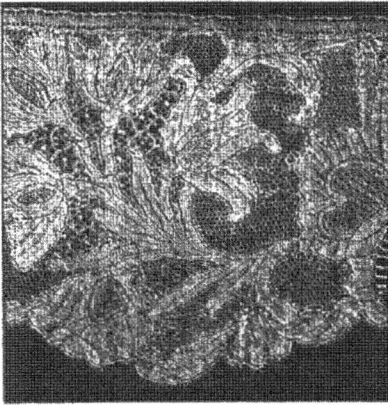

Venetian needle-point lace, "à réseau." 17th century.

XL. Here we have the machine imitation (Fig. 17). In spite of the ribbed appearance of the close portions, the sharp, clear, outlining thread, and the comparative wiry tautness of the ground, and of the little traceries, it is a wonderful piece of imitation.

Fig. 17.

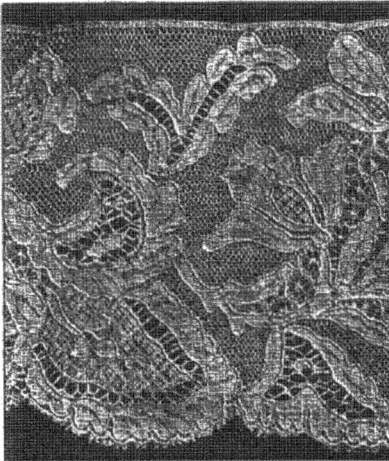

Machine-made imitation of Venetian needle-point lace, "à réseau."

XLI. How much further man's ingenuity may compel mechanism to produce works, delusive counterfeits of handicraft, is a question not to be

easily answered, if answered at all. For anyone desiring to follow the history of the art of lace-making in its literary aspect, there is plenty of ground to be travelled over. But as I said in an earlier lecture, I do not think that this way of proceeding is as instructive as it is entertaining; and I doubt very much if any one adopting it would come even

To know the age and pedigrees,
Of points of Flanders and Venise.

XLII. In the times of the Provence romance writers, French ladies as they worked sang "Chansons à toile." Italian poets have sung the praises of the needle, just as Taylor, our Elizabethan water poet, has lauded the "Needle's excellency." Some verses composed by Jacob Van Eyck, in the 17th century, upon the art of lace-making, and a French epic, entitled, the "Revolte des Passements," appeared about the same time. Pope, Evelyn, Swift, Congreve, and many other writers of the 18th century comment on passing fashions, and refer to laces then in vogue.

XLIII. One of the latest of English poets, who seems to have perceived that patience, perseverance, gentleness, should predominate in the character of a lacemaker, is Mr. Lewis Carroll, who has immortally associated a beaver with the art. A "beaver that paced on the deck, or would set making lace in the bow," was a member of that notable band of personages who went out hunting a snark. But when, as the poet relates,

The Boots and the Broker were sharpening a spade,
Each working the grindstone in turn;
The Beaver went on making lace and displayed
No interest in the concern.

XLIV. The Barrister, another of the hunting party,

Tried to appeal to its pride,
And vainly proceeded to cite—
A number of cases, in which making laces,
Had been proved an infringement of right;
But the Barrister, wearied of proving in vain
That the Beaver's lace-making was wrong—

soon fell asleep, and leaving him in that condition, I will conclude without making further quotations from this strange poem, which may not enlighten us much upon the art of lace-making. As it mellows with time, perhaps it may fall into its place as a stepping-stone in the literary history of lace-making.

XLV. It has been a privilege and pleasure to me to have been permitted to deliver this course of lectures upon the art of lace-making. In offering you my thanks for your forbearance with my shortcomings, as well as for the kind and appreciative attention you have evinced, I can but say that any dreariness which has attended my own personal efforts has, I hope, been relieved to some extent by the excellent illustrations furnished for our instruction and diversion by the authorities of the South Kensington Museum, Captain Abney, F.R.S., Sir William Drake, Mrs. Robert Goff, Mrs. Alfred Morrison, Mrs. Enthoven, Messrs. Hayward, and Messrs. Howell and James.

SOCIETY FOR THE ENCOURAGEMENT

OF

ARTS, MANUFACTURES, AND COMMERCE.

CANTOR LECTURES

ON THE

ARTS OF TAPESTRY-MAKING AND EMBROIDERY.

BY

ALAN S. COLE.

DELIVERED BEFORE THE SOCIETY, APRIL 5TH, 12TH, AND 19TH, 1886.

LONDON:
PRINTED BY W. TROUNCE, 10, GOUGH SQUARE, FLEET STREET, E.C.

1886.

Price One Shilling.

SYLLABUS.

LECTURE I.

Points of resemblance between **Weaving, Tapestry-making and Embroidery**—Special technical peculiarities of **each** process—Ornamental effects as characteristics common to Decorative Textiles—National Styles—Works by Cavemen and Eskimos—Types of Cosmopolitan Ornamental Devices—Coincident similarity between ornaments produced by different **people** at various periods—Imitation as a factor in production of Ornament—Leochare's group of **Ganymede** and Eagle compared with similar compositions in Sassanian Metal-work and Græco-Buddhist Sculpture—Deterioration from, and aspiration to, a given standard of performance in Drawing and Composition—Types of New Zealand Ornament—Types of Scandinavian Ornament—Résumé.

LECTURE II.

Classical allusions to Decorated Hangings—Method of **making Tapestries compared with that** of simple Weaving and Carpet-making—Textiles of Græco-Egyptian, Turcoman, modern Japanese—Ir cations of Commerce, Craft-Guilds, and organised Factors during 1st to 12th Centuries in Europe, Syria, Persia—Application of the Tapestry-making Process to Hangings—Decorated Textiles used in 11th and 12th Centuries—Bayeux Tapestry—Tapestry from St. Gereon, at Cologne—Scheme of its Pattern compared with that shown in Sassanian Metal-work—Sicilian Weavings—Italian and Icelandic Embroideries—Early mentions of Tapicers and Tapissiers—Patronage of the Burgundian Dukes—Influence of Flemish Paintings upon Designs in 14th and 15th Centuries—Spread of Tapestry-making in other European Countries—Petrarch's Triumphs in Books, Furniture, and Tapestries of the late 15th and 16th Centuries—Tapestries in 17th Century—Gobelin's—Mortlake—Résumé.

LECTURE III.

Embroidery—Two Classes : Embroidery on one side of a material ; on both sides—Indications of wide-spread use of Embroidery, and same form of stitches—Long practice of the Art by Mohammedans, Chinese and Japanese—Influence of Christian Ecclesiastical Establishments in developing Embroidery, and Designs for it, in Europe—Importance of considering Embroideries in respect of their workmanship and design—Analysis of Stitches—Simplicity of classification—The numerous names given to works of technical similarity—Specimens of Embroideries of different times in respect of Articles of Use and Costumes—Résumé.

383

ARTS OF TAPESTRY-MAKING AND EMBROIDERY.

BY

ALAN S. COLE.

LECTURE I.—Delivered April 5th, 1886.

The subjects of the Cantor lectures which the Society of Arts have kindly invited me to deliver are Tapestry-making and Embroidery. These are two branches of the comprehensive group of textile manufactures and ornamentation; and although we may perceive some resemblances in methods of execution between the weaving of textiles, the making of tapestries, and certain forms of embroidery, there are sufficiently marked differences to entitle each branch to be separately discussed.

The patterns and ornament of textiles also form a distinct topic, affecting both tapestry-making and embroidery. But in a necessarily limited and preliminary lecture I do not think that one could very usefully try to indicate the classes or groups of ornament peculiar to each process. The closer one looks into the ornamental character of things, the more the conclusion seems to present itself that all ornamentation, in whatever material it may be expressed, is to be viewed as a long chain of many links. The chief part of my lecture this evening will, therefore, relate to a development of pattern.

Certain processes of manufacture have undoubtedly affected the expression of ornamental effects ; and, *vice versâ*, the attempt to produce certain ornamental shapes and effects by methods which have not readily lent themselves to the attempt has sometimes brought about modifications of methods.

Sewing, as used for uniting furs and skins together, may, in some cases, precede weaving in a procession of human crafts ; but weaving in a loom with a shuttle appears to be the senior of processes pertaining to textile manufactures. Embroidery, which is a develop-ment of sewing, comes as a handmaid to weaving. In fact, embroidery postulates weaving, as a rule, since it requires a woven foundation to start from, although the embroidery with horse-hair and beads upon leather, such as the wampam of American Indians, and other tribes in our own hemisphere, is an exception. That, however, does not diminish the significance of the fact that embroidery has been done upon a woven foundation from the earliest known times.

Tapestry-making, as applied to the production of large pieces, is, perhaps, a later process than weaving and embroidery. The apparatus for making tapestry is slightly more involved than that for simple weaving and embroidery. In a genealogy of processes, it would be hardly correct to assign to tapestry-making a position as the offspring of the far older process of carpet-making, which, however, it closely resembles. So far as one can trace it from actual results of the process, tapestry-making in respect of large hangings for use in tents, or buildings, may, perhaps, be considered to be European, and dating from about the 12th century. Before this time, hangings, but probably of light texture, had been put to uses like those to which tapestry came to be devoted. A process analogous to if not identical with that which we shall next Monday see is peculiar to tapestry, had existed for centuries, and had been employed by Oriental people like the Egyptians, Syrians, Tattar, and Tibetan tribes, and possibly Arabs. But distinct evidence that such a process is one of the earliest known to textile makers is not forthcoming in the same way as the indications that simple weaving was one of the necessary and primary human arts or processes amongst people in all parts of the world. As time went on, and goes on, modifications were, and are still, made in the weaving apparatus, the frame, the cylinders, the working of the warp, the number of the shuttles, and so forth; but the main principle of the process has remained the same from all time; and the primitive methods prevail amongst primitive people, as may be gathered from illustrations of weaving which are supplied to us from people such as the natives of Ishogo, a place in that district of West Africa, between the Congo and Gaboon Rivers.

And now turning to the principal subject of my first lecture, I would say that, whilst the ornaments or patterns which have been expressed are very varied, reflecting phases of ingenuous and conventional fancy and rendering for thousands of years, the use of primitive and simple forms of ornament also survives. Not only are there these survivals, but there are recurrent appearances of more elaborate ornament, the elementary components of which are apparently to be traced to simple and primitive forms. It would be misleading were I to exemplify these ornaments merely in respect of tapestries and embroideries, I have, therefore, collected together a few diagrams from various sources, and with these I venture to very slightly suggest a development of patterns.

It is usual to display the history of art and its development by taking records of the earliest historic periods, and attributing to each of the famous nationalities of the world a credit for having produced some distinctive style. Under this method of treatment, we may first discuss that of the Egyptians, then of the Assyrians, then of the Greeks, whose rapid attainment to artistic supremacy seems to isolate them from the Egyptians and Assyrians. The Romans follow the Greeks, and a decline in quality ensues. A somewhat vague Romanesque and Byzantine nationality—though it might more properly be termed "period"—of art is then traced; after which the germs and their blossom of the Renaissance and Gothic styles in Italy, Germany, Flanders, France, England, and Spain are discovered, to be succeeded by developments of antecedent styles, as displayed in certain classes, under titles belonging to royal families and sovereigns, such as Tudor, Elizabethan, Jacobean, Louis XIV., XV., and XVI., Georgian and Empire. To this general scheme, types of Celtic and Scandinavian art, Moorish, Arabic, Syrian, Persian, Indian, Chinese, and Japanese art

either form a sort of supplement, or are occasionally alluded to as circumstances may seem to invite; whilst art, as expressed by people like the natives of the Congo, the New Zealander, and the Toltec or the Aztec of Central America, is dealt with as though it were outside the pale, and possessed a peculiar interest of its own, having virtually nothing in common with the previously named styles.

The term art or skill can be applied to all branches of human work. And in its relation to expressions of form and colour, and to processes or handicrafts, rather than to countries or periods, I propose to consider it in the course of my lectures. For after all what is nationality in art? Is it possible to take any phase of art and maintain that its creation, as distinct from those features which one groups as pertaining to individuality of treatment, is peculiar and due to a single man, and its rearing to a single nation? The greatest geniuses could not have done what they did without work, and the influence of such work, having preceded them. Commerce, in a broad sense, between peoples has from undateable periods distributed the works of human labour and ingenuity, sometimes where wit was keen to act under their influence, sometimes where wit was slow. The rare individual genius carries the art, whatever it may be, a stage further than has previously been reached; whilst others of less ability emulate some chosen example, and in so doing either maintain or obscure the influence of traditions. So far, then, as history of art may be written, and especially perhaps of art in Europe, this practical handing on and modifying of its traditions through retrogressive as well as progressive stages of emulation involves a cosmopolitan survey. Circumstances of isolation, stagnation in custom, and interruption of social arrangements and habits, have been contributory causes to the stereotyping of certain level standards of performance in productions which, through likeness one to another, are subsequently regarded as components of a national style, such for instance as the Assyrian, Egyptian, and Romanesque styles. But national style of art in this sense might be held to be demonstrated by cognate works showing more often a comparative absence than predominance of complete ability. Consequently, to detach and consider by itself some one or other national series of emulative works, impairs the view of development of art for its own sake.

Carlyle writes that the first spiritual want of man is decoration, a statement involving a cosmopolitan aspect of man, and implying a common want and a common response, throughout the period that man has been in the world. Similar conditions of life, according to authorities upon climate, geology, and biology, repeat themselves during the course of hundreds of thousands of years The climate, for instance, of the lower miocene stage prevailed in Europe long before signs of man can be traced; and yet a similar climate now prevails at Louisiana, North Africa, and South China, where man exists. The antiquity of geological records, from which such facts I believe are deduced, is overwhelming in contemplation, as compared with that of the records of human art. Still, if one could adopt a similar view as to the recurrence or succession of marked phases of artistic decorative and ornamental work, the demonstration of an evolution of such work would be possible, although it would, I expect, be a matter of nice discernment to select normal types to fully illustrate it.

Now, decoration as the response to "the first spiritual want of man," may for our present purposes be divided into two broad divisions, the one in which the representation of actual things occurs, the other in which abstract forms are displayed. A line and a dot I may suggest as simple abstract forms, elements that we might expect to find in the first works of decoration. Nevertheless, it is, I think, a striking fact that, chronologically taken, the first specimens of graphic art at present known to us gives us not only representations of animals but also of human habits, like hunting.

These were scratched on bones of animals by cavemen many thousands of years before the Egyptians, of whose skill in representing actual things and abstract forms we have records going back to more than 5,000 years ago. The art or skill in the drawing, as we see by these diagrams thrown on the screen, indicates a facility and fidelity of representation which belong, according to our notions, more to a trained draughtsman than to so presumably barbaric a creature as a caveman. As Mr. Boyd Dawkins points out, a somewhat similar graphic skill displays itself in engravings on bone by the Eskimos of the present time, and it would seem that the conditions of their life are not far removed in likeness from those of the cavemen. But I think it will be allowed that the graphic skill of the cavemen takes a higher position in an evolution of skill than that of the modern Eskimos. From the evidences

furnished by the cavemen, we are not, I think, forced to conclude that pattern making with abstract forms did not co-exist with the power of sketching animals.

And here I would show you a series of simple abstract forms taken from various sources, from the combination of which patterns have arisen.

First we have repeated lines (Fig. 1, A) graven on pre-historic pottery; the zig-zag (B, C, D.), the square (E), the square within a square (F), the cross (G), and what is commonly known as key pattern (H), (Fig. 2, I, J, K, L), are

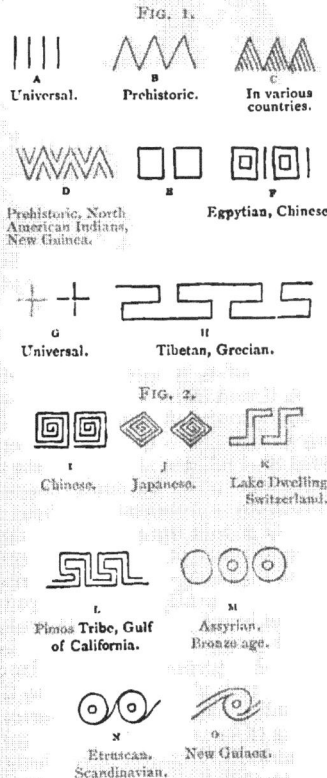

FIG. 1.

| A
Universal. | B
Prehistoric. | C
In various countries. |

| D
Prehistoric, North American Indians, New Guinea. | E | F
Egyptian, Chinese |

| G
Universal. | H
Tibetan, Grecian. |

FIG. 2.

| I
Chinese. | J
Japanese. | K
Lake Dwellings, Switzerland. |

| L
Pimos Tribe, Gulf of California. | M
Assyrian, Bronze age. |

| N
Etruscan, Scandinavian. | O
New Guinea. |

used as simple abstract forms by people of primitive and advanced culture. Certain elaborations of patterns with straight lines are seen as admirably carried out in the fine plaitings and well-ordered carvings of savages as they are in the geometric patterns of the Chinese, Japanese, and those people grouped as Saracenic. Ornament based on circular and curved lines seems to be as early in its appearance as that made with straight lines. The circle and concentric circles are elements in primitive ornaments (M). By the introduction of a curved line between a pair of double concentric circle forms (N) we have the suggestion of a spiral, and this suggestion is carried a stage further by so primitive a being as a native of New Guinea (O). The origin of the spiral (Fig. 3) has, I believe,

FIG. 3.

been a subject of profound discussion, and it seems to be a form not so purely abstract as those we have previously looked at. Some spirals resemble those in shells or the fronds of ferns, others again may have arisen from imitating coils of string or wire, and others from the convolutions on the flesh of fingers. This latter class of spiral is used by New Zealanders for their tattoo ornaments.

Thus the variety of actual things, from representing which an ornament like the spiral may arise, is sufficient probably to account, if need be, for a number of independent appearances of apparently the same ornament. The same sort of remark applies to many other ornamental forms. As the study of ornament proceeds, forms having an apparent likeness to one another can be grouped together as generic types in one large family ; and the influence of dimensions of space— length and breadth—is seen to have effected the use of such types in the making of patterns. A sense of length has operated in producing horizontal patterns, whilst breadth or height has assisted in producing perpendicular ornament. A sense of surface, limited by length and breadth, has helped to generate the scattering of forms in horizontal and perpendicular series, an arrangement very noticeable in diapers, such, for instance, as we observe in this Assyrian King's costume. The diagram shown on the screen is taken from a drawing of a sculpture done about 800 years B.C. Another example of the use of ornamental diapering is to be seen in a sculpture from the Usumacinta River, in Central America, possibly carved by an Aztec artist of the 13th or 14th century.

I hope that these suggestions may have been sufficient to establish the fact that schemes of arrangement are to be deduced from the simplest of patterns, and that although these schemes have a relationship one to another, they may possibly and probably, like the representation of forms, have grown into usage quite independently of any such factor as interimitation.

But a vast quantity of patterns has been made which have been imitated and adapted from one to another. The opportunities of imitation, such as those furnished by intercourse, whether arising from peaceful or warlike conditions, have recurred from the earliest of times. It is, therefore, an almost hopeless task to discover absolute originality in any production. Theorising upon the development of pattern, one seems to see that monotony of symmetry, for instance, educes a desire for contrast of some sort. Both symmetry and its contrast are conspicuous in elaborated details and masses of ornament compounded of abstract forms and quasi-representation of actual things. When certain ornamental effects are attempted, the unconstrained representation of the actual appearance of things is affected by conditions such as those which arise from the nature of the material in which these effects are to be rendered, the use of the object, and the shape of the whole or that part of it which it is intended to decorate. For instance, from the method of cross stitch embroidery, which is usually regulated by the rectangular lines of the woven material upon which the embroidery is done, rectangular rendering of things ensues, as in this specimen (Fig. 4, p. 5) (made perhaps in Germany during the 16th or 17th centuries), where it was suggested that some Persian characters were depicted. The suggestion, however, does not bear the test of close scrutiny, since we trace bird forms in the device, which is repeated and scattered in a diapering pattern over the main portion of the specimen. We see that the device itself is made up of an oblong body resting on two feet; a neck with square head and straight beak, is bent backwards over the body—as in the gait of a waddling duck— whilst from the extremity of the back rises a device suggestive of an upturned tail. This, then, whatever may be its origin, is no mere arrangement of lines to produce an abstract form; it possesses a distinct meaning, notwithstanding that its value in representing a bird is somewhat obscured. Similar rectangular renderings of animals is furnished by tent stitch embroidery from

Anatolia. Many shapes in woven textiles and carpets from Tartar tribes have become so contorted by the special process in which they have been rendered, that one loses trace of their having started originally from abstract forms or from the representation of actual things. The same characteristic is observable in certain classes of ornament made by strict Mohammedans, whose reverence for religious doctrines prevents them from actually depicting living objects. The orderly arrangement of the odd-shaped details, however, predominates, and gives them value as patterns.

But reverting to the monotony which makes

North German Embroidery, 16th Century.

one wish for change, and applying this feeling in respect of a primitive ornamentist who had got as far as making a pattern like A of Fig. 5, we

FIG. 5.

might fairly, I think, suppose that he would seek to make some change by introducing some additional lines. In such a pattern, then, as B, his pleasure in radiation of lines evidently rules him. But the slight alteration he had thus made might not satisfy him ; and as his power of drawing might not be limited to straight lines only, he might use curved lines ; and by adding curved lines to the ends of his radiating lines, he might make a more complete looking figure, such as C. Palm trees spread their leaves out in a radiating manner ; so that a pattern maker, dominated by the pleasure of seeing radiations, might, in his ambition to make forms, be influenced by the appearance of the palm. From very early times the palm has been venerated in the Eas

as a holy tree. An early Assyrian symbolical ornament, simple or primitive in construction, was produced by a pattern maker who may or may not have been able to analyse his sense of radiating shapes. The likeness between the radiating motives in this symbolical ornament and the pictorial representation of palms may be seen if we refer to an Assyrian bas-relief from Nineveh, in which a row of palm trees appears at the back of a procession of water-carriers. Some centuries earlier Solomon uses the palm as an ornamental detail for adorning the Temple (see 1 Kings, vi. 29).

The veneration of symbols such as the palm ornament with its radiating lines, helped to fix the use of such symbols for many centuries (quite apart from sense of their æsthetic fitness). The same condition occurred in Egypt, in regard to the lotus plant and flower, of which ornamental renderings became fixed by religious discipline. Thus types of ornament pervaded such countries ; and it was not until desire for variety went beyond a conservative power of religious doctrine, as for instance in the Greeks, that new shapes, apparently based upon a perception of those previously used, arose, and the "anthemion," or honeysuckle, as it is termed, was designed (Fig. 6). In this the essential feature of radiating lines is prominent, no matter whether the forms are like details in the honeysuckle blossom or not.

FIG. 6.

Another example of motive and arrangement of motive in design, which was adhered to a good deal in consequence of an associated religious value, has been discussed by Sir George Birdwood. This motive consists of a bud and blossom in repeated alternations, and is known as the knop and flower ornament. A sense of alternation, as an effective and simple means of contrast, seems to be universal amongst ornamentists, so that such a motive as this blossom and bud arrangement may

spring into existence and be adopted, apart from the influence of sectarian doctrines.

The pine cone, the Jerusalem artichoke, the pineapple, and such like, have a common resemblance to one another, in appearance of successive diamond shapes, presented by the overlapping of their leaves or scales within a tapering oval shape. And this device, which relies for its effect upon a sort of radiation, has educed inventiveness in pattern makers. The vogue which this cone or pine motive with radiating cross lines has had in a long series of variations, may no doubt have been influenced by the religious significance with which it was invested thousands of years ago in the East. But I venture to think that the attractiveness of radiating lines has had as much to say to its later adoption as its symbolism had to its earlier wide-spread use.

Such motives are well known in patterns for surfaces, for European costumes and hangings of the 15th and 16th century, as well as for woven fabrics, some of which, nominally made at Venice, are evidently very close reproductions of similar stuffs, if not the originals, made in the East. Here, again, are a few diagrams of ornaments in which the radiation of lines upon the plan of the Greek anthemion is an essential feature common to them all.

The ornament from Ispahan (C of Fig. 7) of the 5th century, with a central fruit form, may in

FIG. 7.

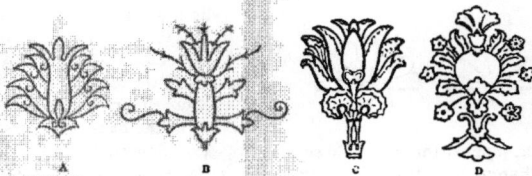

some distant way be related to D, the Italian ornament of the 16th century in which the fruit form is more pronounced, whilst B, the so-called English ornament of the 14th century, seems also to be connected in likeness with them and with A, the Chinese specimen as well.

Coincidences like these are interesting. We find counterparts of them in other results of human labour and thought, such as literature, or the art of writing and telling about things as distinguished from the art of depicting them; and a small book, entitled "Customs and Myth," written by Mr. Andrew Lang, abounds

with them. Mythology and history have had a considerable effect upon producers of works of art. Scarcely a Greek sculpture exists that is not discovered to illustrate some event or personage of mythology and history. Here, for instance, we have a photograph of the group of Jove's eagle carrying off a youth— Ganymede—to serve as cup-bearer to the gods. It is considered to be the work of Leochares, the famous Greek sculptor, about 350 years B.C.

Here is evidently another version of the same sort of story. This, as we see, is part of the decoration of a golden jug or vase, which, with other treasures, was discovered in 1799 in Hungary, in a district associated with the warlike tribe of Gepidæ, which settled on the banks of the Danube. But whether this vase was the work of an artificer working under the influence of Perso-Roman or Sassanian ideas, of Scythic or of Græco-Asiatic thought, it has not yet been decided by the learned in these matters. Still, there is a justifiable feeling that this jug was made about the third or fourth centuries A.D., though somewhat similar style and design appear in European works of later centuries.

Now, on another vase of the same time we find a somewhat similar group of a human being in the clutches of an eagle; but the human being, upon inspection, is a woman, so that this second incident depicted clearly does not relate to Ganymede.

From this specimen I pass to a photograph of a sculpture lately discovered with many others at Sanghao, in a north-western district of India. I have taken this from one of a series of interesting monographs beautifully illustrated, published, under the supervision of my brother, Major Cole, R.E., by the Government of India. According to archæologists, the event here shown belongs not to Greek mythology but to that of Buddhism. The woman is said to be the mother of Buddha Sakya Muni, who was carried up to the Trayastrinsha heavens, to be there regenerated after her death. This sculpture may perhaps be regarded as the work of a carver about on a par, in quality of design and workmanship, with the producer of the Scythic or Græco-Asiatic vase. Both workers are removed from each other by great lapses of time. The carver of the Buddistic episode presumably worked about the beginning of the Christian era, and, as I have said, in a north-western corner of India, at Sanghao. This place is some three or four hundred miles from the ancient Sogdiana, where Alexander the Great 300 B.C. settled for a few months, during his expedition into Bactria. Architectural remains and pieces of sculpture have been found in north-western districts of India, and are often spoken of as Græco-Bactrian, and Græco-Buddhist. As evidences in expounding a development of art, the Græco-Asiatic and Græco-Buddhist figures might fairly be classed together as illustrative of a phase of attainment much in the same way as we classed the simple ornamental arrangements we looked at during the earlier portion of the lecture. Both indicate a lower level in performance than that of Leochares' work, and might be regarded

either as deteriorations from that level or as aspirations to attain to it.

Deterioration from or aspiration to something better, are extremely interesting qualities to detect in a development of art, and in this connection I propose to refer to samples of the artistic expressions of the New Zealander; not, however, that I can in any way suggest the stage of development to or from which this type of ornament may be ascending or descending. Broadly speaking, two foremost motives in ornament from New Zealand are the human figure and spirals. But the New Zealanders, like many other people whose condition of life and habits is different from our own, make both realistic imitations of things and ornamental devices based on abstract and other forms. The quality of their realistic works is shown in carved heads like these (Fig. 8) which

Fig. 8.

have, I believe, the prime purpose of displaying portraits, the one of a man not tattooed, the other of one tattooed.

We may look at a piece of ornamented pierced work in which spirals are alternated with human figures, and therein detect how the New Zealander's appreciation of contrast and of balancing forms affects his patterns. And now we pass to a canoe prow (Fig. 9, p. 8).* The main lines of the prow are emphasised, and separate the various portions which are ornamented. Two spirals corres-

---

* This specimen belongs to H.R.H. the Duke of Edinburgh, who kindly allowed it to be photographed.

ponding with one another are so arranged as to give another proof of the New Zealander's sense of balance of form. Between them are other shapes, also arranged in an orderly manner, and again expressing his sense of balance of form. Below is a narrow space filled in with curves producing contrast with the rigid boundary lines of the space itself. It is evident, I think, from the way in which the curvings and other forms are grouped into this space of irregular shape, that the limits of space have affected the arrangement of the details in such a way that the meaning of them is well nigh lost. This squeezing in of details to fill a given space is a practice often demonstrated in other varieties of ornament. Beginning with this lower right hand corner of the prow, we may distinguish a grotesque human figure. Its head is set nearly at right angles to its body. Its eyes gleam from beneath two angular brows—the forehead is low—the nose small. A large broad lipped oval forms the mouth, into which is thrust three fingers which do duty for the whole hand. Then comes the arm of this hand, starting abruptly from a plum-shaped body. Across the body we see three fingers like those in the mouth, and the arm belonging to them is set a-kimbo, the two legs are straddled outwards. This odd rendering of the human figure constantly recurs in New Zealand ornament. The pattern on its surface perhaps represents tatoo marks. Beyond the human figure are horn-shaped and twisting details, also covered with tatoo marks. Upon some of them we see the three fingers. Now, if we look at the device set between the two spirals in the upper part of the canoe head, the three finger device, thrust into an open oval and a pair of eyes will be found; thus indicating—obscurely perhaps—that the motive of this open pattern is the human head. In a second similar New Zealand prow

FIG. 9.

we find the human figure in the lower space more grotesque through distortion than in the corresponding space of the first prow we looked at, and this distortion in the second prow arises no doubt from the artist of this piece being less skilful than the artist of the first. Nevertheless, in this second piece we recognise the same general characteristics which, as it were, give a style to this method of using and depicting forms. It is likely that both were wrought during the present century, though I am not aware of any circumstances why they might not have been produced in previous centuries. It is allowable, I think, to conceive that, in the course of years, as other New Zealanders imitate with variations what has gone before, at the same time developing their compliance with rules as to balance of forms in arrangement, contrast, and so forth, a perfectly different style of ornament may arise in which there will be little, if any, trace of the distorted human figure.

Now distortion in representing figures and their arrangement may be observed in other phases of ornament with which New Zealanders have apparently no connection, and by way of illustration we may refer to one or two examples of Scandinavian design emanating

FIG. 10.

from the earlier iron age, which for convenience one may roughly date between the 4th and 11th centuries of the Christian era. Here is a specimen of ornament (Fig. 10) from Scandinavia, the grotesqueness of which is not very remote from that of the New Zealander's. The subject here is animal form ; two figures with goggle eyes, pointed snout, and almost human paws, are figured opposite to one another. The tail of each curls up towards the back of the head. The shape of the space into which these details have been grouped has affected their general arrangement. The idea of animals placed *vis-a-vis* is very ancient in its connection with pattern, and long before this grotesque rendering (Fig. 10, p. 8) of that idea was made, other more perfect renderings had been produced. It may not, therefore, surprise you to hear that Dr. Hans Hildebrand, Royal Antiquary of Sweden,

FIG. 11.

considers this pattern to represent two lions *couchants*. Lions *couchants* and *vis-a-vis* often appear in Roman ornament, as well, indeed, as in many other types of ornament, and this motive has been adopted by Teutonic tribes, who have remodelled it according to the exigencies of their taste, or as far as their limited skill permitted them.

A further transformation of the lion motive, gives us the so-called lion shapes intersecting one another, and, as it were, squeezed up to fit a square space (Fig. 11). The corrupted representation of the animals has become still more

FIG. 12.

unlike the Roman rendering— the forms are no longer *vis-a-vis* to one another, but are interlaced. A likeness in details between this and the first of the Scandinavian renderings is, however, noticeable. Symmetrical distribution and balance of forms grow in emphasis, as the likeness to animal forms—always obscure—declines (Fig. 12). Other and later specimens

show further developments of the two lion subjects. The increased elaboration in interlacing the forms marks a still further developed skill on the part of the designers in symmetrically arranging forms in a given space (Fig. 13).

FIG. 13.

Before leaving such Scandinavian types of ornament and their kinship to New Zealand types, I wish to recall the detail in the New Zealand ornament, which we found to be three fingers clasping a body or a curved form. Here is a diagram (Fig. 14) of a Scandinavian clasp, buckle, or fibula, which dates from after the 11th century. In it is a motive of three fingers or claws clasping forms. This is repeated in an orderly way, so that a well-devised pattern is the result. I do not suggest that this coincidence of the three fingers confirms any

FIG. 14.

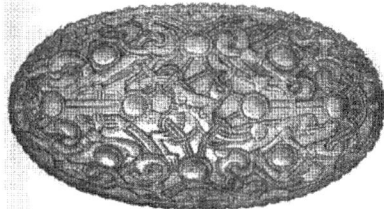

sort of imitation or trace of inter-influence between the 11th century Scandinavian work and New Zealand work of the 19th century. It seems to demonstrate that gradual developments of pattern-making may be apparently independent of one another, and yet exhibit in a remarkable way a common similarity of perceptions, cosmopolitan in existence, but with variations in growth and application.

Briefly recapitulating the points in this matter of ornament and pattern-making which I ventured to bring before you, we find, first, that a graphic power in some degree is an attribute of man ; next, that this power exhibits

D

itself in rendering imitations of actual things, abstract forms and forms compounded from a mixture of both. These are then repeated to fill a space, and the placing and distribution of them are subject to an appreciation of length and breadth. From this grow repetition and contrast, balance of forms and symmetrical arrangement. The actual expression of patterns varies with the ability of the pattern - maker. If one takes note of such factors as these in a development of ornament and pattern, I think that one learns to perceive the intrinsic charm in works of art, and to become proof against those alluring incidents relating to country and period which have little to do with the cultivation of our respect for skill in performance.

I can but feel sensible that there must be many deficiencies in my attempt to cope with my subject this evening. If any value attaches to my remarks, it has certainly been very much enhanced by the diagrams I have shown. These have been made in Captain Abney's laboratory, and to him both you and I are, I venture to think, equally indebted. For myself I have to thank you for your patient attention.

Next Monday evening my lecture will be about tapestry-making, and I propose then to speak about the special process and its employment in the production of other things than great hangings, as well as about patterns which have been made with it, and their relationship to similar patterns wrought by other means.

[This lecture was illustrated by a series of diagrams thrown upon the screen by means of the electric light].

LECTURE II.—DELIVERED APRIL 12TH, 1886.

My lecture this evening is to be upon tapestry - making. The word tapestry has grown to be used in two senses, from which a good deal of confusion and some uncertainties have ensued. From a general and non-technical point of view, the word tapestry has been used to indicate any sort of decorated hanging. Thus early mentions of tapestry have been accepted as proofs positive that the special process which is now identified with tapestry-making was in question. But this assumption is not, I believe, correct. The special and technical meaning of the word "tapestry," in its indication of a peculiar process, will, I hope, become clear as the lecture proceeds.

Various books upon tapestries and textiles—and one or two have been lately published in France of remarkable completeness—contain abundant quotations from old writings to prove the use of decorated textile fabrics for hangings and curtains, at the times of the Egyptians, the Assyrians, the Greeks and Romans. And as this particular branch of the investigation seems to have been pretty fully dealt with, I do not propose to further follow it. It may probably be taken as certain that actual specimens are not likely to be forthcoming of the curtains with cherubs' heads, used for the Tabernacle of the Ark, of the cloths adorned with animals and episodes which are mentioned in the Iliad, or of the hangings decorated with illustrations of Greek myths and victories which Apollonius of Tyana is said to have seen at Babylon. Whether these were embroideries, or woven and painted cloths, it is impossible to say. It is, however, I think, more than probable that they were not made as tapestries, say from the 12th century, have been.

Remains of other textiles, mummy cloths, portions of costumes used in ancient Egypt, and woollen stuff of the Bronze Age in Scan-dinavia prior to the Christian era, have been discovered, and their methods of production duly verified. The majority, if not all, of such witnesses to the antiquity of well-wrought weavings and sorts of embroidery, have been preserved for centuries in subterranean burial places in coffins of wood and stone, whence they have been exhumed by the modern explorer; but hangings and large pieces of stuff to decorate buildings have not, apparently, been so deposited as to insure their existence for long periods. Other causes, too, have helped to efface traces which would be of value in demonstrating an evolution in the use of decorative hangings. The depredations of fanatical iconoclasts, not only in Europe, but also in continents like India, are too well known to now require more than a note. The effects of earlier sectarian repugnance for decorative works may be inferred from such letters as St. Epiphanius, Bishop of Salamis, wrote to John, Bishop of Jerusalem, in the 4th century Although this letter has often been quoted, I venture to give an extract from it. The bishop writes:—

"On my journey through Anablata, a village in Palestine, I found a curtain at the door of the church, on which was painted a figure of Christ, or some saint, I forget which. As I saw it was the image of a man, which is against the command of the Scriptures, I tore it down, and gave it to the church authorities with the advice to use it as a winding-sheet for the next poor person who might have occasion for one, and bury it."

Speculations, however, as to the probable recovery of this curtain, or any earlier decorated wall-hanging or curtain, need not perhaps occupy our attention.

The question what then is tapestry seems to me to require an early answer. To the French word *tapisserie*, an off-shoot of *tapis* (carpet) we are no doubt mainly indebted for our word, in which, however, we have a second "t" deriving it from the Latin word *tapètum*, a source common both to French and English words. As early as 1250, French regulations of the artisans of Paris contain mention of *tapissier sarrazinois* and *tapissier nostrez*—and sixty years later, "tapicers" are named in ordinances concerning such craftsmen established in London. Last Monday I suggested that tapestry-making was more like certain forms of carpet-making than any other special branch of textile manufacture. It is possible that the 13th and 14th century *tapissiers* and *tapicers* were men engaged in producing coverings and stuffs for use as carpets and hangings—woven either in the ordinary way, or done according to the special processes of carpet and tapestry-making. Although there is scarcely any evidence to show that tapestry hangings, in the technical sense, were made in Europe before the 12th century—the actual process which came to be identified with such articles was well known in the Saracenic countries of that and earlier times. It would appear that this process was used in respect of trimmings to dresses. On the other hand, Tartar and Turcoman people appear to have used an identical process for making carpets and such like. I do not think anyone has been able to decide the question as to the actual difference in craft between the *tapissier sarrazinois* and the *tapissier nostrez*. The latter is thought to have produced some home manufacture as distinct from an imitation of Saracenic manufacture. However this may be, I will now submit certain diagrams by which I hope to show the difference in process between weaving and tapestry and carpet-making.

Woven fabrics made by hand are produced, as this diagram indicates, by passing a shuttle charged with thread, thrown across and in between alternate threads stretched in two ranks. The two ranks can be raised above or brought beneath one another by two frames, each of which operates in respect of one rank of threads only. These frames are moved by pedals. When the shuttle with its thread has been thrown across the width of the two ranks of warp, a comblike instrument is brought against the interweaving thus made, so as to compact the thread of the shuttle between those of the warp. The textile as made is wound round a cylinder, and the weft and the warp threads are equally visible on both sides of the fabric.

Now for carpet-making by hand, a stretched rank of warp threads is also necessary. But these warp threads plays no visible part in the face of the carpet. They are covered round with weft threads. Instead of a shuttle with a weft, as in weaving, you use various sets of thread, which you loop, knot, and intertwist on the warp threads. In making carpets with a pile, you cut the ends of the threads which have been knotted on to the warp. From above these knotted threads, and across and in between the warp, a stout thread is thrown. This is pressed down with a comb, so as to compact the whole fabric. A fresh series of knottings is then made, and the above-named operations repeated. The weaving diagram showed that the warp-threads lay in a horizontal position. In carpet-making the warp-threads are usually in an upright position. Here I show a sketch of some Indian workmen making a carpet upon upright warp-threads. On an upper cord, above the heads of the workmen sitting in front of the warp, are hung bunches of thread, which may be of silk, wool, goats, or other hair. The sticks within easy reach of the workmen are attached to a set of strings which are fastened to alternate warp-threads. By moving the sticks, half of the warp threads can be pulled forward so as to divide the warp into two ranks, between which the cord may be thrown above each series of knottings. To the left of one worker is a small pronged instrument, like a comb with a long handle. This is used for pressing down the work. To the right of the other workman is a pair of scissors, with which he clips the ends of the knotted threads and trims the piled surface of the fabric. This method and apparatus has probably been in use for many centuries in the East. And rough and ready as they appear to be, highly finished carpets with one side of close sheeny pile, lovely in pattern, colour, and texture, have been made with them.

But there is another closely-allied process for making carpets and hangings. This is one in which no stout cord is thrown across and in between the warp; no scissors to cut the ends of knotted weft-threads are used, and no pile is produced. Both sides of the textile so made are often alike. This process requires that the variously-coloured wefts shall be intertwisted between groups of the warp-threads. In this respect it is almost identical with that particular process which is known as tapestry-making; tapestries, however, are finished for display on one side only.

By the help of a few plates which have

been photographed from a standard French Dictionary of Manufactures, published in the last century, I hope to present you with the leading features of tapestry-making. My first illustration gives a considerable framework, containing a wide range of warp-threads, upon the lower portion of which is seen the face of the tapestry, with completed parts of the design. The workman is at the back of these warp-threads, and his design is placed upon the board, leaning outwards, in front; this he sees through the warp-threads. Here he is at work. The numerous pegs or slays are wound round with coloured threads; the attachments of strings, some of which he is pulling, operate upon the warp-threads. He can thus pick out and pull forward the particular warp-threads between which he has to intertwist the thread of a particular slay. In the pile carpet-making processes slays are not used. Another diagram gives us an idea of how the comb is used.

Tapestries are made not only upon vertical threads, in the manner roughly described, but also upon horizontal threads. These two illustrations indicate the use of the process in its connection with horizontally ranged threads. In the upper one we have the worker intertwisting his slay of weft-threads, whilst in the lower he is using the comb to compress his work. Tapestries made upon vertical warps are termed high warp, or *haute lisse* tapestries. Those made on horizontal warp are called low warp, or *basse lisse*. But the results of both methods are virtually identical, so that it is almost impossible to detect any peculiarity which shall distinguish the *haute lisse* tapestries from those of the *basse lisse*. In weaving, you may have, as I mentioned, the warps either vertical or horizontal; and this is not unimportant in regard to the conclusions which some inquirers have arrived at, that the mention of high and low warp, *haute* and *basse lisse*, must imply one or the other of the tapestry-making processes.

Sir Gardner Wilkinson gives a drawing from sculptures 3000 B.C., of Egyptians at work upon a small high warp frame, and the arrangements for pulling forward the vertical warp-threads establish an idea that a tapestry-making process is being used by them. This process is, as I have said, of great antiquity, and of wide-spread employment. As to its antiquity, I have a specimen, Fig. 15 (p. 14), now preserved at the British Museum. It was exhumed from some tomb near Sakkarah, an Arab village near Memphis. I believe that the

late Dr. Birch considered that it was pre-Christian in date, possibly belonging to the period of Greek colonisations in Egypt. It is possible that the corselet mentioned by Herodotus as having been captured by the Samians, in the course of its transit from Amasis, King of Egypt, who sent it as a present to the Lacedemonians, was ornamented with such work as that now before us. The date of that corselet was probably about 530 B.C. Herodotus describes it as made of linen, "with many figures of animals inwrought and adorned with gold and cotton wool, and on this account," he says, "each of its threads make it worthy of admiration. For though it is fine, it contains 360 threads, all distinct." These 360 threads might be the warp-threads. In the specimen before us there are, in the width of 8¼ inches, upwards of 184 warp-threads, and the number of crossing wefts on each warp-thread of 11 inches long, is 600. Possibly that portion of the linen corselet which excited the admiration of Herodotus may have been a panel of ornamental work about 17 inches in width, which would not be too large to serve on the front of the corselet. It might, indeed, have been a sort of ephod—like the linen ephod, perhaps, which David wore when he danced with all his might. I make these suggestions with much deference, relying very much upon what I have gathered to be the opinion of the late Dr. Birch as to the date of the actual specimen before us. He has described it as a rectangular fragment. In the centre is a square of green ground, upon which appears in white with red outline, blue eyes and armlets, a nude figure of Aphrodite, in front of whom is a swan flying. This compartment is about 3¼ inches square. Round it is a broad border, on which in red, blue, and white are ten draped female figures standing—the left hand and arm of each is raised—whilst the right arm hangs pendent. The four figures on the upper and the four on the lower part of this border are full face; the figures at each of the other parts appear to wear head dresses and face to the left. The drapery of the figures exhibits on the skirts a pattern of three diamonds, in one of which is a cross in the other two are circles. The ground above these figures is strewn with blue and white spots or flowers. The whole rectangular fragment has been surrounded with a blue and red border between white lines. The outer edging of all is a rude rendering of the bud and blossom device. As may have been noticed, the drawing of the various forms is quite archaic or primitive.

It is evidently done by someone possessing but little skill in realising and depicting the subject. Similar quality of drawing is to be seen in other relics of this class of work, which have recently been rescued from tombs, probably of Christians of the Coptic sect. In such, the figures pourtrayed wear *nimbi* like those of Christian saints. Specimens of these robe ornaments have recently been

acquired for the South Kensington Museum from Egypt. From some parts the coloured threads have completely disappeared, leaving, however, the warp-threads, thus furnishing a key to the manner in which the work was done. It is probable that small slays were employed, the warp-threads being stretched in a handy frame of some sort. When the work was finished, it was stitched to the coarse

FIG. 15.

Panel of Tapestry-Weaving for the decoration of a Dress rom Sakkarah, near Memphi Græco-Egyptian, 2nd or 3rd century B.C. (?)

linen robe. This tapestry-making process for making costume ornament, upon a small scale, has not, I believe, been used in Europe. It is known, however, to Peruvians and natives of Borneo. Specimens of tapestry-making, in which the weft is silk throughout, are made, on a small scale, in the public school for females at Kiyoto Fu, in Japan. The Japanese seem to regard them

as displaying a new sort of work which they have lately invented, and accordingly named Tsu-zu-re-ori. But this specimen, which is about a foot high, shows that the process is identical with tapestry-making as already described. I have little doubt that the Japanese adapter derived his idea of the method, perhaps, from some bit of European tapestry, or from a Turcoman, Central Asiatic, or Mongolian carpet, produced in this way (Fig. 16). So much, then, for the process of tapestry-making and some of the peculiar uses to which it has been put.

Its celebrity, however, in Europe, arises from its use in connection with hangings, the larger quantity of which has been made with strong warp-threads or strings, usually over-worked with worsted, sometimes with worsted and silk. In such form we seem to have no data upon which to found a statement that this class of work appears in Europe before the 13th century. But at this date we get indications of the special application of the process to the production of stuffs to be used as hangings, and such like.

Of hangings, without regard to their particular make, we have representations such as this diagram furnishes. It is engraved in

FIG. 16.

Corner of a Curtain or Carpet or Tapestry Weaving; Turkoman manufacture.

M. Muntz's excellent work on "Tapestries," aad displays a corridor of the Emperor Theodoric's palace at Ravenna, the seat of the later Roman Government. The curtains, looped under the arcades, were probably of ordinary woven material, far thinner and lighter in texture than tapestry-made hangings. The ornament upon them may have been painted, embroidered, or woven into them. It may, indeed, have been done by the tapestry process on the small scale of the Egypto-Coptic specimens; but of this we know nothing with certainty.

The diagram, however, may give us ground to surmise that the influence of Rome and her

Oriental connections, which had been protracted through centuries, affected the adornment of palaces long before the times of Theodoric. And as the organisation of the Christian Church, with its ramifications in the East, spread itself about Europe, fashion, in the use of decorated textiles, was widely disseminated. One or two instances will suffice. Withlaf, a king of Mercia, in 833, presented a cloth of gold displaying the destruction of Troy to the Convent of Croyland in England; and in 992 Abbot Egelric (the second of that name) gave the same establishment two large foot cloths, woven with lions, to be laid before the high altar on great festivals. Possibly these articles were of wool. Now from the first century "coarse wool, woven in Belgium, found a greedy market in Rome," according to Signor L. Brentano, and the industry was extensively practised during succeeding centuries by the noted weavers of Flanders and Brabant. We have little to guide us as to the sorts of patterns which may have been wrought in these fabrics, but I hope I shall not be charged with overtaxing your credulity if I suggest that perhaps in the 10th and 11th centuries some such patterns as this like this specimen may have been used. This character of pattern appears also in more delicate textiles, which are generally thought to have emanated from Greece and Sicily between the 10th and 13th centuries.

Besides indicating conditions consequent upon the desire of the rich and powerful to be supplied with the best obtainable articles produced by artistic man, history also points to the effect which has followed upon the efforts of handicraftsmen from the earliest of times, to perpetuate a supply of wonder-stirring works, the sight of which gave birth and life to demand. Commerce in such works ensued. To instance early commerce, I need not go so far back as the almost prehistoric amber trade of the Phœnicians with North Europeans; but as the period when the patterned stuffs of which I last spoke belongs to years between the 9th and 13th centuries, of which we are generally considered to know but little, I thought I might place before you a few items illustrative of the spread of commerce, the specialising of crafts in the formation of craft gilds, and the establishment of organised factories about that time.

The constitution of craft gilds is said to have been adopted from the more ancient religious gilds. The late Mr. Toulmin Smith's book on "English Gilds" gives much information about them. And, as germane to our subject, it is interesting to read that "foremost amongst the free handicraftsmen of the Germanic States, for some centuries before the 11th century, were the weavers." They formed a kind of middle class between the patricians and the bond craftsmen. "Whilst the other craftsmen worked to supply mere local demands, the weavers' manufactures found markets in the most distant countries, which fact naturally invested them with greater personal importance." Accordingly, in all the manufacturing countries of that time, in England, Flanders, Brabant, as well as in the Rhenish towns, the most ancient gilds were those of the weavers. The Gild of London Weavers was chartered by Henry I., and so was that of the Oxford weavers. In Germany the Woolweavers' Gild of Cologne arose as early as the 11th century. At Spire, the Gild of the Woolweavers existed at the beginning of the 12th century. At Mayence, the weavers are mentioned as early as 1099. Corresponding organisations in the East—in Persia, in Syria, and Byzantium certainly existed at these times and earlier. Apart from the indications one finds in the Bible, dating from hundreds of years before Christ, the fact that splendid textiles were made in Syria particularly is brought out in Washington Irving's "Successors of Mahomet"—and, of course, by Gibbon previously. The Saracens or Moslems at the beginning of Mohammedanism levied from the towns of their early conquests in Syria, tribute, which in great measure consisted of fine textiles. Damascus, famous in the 7th century for its silk weaving, was taken by the Saracens. These conquerors allowed the supposed daughter of the Roman Emperor Heraclius, who was married to Thomas, a noble Greek in Damascus, to leave, taking with her three hundred boxes containing costly silks and cloths of gold. Nevertheless much similar booty was left for the Moslems when they entered and sacked the town.

How far the Persians, who were subsequently vanquished by the Saracens, had encouraged costly productions, may be inferred from the detailed description of a large and sumptuous carpet used in the palace of the king, Yezdegird. This carpet was of silk. In design, —suggestive of Vathek's mountain paradise— it represented a parterre of flowers embroidered in their natural colours, and overlaid with jewels; the fountains playing amongst the flowers were wrought with diamonds and sapphires, to represent the sparkling waters.

The value of the whole was beyond calculation. The carpet was taken from the palace at Madayn, and brought to Caliph Omar at Medina. The caliph ordered it to be cut up and a piece given to each of his chiefs, one of whom sold his portion for eight thousand dirhems of silver. It was at this time that the port of Amalfi in Southern Italy grew to importance. According to Gibbon, it was for 300 years a principal centre for supplying the Western world with the manufactures of the East. Before the 8th century, even, we get an idea of the wide scope of Oriental commercial relations with France, in the mention of certain Greek and Syrian merchants who established a centre, for their operations in the silk trade, at Paris during the 6th century. That they gained popularity is attested by one of them becoming Bishop of Paris.

A mention of the establishment of silk-weaving looms in Sicily may illustrate my reference to organised factories. In the 11th century, the Normans from the north of France came in contact with the Saracens, who were then in Southern Italy and Sicily. A Norman expedition went to Greece. Under the domination of chiefs like Robert and Roger Guiscard, the manufacture and weaving of silk were developed in Palermo. Gibbon relates that, after sacking Corinth, Athens, and Thebes, Count Roger despatched his lieutenants for Sicily "with a captive train of weavers and artificers of both sexes. A stately edifice in the Palace of Palermo was erected for the use of the industrious colony; and the art was propagated by their children and disciples to satisfy the increasing demand of the Western world." This establishment is mentioned by contemporary writers as the Hotel des Tiraz. "The decay of the looms in Sicily may be described to the troubles of the island and the competition of the Italian cities."

From these foregoing indications we may perceive that, at the 8th century, in Europe there was considerable activity in producing articles of artistic manufacture cognate, in their use at least, to that of tapestry-made work. Now the earliest piece of hanging made by the method corresponding with that of the old Egyptian costume trimming we looked at dates probably from the 12th or 13th century. It is comparatively narrow, and was of some length. This character of shape is distinctive in hangings of lighter stuff, as well as with early tapestry hangings. Larger and squarer tapestries are of later date. There is much discussion as to where this early piece of tapestry, a portion of which I show, was made. Some have thought it was made in Syria, others in Germany, and this latter country, I think, establishes a better claim to it, though, in some respects, France might prefer an equally strong claim to having produced it. The larger portion of it is preserved in the museum at Lyons. Another piece is in the museum at Nuremburg. And a bit of the border is in the South Kensington Museum. Here is a photograph of this bit, in which the twisting of the threads may be clearly followed. The tapestry is made of woollen threads, chiefly greens and blues, twisted around stout flax strings or warps. When intact, the whole piece belonged to the Church of St. Gereon at Cologne. The scheme of the pattern consists of a series of repeated ornamental circular bands, within which are figured chimerical birds and beasts. This device occurs in Oriental ornament, and is frequent in ivory carvings, metal works, and embroideries of the 12th and 13th centuries. But here is an earlier example of the principal motive in the pattern. This gold vase is considered to be Scythic, Perso-Roman, or Græco-Asiatic work of the 4th century A.D. A scheme of pattern in which the repeating circular bands surrounding birds and creatures are used, may also be noticed in the chasuble of Pope Boniface VIII. This is a photograph of the back of it. The chasuble is entered in the inventory of the Pope's possessions, dated 1294. This character of ornament is vaguely called Oriental and Byzantine. But imitations of it have been produced far and wide. We may find it in modern Japanese weavings, and what may strike us as even more remarkable, we have it in Icelandic embroidery which dates from the 16th century. Through the kindness of Mr. William Morris, I am able to show you a diagram of the Icelandic specimen (Fig. 17). This is a coarse linen hanging composed of two bands of linen joined together. It is embroidered with wools in a running or darning stitch. The scheme of repeated circles inclosing chimerical creatures plays as we see the principal part of its pattern. The indications of the circles are indistinct, though sufficient for the purpose of tracing the use of this character of design. The legends are in a sort of Gothic black letter. Kindred pattern is to be seen in weavings of the 12th or 13th century from Sicily or Italy. So much, then, for this particular motive and pattern, the modifications of

which could furnish matter enough for a single lecture.

Returning now to the length and narrow width of the early tapestries, it is to be noted that they were used as frieze-like decorations or bands to be hung along the walls of churches and buildings. A remarkable instance of such long hangings is given us in the famous linen band embroidered in wools, with over seventy different scenes connected with the Norman conquest. Mr. Fowke's book on this precious relic of 11th century art exhausts all that has to be said about it. The portion I show displays a part of the king's palace; then comes a view of an interior, where Edward the Confessor, seated, is in coversation with two personages, of whom one—the taller one at the

FIG. 17.

Icelandic Embroidery in Worsted upon Linen ; probably of the 16th century.

back with the moustache—is probably Harold. Then we have a troup of horsemen led by Harold, upon whose left hand is a hawk. Harold is riding, as the legend tells us, to Bosham. In front of the cavalcade are hounds. The building they approach is a church, with two men kneeling at its entrance. Along the border we have repeated pairs of beasts and birds, reminding us of the like devices which occurred in some of the roundels previously seen. This long linen hanging—measuring some 230 feet by 20 inches—is celebrated as the Bayeux Tapestry. But the term tapestry applies solely to its use, and not, of course, to its make, which, as has been said, is of embroidery. That it may have been wrought at Bayeux is

c

possible. The earliest mention of it occurs, I believe, in an inventory of the contents of Bayeux Cathedral, dated 1476, where it is accurately described as a "tente très longue et etroite a broderie." In the 16th century it is again entered as a *toile à broderie*; but the name *tapisserie* having been given to it, has caused occasional misapprehension as to its technical character.

The next few bits of real tapestry I have to show, further demonstrate the long and narrow shape of early tapestries which survived into the times when larger and squarer specimens were produced. Here is a strip of the early 15th century tapestry work, made perhaps in South Germany. It represents the wooing of a princess by two suitors; comparatively rude in drawing—it must have been rich in colour. The threads in it are of wool, but small portions are also worked with gold thread—now almost black. A conventional treatment of renderings is marked, in the use of black threads out-lining many of the details — a characteristic of many early tapestry designs. Scrolls with legends upon this are introduced amongst the various groups of figures. This feature constantly recurs in tapestry designs of the 14th century. Examples of it are in the Church of Saint Laurent, at Nuremberg, and in the National Museum, at Munich. Here again we have a frieze-like tapestry, in which is figured the admission of a young lady into a sisterhood.

Tapestries such as these, then, form the connecting link, as it were, between the circular band and animal pattern of the Cologne 12th century tapestry, and the patterns of figure subjects depicted from the 14th century onwards. The tapestries of early times, *i.e.*, 13th and 14th centuries, are thought to have been almost exclusively made in small frames, in which the ranks of warp were stretched horizontally—and this, as I have previously mentioned, is known as low warp, or *basse lisse* process. There seems, however, no particularly good reason why upright frames with vertical warp (*haute lisse*) should not have been in use concurrently. But this is a point of anxious dispute amongst those to whom it is of importance. One fact may be noticed here, and that is that in the evolution of the method of tapestry-making, the production of larger pieces than those we have seen as types of early European tapestry, necessitated the use of wider and better constructed high or low warp frames. In these larger frames designs

of correspondingly increased size were wrought in tapestry.

From the 13th century, the decoration of walls in Italy and the South was reviving and becoming wide-spread in the use of fresco-painting. And to some extent one traces in the tapestries of the northern and more weather-wearing countries a companion fashion to that of the southern frescos. There can, however, be no doubt that, without the revival of painting in Italy and its necessary influence, painting in the North would not of itself have put forth the great figure-designs for tapestries, such as began to appear in the 14th century. From this period onwards, we have frequent indications and evidences of notable bodies of craftsmen known as "tapissiers," and in England as "tapicers." In the first instance, they may not have particularly identified themselves with the tapestry-making process. Their business was always in connection with stuffs like carpets and hangings, which were originally woven. Subsequently some were made according to the special process, by which the workman was able to produce a wider range of effects. I believe that the number of colours of the earlier tapestries was restricted in a way which reminds one of the limited number of tones at the disposal of the water-colour painter a hundred years ago. And it is not until the tapestry-making craft is well established, that the employment of a more generous scheme of colours occurs. This has developed in such a way that it is a boast now at the famous Gobelins factory that they have upwards of 14,400 tones of colours in dyes for threads. But 300 years before the establishment of the Gobelins factory, under the patronage of Henry IV., the peculiar process and its practice had been encouraged very considerably by the Dukes of Burgundy. The far smaller number of colours available for use engendered a simpler rendering of designs than that which marks the tapestries of late 16th and succeeding centuries. Although the Dukes of Burgundy, early in the 14th century, are historically conspicuous as promoters of tapestry-making, it should not be inferred that the manufacture secluded itself solely under their auspices. Amongst the mysteries of craftsmen there are records of some applying to "tapicers" in England at this time. These workmen were influenced by works possibly more splendid than they themselves were accustomed to make. The French Sovereign presented handsome tapestries, made in Paris and Angers, to Edward II. and Edward III., and no doubt many other foreign specimens were imported into England.

Monsieur Guiffrey has cited some interesting facts concerning a prominent tapestry worker of whom he has found records dating from the 14th century. This craftsman was named Nicholas Bataille. At one time he was valet to the Duke of Anjou, and in the cathedral of Angers there are specimens of the tapestry hangings produced under his supervision when he was in the service of the Duke of Anjou. The Register of the Treasury of the Duke of Anjou shows that in one case the Duke borrowed from his brother, Charles V. King of France, a MS. illuminated with scenes from the Apocalypse. An artist of repute, Hennequin or John of Bruges, was charged to make enlarged copies of these illuminations. These enlargements were then worked out by Nicholas Bataille and his staff. That the Duke of Anjou should have had the perception to cause an illumination to be thus enlarged, marks a taste no doubt inherited from his ancestor Charles of Anjou, who, on his journey in 1266 to assume the kingship of Naples, is said to have stopped at Florence, and visited Cimabue, then at work painting a Madonna for the Church of Santa Maria Novella.

The more notable tapestries of the 14th and 15th centuries appear to have been worked after designs from Flemish artists, who, as a group, were more able and distinguished at that time than their brethren in France. Gold and silver threads and silks were frequently and lavishly intermingled with wools for such hangings—with effects on a large scale similar to those of the small golden and glowing missal illuminations. We lose the effulgence and splendid colour of such works in photographs of them, which, however, give us the means of obtaining an impression of the careful study and drawing of the faces and draperies, as for instance in this diagram taken from a tapestry of the late 15th century. In this group we have a variety of faces displaying different expressions, depicted within the limits of this phase of art, as well almost as one could expect. Inequalities in scale and absence of perspective need not of course be particularised. Such features belong to the phase of work. They are often spoken of as elements giving the stamp of style; it should, however, be remembered that the designers did not work differently. They probably had

no thought for "proprieties of style" such as we sometimes pretend to insist upon. Style, indeed, is a term which has grown into a respectful usage, through its repetition by persons belonging to a much later date. Good style or bad style serves as a general term to sum up excellencies and deficiences in groups of kindred works.

At the time that such a piece as this was made, the practice of tapestry-making had taken root in many parts of Europe—in France and Flanders especially as, in a less degree, in England, Spain, and Italy. Flanders, however, seems to have been the district to which great patrons of art looked for the best work. A friend of mine has kindly referred me to Gaye's "Carteggio inedito artisti," &c. This contains reprints of interesting documents, amongst which is a letter written by Fruoxino, apparently a travelling agent of the Medici merchants. Dated from Bruges, 22nd June, 1448, it is addressed to Giovanni de Medici, a son of Lorenzo de Medici, who, with his brother Lorenzo, had, as leading members of the firm, carried on a very extensive trade. This letter relates to the efforts which the agent had made to buy some tapestries for his employer. The agent had been to Antwerp, but had met with little success there in getting what was wanted. He had seen a set of tapestries illustrating the story of Samson, but these, he says, would, from their size, be difficult to "hang in your chamber." The tapestry-makers worked, as a rule, to order; so Fruoxino advises Giovanni de Medici to send the exact size of the hanging he wants, and to name the subject which may be specially designed and worked for him.

It would not be possible for me to attempt giving you a brief account of all the known tapestry-making centres which flourished, with varying fortunes, during the 15th century. Sovereigns, pontiffs, and nobles did what they could to stimulate competition in the art. Paris and Arras had rivalled one another, and after the overthrow of Charles the Bold, Brussels came to the fore; Lille, Tournay, and Bruges, had also been and were to the fore. M. Muntz's excellent book on tapestry is replete with incidents of the rises, falls, and migrations of the art. From 1420 to 1500, swarms of tapestry workers, natives of Arras, Lille, Bruges, Tournay, and Brussels, swooped (as he says) down on the territories of the Marquis of Mantua, the Duke of Ferrara, the Duke of Urbino, on Venetia, Tuscany, and Umbria. The oldest Italian workshop hitherto known is that of Mantua. From 1419 a French tapestry worker remained in the service of the Gonzagas till about 1442. He was succeeded by other French and Italian workers. Thus, to a large extent, tapestry-making in Italy was indebted to an influx of Flemish and French workers.

On the other hand, an interchange of talent is indicated when cartoons by Cosimo Tura, Mantegna, and Leonardo da Vinci, were sent by the Medicis and others to be wrought in tapestry by the workers at Bruges. Vasari gives a minute description of a cartoon by Leonardo da Vinci for tapestry, which was to have been worked in Flanders, and presented to the King of Portugal. This intention was not fulfilled, and the cartoon alone was produced.

M. Muntz has closely tracked his subject. He gives much that is interesting about Italian tapestry works. He puts at rest a frequently accepted idea that Pope Leo X. caused Raphael's cartoons displaying the Acts of the Apostles to be worked at Arras; the fact being that the Arras works had collapsed some 36 years before the artist received his commission.

Before offering any remarks upon changes in design which developed soon after the commencement of the 16th century, I would show you a diagram of a closely filled design of the late 15th century, the tapestry worked from which is preserved at Rheims. We have here the coronation of Clovis, King of the Franks, in 481. The second incident represented is the siege of Soissons, five years later. This city was in the possession of the Roman King Syagrius. Further on is Clovis, with uplifted sword. He is no doubt engaged in combat with Syagrius, who was defeated and fled. The splendour of knightly panoplies, rich with resplendent armour, jewels, and sumptuous stuffs can almost be taken for granted even from this diagram. The composition with all its elaborated details reflects the later 15th century ideal of such feats of arms—performed by warriors led by Clovis; of whom, however, with a closer regard for truth than romance, it is written, that, "when he first took the field, he had neither gold and silver in his coffers, nor wine and corn in his granaries." Sets of great pieces like this of the Siege of Soissons, which is some 10 ft. or 11 ft. in height and 20 ft. in length, were taken about from place to place when their royal or noble owners changed residence. A waggon drawn by five horses carried the tapestries of Louis XI. on such

occasions. The tents of Charles the Bold, Duke of Burgundy, were hung with great tapestries. Some of them are now preserved at Berne, having been captured in 1486 at the Battle of Gransons.

The quality of flatness, due to comparative absence of perspective, and the fullness of details so arranged as to produce a complex pattern, are features in finished designs wrought in tapestry during the later 15th and early 16th centuries. But these features rather quickly disappeared after the entry of Raphael and other Italian artists, upon the scene as designers for tapestry.

Henceforward, an impulse was given to the production of designs which the tapestry worker should render with as near an approach to realistic effects of light, shade, relief, and distance, as his fixed warps and bunches of coloured threads would allow him. This tendency to give tapestries a likeness to paintings has been, and is still developed, at the Gobelins factory. The steps leading to it from the simpler and flatter looking designs of the 15th century are many, but not, I think, peculiarly interesting. Here, however, is a type of design which found much favour when produced in the 16th century. And here is another sort of type specimen of the 17th century. At the famous Mortlake tapestry factory, which was founded by James I. early in the 17th century, designs after Raphael, Rubens, and Vandyck, were worked, in which pictorial, as distinct from Gothic, effects predominate.

In conclusion, I return once more to the designs of the late 15th century, in order to place before you diagrams of a few remarkable specimens illustrative of the Triumphs of Petrarch. In connection with them I may refer to one or two specimens of other decorative work. These indicate the adoption by designers of allegories in illustration of which they made compositions of stately processions rich in ornamental detail. Mantegna's cartoons of the Triumph of Cæsar are preserved at Hampton Court, and are pre-eminently interesting in this respect. Here, taken from the Aldine print (of 1499) known as the dream of Poliphilo, are two cuts displaying the Triumph of Europa. From a decorated wedding robe chest or *cassone* (1480), I have taken the front panel, upon which, in the original, are painted the Triumphs of Love, Chastity, and Death.

As is well known, Petrarch wrote a series of allegorical triumphs, about the middle of the

14th century. The subjects of these are, the Triumphs of Love, Chastity, Death, Fame, Time, and Eternity. They are full of suggestions, but are much too long to quote on the present occasion. They, and the designs made a full hundred years later, are replete with detail; and the designs indicate that the poems were certainly known to the designers. Cupid is invariably represented as Petrarch describes, in a fiery chariot drawn by four snowy steeds. Chastity, in her white robe, bears "a fair pillar." Death is spoken of by the poet as a "lady clothed in black," and designers select Atropos to represent her.

The scheme adopted by the designer of the tapestries of which I have two diagrams, gives two episodes to each tapestry. These episodes mark the triumph of the particular virtue or fatality which is preceded by the overthrow of the alien fate or antagonistic influence. These hangings measure 26 ft. in length and 14 ft. in height. In the case of the Triumph of Death, we have the overthrow of Chastity by Atropos. Then comes the actual Triumph of Death as typified by the "three fatal sisters of Destenye" seated in a car in which lies, dead, Chastity. Bullocks draw this car over a mass of dead and dying. A knight heralding the extinction of life and bearing two lances, one labelled Fortitudo and the other Malheur, cleaves a path through the crowd of illustrious defunct.

The second diagram is of the Triumph of Time (Fig. 18, p. 22). This is rather different in treatment from that of the previous tapestry. Massed in groups without much indication of feeling for perspective, the magnificence of terrestrial glories, historic facts, and ingenious materialisations have been pressed into the service for that; but now the designer, for his Triumph of Time, draws upon his imagination of ætherial entities, and as a salient feature of the upper part of his composition uses a semicircular arrangement of figures robed in white flowing folds typical of the hours, and floating before the zodiacal signs Gemini, Cancer, and Leo, into which the sun is entering. The first group on the left indicates Fame overthrown, whilst the second near the centre of the design is the triumph of advancing Time, an old winged cripple supporting himself with a crutch; the left crutch he carries in his hand, and he stands in a bent attitude over Fame vanquished. Both figures are on a car dragged by winged horses, into air over a wide-spreading landscape.

Late 15th century tapestries of the Triumph

of Chastity, Death, and Fame, are in the South Kensington Museum. Corresponding tapestries of the Triumph of Death, Chastity, and Time, are at Hampton Court Palace, and have lately been admirably repaired. There are other very remarkable tapestries in the palace, but I cannot venture to speak of them now. Besides those at Rheims and Berne, to which I have referred, examples of these closely filled figure compositions are to be found at the Cluny Museum in Paris, and in great splendour at the Museum at Madrid. Some very remarkable specimens of the middle 15th century, which had belonged to the Chevalier Bayard, are in the collection of the late M. Achille Jubinal, whose writings on tapestries must always command respect. The tapestries in the Uffizi Palace at Florence, at the Vatican at Rome, and in the Garde Meuble in Paris, are extremely numerous, and generally of a later period. Scriptural, ecclesiastical, and natural history, classical mythology, middle age, and Provençal romance, poetry, and allegory, have influenced designers for tapestries from the 14th century onwards. Whilst pastoral, domestic, and sporting scenes have, in the 17th and 18th centuries, been reproduced in tapestries, sometimes even from the small cabinet paintings of artists, who probably had no idea that the perpetration of such doubtful compliments would be contemplated, much less carried out.

Now the points which I have endeavoured to establish are, briefly, that the term tapestry may be read in two senses; the one in which at all times it refers to hangings generally; the second in which it implies a special method of producing a textile fabric. The earlier hangings, although pains have been taken to prove that they were in a large degree made by this special process, appear, on the whole, to have been of lighter material than that of the special fabric; and the ornamentation on them was rendered by weaving, embroidery, or painting. Indications that the special process was known in early times have been given, but it was then applied to making small ornamental trimmings of costume. The application of the special process to the making of works on a much larger scale than that of such trimmings, seems to occur in the 12th or 13th centuries, although in old Asiatic civilisations it had probably been employed for carpets, the patterns of which were composed of formal, somewhat geometric devices, arranged symmetrically. The fame of tapestry hangings made by the special process rests

FIG. 18.

Tapestry of the Triumph of Time.

23

upon the renderings of great figure subjects designed in the 15th century. The drawing, arrangement, and colouring of such, invest their application to textile hangings with an appropriateness of surface pattern. This cannot be conceded in respect of the later results of the special process when the rendering of subtle painting effects are attempted by the tapestry maker. In such phases of the art, regard to the peculiar use of the textile hanging, as well as to the limitations in employment of materials, is probably as unconsciously put aside as it was equally uncon-

sciously displayed in the antecedent works of the 15th century.

It was out of my power to get my diagrams coloured ; but to make up for this grave deficiency, the authorities of the South Kensington Museum have kindly lent the specimens exhibited in this room. Each is labelled, and I hope that the sight of them, coupled with the information I have had the honour of laying before you, may lead you to recognise the high interest which attaches to a study of tapestry in respect of its use, its designs, and its method of production.

LCETURE III.—DELIVERED APRIL 19TH, 1886.

It will, I think, be convenient for me to commence my lecture this evening by shortly stating what I understand by the term "embroidery." In the first place, it applies to the ornamental enrichment, by needlework, of a material. Such enrichment may be produced with various materials, similar to or quite different from that into which it may be worked. In many instances, the enriching material is more costly than that to which it is applied; though works beautiful in effect have been made in which the embroidery is of the same material as its ground or foundation. We may notice instances of these as we proceed. Under the definition just given, embroidery may be classed into two broad divisions; the one of embroidery done on one side only of a material; the other of embroidery done with equal finish and effect on both sides.

Ever since man has been known to exist, needlework of some sort has been done. The needle, as successively made of bone, wood, and metal, is many thousands of years old. When, therefore, we begin to investigate the embroidery of the first historic nation, it is not surprising to find it well established as an art, more or less, of common practice. As we proceed, we find that almost the same character of conditions which have favoured the practice of embroidery has repeated itself throughout the world.

Some notion of this repetition may, perhaps, be gleaned by comparing the work done by the civilised child with the work of an adult belonging to a race or nation in comparative primitiveness. The likeness which may often be traced between such work marks an approximate equality in ability. And, as we go through history, we seem to find that the habits and practices of the earliest historic nations more or less correspond with those of people at the present day who are regarded by us as being in a primitive stage of civilisation. But the small indications which I have hastily perceived, and inadequately followed up, in regard to this matter, convince me that it is far too large to be fitly discussed now. In illustration of the relationship which establishes itself between, say, the work of a school child under discipline and that of a peasant who has little or no instigation to rise above a certain standard of performance, I would suggest your looking at samples worked by 17th century school children of twelve and fourteen years of age, and 19th century peasant embroideries, say, from remote villages in Norway. The designs represented differ but slightly, whilst the quality of performance is fairly level. Again, we may examine specimens made by other people quite remote from one another, but apparently subject to one and the same sort of influence. And as exemplifying similar character of design, all of them suggestive in composition, stitchery and colour, actual specimens of Spanish, Persian, and Cretan embroideries are exhibited. In patterns on specimens from Crete we find signs of the influence of a mixture of ideas. Here (Fig. 19, p. 25) for instance is a borderfor a petticoat, of canvas embroidered, in the 17th century, with many coloured silks in various stitches—chief amongst which is a sort of long, cross, twisted-thread stitch. This stitch is much affected by the mixed races of the Grecian Archipelago.

The pattern of this border consists of a band with floriated scrolls springing from each side of a central device, above which is a series of vase or basket motives. Out of these come bunches of carnations; between these appear double eagles and symmetrical arrangements of variegated carnations. In the lower portion of the pattern are s shapes, terminating in carnation blossoms. Birds of an archaic type are also introduced. Incidentally, I may say that the double-headed eagle occurs as a device upon Karamanian coins of the 10th century, and upon pre-Mohammedan coins. Mr. Purdon Clarke tells me that the bird with two heads is as often introduced into ornament in the south of India as it is in ornament from Tibet and in cloths from Yarkund. He believes its use to date from classic periods. The double-headed eagle of Charles V.'s time is thus comparatively quite modern. The same sort of motive of course appears in embroideries from Persia—of which there are designs wrought in a way similar to those of the specimens shown, wherein the carnation blossom is a prominent feature. Again, in Spanish embroidery of the 17th century, the double-headed eagle is naturally a usual device. In this specimen of Spanish work one may trace a kinship, its crowded and orderly arranged ornament, and its somewhat startling colours claim with those of patterns to be seen in work from Crete. The class of flowers, chiefly tulips, in the Spanish specimen, the real forms of which are somewhat obscured by ornamental treatment, is, however, quite different from that of the Cretan patterns. Still, carnation forms are abundant in patterns, not only Spanish, but also Italian and German of the 17th century, and the ornaments made with them recalls that to be

FIG. 19.

Silk Embroidery on Linen of Cretan workmanship. Probably 17th century.

noticed in Cretan, Syrian, and Persian specimens.

For the most part, the embroideries to which I have been alluding might be grouped as peasant work; and the facts I have suggested go towards confirming the likeness which exists between the works of similarly circumstanced people, who have produced works of similar ornamental character and needlework quality.

On the occasion of my first lecture, I attempted to bring forward some rather well-known points in connection with the development of designs and patterns. The specimens we have before us, and those I propose to show, will suggest a multiplicity of considerations concerning motives and their treatment in making patterns. Time will not permit me to do more than glance at such considerations, however, and I propose to devote the greater part of this lecture to an examination of the stitches.

Broadly speaking, the more complete and finished embroideries are such as have been made by workers who have given themselves up to the craft as to a life-long profession; at

D

the same time, specimens of needlework of great excellence often issue from the hands of those who possess a dexterity which they exercise for occasional enjoyment rather than from regular necessity. Groups of embroiderers, pursuing their art with regularity and under conditions of organisation—a natural necessity of thriving crafts—are to be met with in many countries and at various periods. With Eastern people like the Chinese, Japanese, and Mohammedan races, embroidery rises to a degree of perfected practice bespeaking a sort of second nature centuries old. In Western and Central Europe there seems to have been no such pronounced settlement of practice. Certain phases occur, as when a domination of ecclesiastical authority is apparent, and, later on, when a fashion was maintained in making imitations of the imported Oriental work, and again when embroidered costumes were in vogue. In Polynesia, Africa, and the New World, embroidery has been an art with tribes slow in changing their customs, or, so to speak, in passing up the ladder of civilisation. In this regard, they resemble the peasant peoples in other more civilised parts of the world. As a domestic or home industry, embroidery is frequently distinguished by admirable skill, although the patterns depicted may not indicate any corresponding quality of trained perception in drawing, selection of colours, and arrangement. The constant regular employment which is possible in workrooms specially devoted to the purpose, in religious houses, or in Eastern harems, has naturally left its mark upon the work produced within them. So, too, has that conservative quality of keeping things in families, as with a tribe or village of peasants, who adhere to a particular sort of stitch or style of design, and acquire great skill in doing it.

But the modern system of human industry aided by machinery inevitably affects the recurrence or prolonged existence of such circumstances as those glanced at. As the modern system gradually extends its scope, people adopt new processes and new habits for the old, and, except under special provisions, embroidery by hand is not likely to be exempted from its effect. Such as perceive the charms of embroidery, and are willing to pay the rate of wages which shall induce workers to keep to the handicraft, may contribute to the maintenance of this art; but unless a revolution in the influence and spread of machine-aided industry takes place, it is

hardly likely that embroidery will take such a position in the future as it has held in the past.

One usually associates women with the art, but it must not be forgotten that men have been, and still are, amongst its foremost adepts. In India, China, and Japan, the art owes its best expressions to men. In Europe, it probably owes more to women, though members of religious communities, like Benedictine monks in past times, have excelled in the use of the needle. Abbot Wygmore, of the 14th century, was a proficient embroiderer, and the brethren at Woolsthorpe, in the 16th century, wrought much excellent needlework. Similar instances could no doubt be quoted of other countries.

In dealing with tapestry-making last Monday, I adopted the method of chronologically showing a rise and development of that art. I might, perhaps, discuss embroidery somewhat differently, dealing with it as it appears in various countries. To do so, however, would, I find, involve duplication of remarks. I, therefore, propose to avoid this as far as possible, by grouping together similar features as we find them, and speaking of them without much digression as to country and period of production.

In the first place, stitches, I think, should claim attention, although designs and patterns are equally important; but the time at our disposal makes it impossible for me to fairly deal, even briefly, with both of them. Designs and patterns frequently conjure up a variety of interesting topics, apart from their demonstrating suitable selection of subjects, composition, drawing of forms, and mingling of colours. The subjects pourtrayed often attract one to enter into considerations of history; the probable date of production is usually a fertile source of discussion; whilst ethnography, in its attempts to determine national characteristics, perplexing and attractive as are its ramifications, not infrequently throws a cloak of excuse over absence of skill in craft and design, and a work of doubtful art becomes elevated to an importance the significance of which is not always intelligible.

The late Canon Rock, who has written with enthusiasm upon textile fabrics and embroidery, made out a classification of sketches by means of certain titles which he found in Dugdale's "History of St. Paul's." There, as well as in old records, inventories, and such like, he found mention of classes of work, such as *opus anglicum, opus plumarium, opus pulvinarium*, *opus pectineum*, and *opus consutum*. Following his suggestions, I adopted these classifications for a catalogue of a large and unique collection of decorative needleworks which was exhibited in 1873 at South Kensington Museum. Since then, however, closer scrutiny of the precise meaning of these Latin titles seems to me to have demonstrated their comparative uselessness in conveying definite technical information. No authorities clearly show what the *opus anglicum*, for instance, really was, whether it was a chain or a split-thread stitch, or, as Dr Bock, of Aix-la-Chapelle, suggests, beadwork(!) and I say this with some deference in view of opinions given in a large book upon needlework recently written by Lady Marian Alford, who has done so much to further practice of the art. The term seems to imply that at a certain time – about the 13th and 14th centuries —English embroidery, especially on ecclesiastical vestments, was in high repute. But a number of specimens of the same character as that attributed to the *opus anglicum* were made abroad, and hence a doubt is thrown upon the peculiarly English nature or style of this embroidery. The temptation to closely investigate the special and technical distinction of *opus anglicum* is strong; but it would obviously take one far away from examining embroidery, and from arriving at a knowledge of stitches generally.

Earlier in my lecture I said that we might divide embroidery into two classes—the one in which the work is made for display on one side of the material; the other in which it is equally finished on both sides.

In respect of the first of these classes, I have diagrams of stitches (Fig. 20, p. 28) some of which are made for display on one side of a material. They are worked by drawing the needle with its thread in one sweep through two or more places along the surface of the material. The simpler of such stitches are—long and short stitch—as here. Then there is a stem stitch. This, as shown here, merely implies an oblique arrangement of short stitches. Feather stitch, or *opus plumarium*, is another term used in embroidery, but here again we find that it may mean an arrangement of long and short stitches, so taken as to completely cover a portion of the surface being worked upon. In plain needlework, however, as distinct from embroidery, there is another arrangement of long and short stitches for seams, to which the name of "feather" stitching has been also applied.

Running and darning (closely similar in effect on both sides of the material) may involve the use of long and short stitches, but instead of the needle passing at one sweep through two places only, it has to be stealthily worked through half a dozen or more. Chain stitching involves the looping of the needle's thread in the progress of the stitch. Sometimes, instead of making a loop, the point of the needle is made to split the thread, thus giving a looped character to the stitch. Knotting stitch is another development of the looped stitch. In this case the needle makes a passage down through the material, and not along it, and a knot is so formed on its surface. Tent, cross, and cushion stitches are often worked upon an open reticulated ground, such as canvas. They are supposed to constitute the group of *opus pulvinarium*. But we find tent and cross stitch are the principal stitches used, with marvellous patience, by Mohammedan embroiderers in the intricate and richly-coloured ornamentation of leggings for ladies, the material of which is of closely-woven linen or canvas. Here, for instance, is an employment of red silk worked in cross-stitches to cover the ground about a pattern, the leading forms of which are of the linen fabric which the embroidery ornaments. This is sometimes called Italian work of the 16th and 17th centuries, sometimes Spanish. Specimens have also come from Albania, and from one or other of the Cyclades.

The making of tent, cross, and cushion stitches differs from that of the long, short, and looped stitches. The needle is passed up through the material, and then down again through its face. In cushion stitch the Germans have much delighted. Berlin wool work is often done with cushion stitch. The Swedish have distinguished themselves for some centuries in such work, the patterns or which are primitive in form and garish in colour. Such works are not, however, of such pretentiousness as the *tapisserie au petit point* of the French. Here is a specimen of such tent and cross-stitch work of the 16th century. The fashion for it found followers in Italy and England. The stitches we have so far considered are chiefly for decorating one side of a material only.

Now, the second class for obtaining equal effects on both sides, includes satin stitch and tapestry stitch, which latter is not to be confounded with the *tapisserie au petit point* previously named. As shown in the diagram (Fig. 20, p. 28), satin stitch may be of long and short stitches. From Italy and the Greek Archipelago come specimens wrought with much finish in this stitch. This specimen is simple in its pattern of leaves and branches with horizontal, perpendicular, and oblique satin stitches worked across the

FIG. 20.

STITCHES	FRONT	BACK
Short.		
Long.		
Stem.		
Arrangement of Short and Long Stitches. *Sometimes called Feather Stitch.*		
Chain or Looped Stitch.		
Running.		
Darning.		
Tent.		
Cross.		
Cushion.		
Satin. *(Short)*		
Satin. *(Long)*		
Looped *on edge* or Button Hole.		

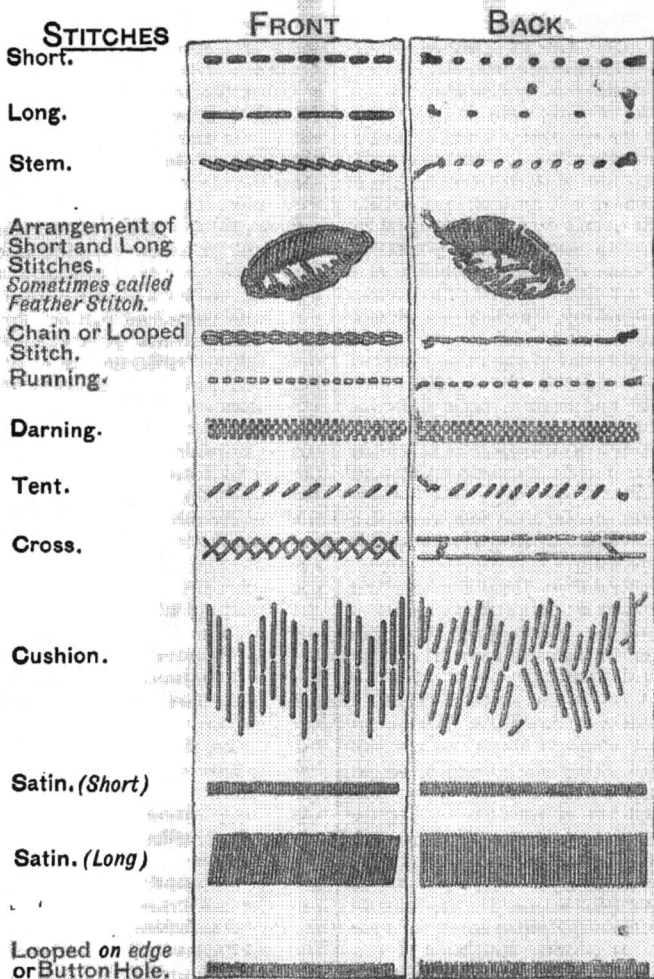

Diagram of Stitches : showing their effect upon the front and back of the material into which they are worked.

various forms. The colours, which I regret cannot be displayed, are of light blue, salmon, and golden-hued tones. The French speak of this satin stitch as *au passé*, and as *sans envers*. The owner of this specimen considered that it was of Venetian workmanship, dating from the 16th century. But other authorities declared that it was Turkish of the 19th century. The controversy does not diminish the virtue of the specimen as a finished piece of work.

Returning once more to the diagram of stitches, I wish to direct your notice to the form of looped stitching which has been done upon the edge. This is called button-hole stitch. It may also be done upon a thread. Here is a diagram of it made upon a couple of threads. When used in this way to render a pattern, the result of the work is needlepoint lace.

We have thus briefly glanced at some thirteen or fourteen stitches, five of which classify themselves into a single group, as long or short stitches; four as looped stitches; whilst the three stitches known as tent, cross, and cushion are virtually the same, and so may come under one heading; satin stitch differs from all of them, and therefore takes a place by itself. Thus we have not more than four distinctive group of stitches. And now, turning to the tapestry stitch, it is, I find, supposed to be a peculiarity of the *opus pectineum*, or work done in a loom or frame, and in the process a comb is used. This implement, as we noticed last Monday, is one of importance to the tapestry maker. Tapestry stitch, however, as wrought with a needle, does not require the employment of a comb to compress the intertwisted threads together. Here is a specimen of work from Skåne in Sweden. The original specimen, to be seen below, is square. Only half of it is shown. The specimen is made up of bands of needlework and lace called " Klutaband." These are first used by peasants for the broad ends of cap-lappets, subsequently they are joined together into squares. The bands of geometrical pattern—flanking the lace insertion— are those worked in tapestry stitch ; the threads, corresponding to the warp of regular tapestry, are such as have been left of a strip of linen from which a number of warp and weft-threads have been withdrawn in a certain space. The tapestry stitching has then been worked in and out and between these threads, and is so managed that both sides are alike. In regular tapestry-making only one side of the production is presentable. From Persia come squares dating from the 17th century, very often of extraordinary minute needlework, done on loosely woven linen or cotton, in which a tapestry stitch identical with the Swedish is done. Work for the decoration of robes by

Egyptian Coptics was not needlework. It was done with a small "slay," such as the tapestry maker uses. And this work is the same in process as that of tapestry-making. Here is a specimen of Egyptian Coptic work, probably of the 4th century of the Christian era. This, however, like tapestry, is presentable on one side only.

In connection with the Swedish and Persian needle version of tapestry making, I spoke of withdrawing threads from the material. There is a considerable group of embroidery known as drawn work, the essential feature of which is the withdrawing of threads in order to obtain open devices in patterns. Here is a specimen of such work taken from an Italian shirt of the 16th century.

A reversed counterpart of such drawn thread work is embroidery done with a darning or running stitch upon an open reticulated ground or net—as in this example, which is probably either French or Italian of the late 16th or early 17th century. A phase of this work survives in the embroidery on net of many countries ; in Ireland, amongst others, where it is called Limerick lace or run-work.

Running, done in close material, results of course in quite a different effect from that of running on an open ground. Here is a specimen of worsteds run into a linen. It is an Icelandic work of the 16th or 17th century. Here is a fragment of similar work, very simple in pattern, which came from a tomb at Sak-karah, in Lower Egypt, and may be of the 4th century.

Thus from *opus pectineum* we have been led to note certain ways of dealing with materials of close and open fabric into which embroidery is worked. We have not, however, increased the number of distinctive groups of stitchery, although their application has been varied. With some fancy, a Latin name has been assigned to the drawn threadwork, and it has been called the *opus araneum* or *filatorium*. But both denominations are valueless from a technical point of view.

The *opus consutum* has now to be referred to. The term applies to the cutting of materials into ornamental shapes, which are afterwards worked with stitchery of some sort. Here, for instance, is another part of the Italian shirt already referred to, in which simple details in a pattern are produced by cutting out bits of the ground.

Another sort of cut work consists of cutting away the ground about a pattern, first outlined with a cord or thread, and, where necessary, inserting little bars or tyes between the portions of the pattern. This work has been done hundreds of years ago in Italy, and is done in Ireland at the present time, at Carrickmacross. Here is a specimen of the cut work from Carrickmacross. With your permission, I should like to digress here to allude to a movement which has been made towards the improvement of patterns used by the Irish lace workers. In a sense, this movement owes something, I think, to this Society, for having given me the opportunity, in 1881, of delivering some lectures on lace-making and lace patterns. In the following year I was called upon to give similar lectures elsewhere, and, amongst other places, I lectured at Limerick, Cork, Dublin, and Belfast. The outcome of these lectures in Ireland has been the movement I referred to. A competition amongst pattern designers was held last year. Prizes were awarded to the value of £74 for some forty designs. Of these, a dozen or more are now being worked at some six or eight lace-making centres, schools and convents in Ireland. One has been finished for her Majesty the Queen, who was graciously pleased to give a commission for it and other prize patterns. Here is a specimen of the new piece of Carrickmacross cut work made for her Majesty. In the course of a few months, I hope that a sufficient number of needlepoint laces, embroideries upon net, and cut works will have been produced by the Irish workers to form a collection for public exhibition, and, at least, to demonstrate that the sale of Irish lace need not be entirely dependent, as it too often has been, upon a sort of philanthropic patronage.

Returning now to our review of cut works, we may note a variety kindred to the last sort of work. Here, again, the ground has been cut away, and the pattern left. But the pattern is so planned that the details composing it touch one another in places, thus getting rid of any necessity for inserting bars or tyes. The edge in the original of this border is enriched with gold thread. The pattern itself appears in one of the numerous Italian pattern books of the 16th century, without a full reference to which no history of embroidery is complete. They are often held to be lace pattern books. This is a mistake; a great number of the patterns are for many classes of decorative work besides lace.

Two more groups of cut work have to be noticed. The oldest of these appears to be patchwork. This is often associated in one's mind's eye with quilts made of hexagons in pink, and white, and lilac, such as one occasionally sees in peasants' cottages, or floating upon clothes lines in back gardens. From these, however, I have now to take a great step. In 1881, excavations at Deir-el-Bahari, in Egypt, brought to light a canopy, of which Mr. Villiers Stuart, in his book entitled "The Funeral Tent of an Egyptian Queen," has given a highly interesting and large coloured plate. He speaks of this canopy as a perfectly unique example of Egyptian tapestry, using the term as implying a hanging or covering of some sort, and not as involving any technical process. For, of the actual technical character of this canopy, Mr. Villiers Stuart tells us it may be described as a mosaic of leather work, consisting of thousands of pieces of gazelle hide stitched together with coloured threads to match. It is, in fact, a patchwork. The colours of the pieces of leather thus stitched and patched together, consist of bright pink, deep golden yellow, pale primrose, bluish green, and pale blue. Vultures, hieroglyphics, with diaperings of daisy blossoms, and borders containing goats, scarabs, and repeated fringe device, are the principal details to which the bits of gazelle hide have been shaped. Arranged in formal order, they make the pattern of this canopy. Mr. Stuart was able, from various data, to fix the period, when this patchwork was made, at 980 B.C. It was wrought for a queen who was mother-in-law to the Shishak who besieged and took Jerusalem three or four years after the death of Solomon. Made in a very similar way to the Egyptian queen's canopy, but of different materials, is a French hanging of the 13th or 14th century. Here is a photograph of it. The design represents various incidents in a knight's encounter with a dragon. The details are cut out of different coloured cloths. These have then been sewn or patched together, and then applied to the ground; the seams between the patches being overlaid with narrow strips of leather. These latter were whipped round with fine golden strips suggestive, as Canon Rock says, of the lead lines in stained glass. In stained glass, the leading is necessary to hold the bits of glass together, whilst in this patchwork the corresponding lines are used for decorative effect, and are not constructive necessities.

From Persia at the present time (doubtless an inheritance of old practice) come gaudy patchworks (of Resht) done with much elaboration in pattern. Here is part of a large cover wrought in this way. The enrichments to the simple patchwork are worked in chain stitch with silks.

Amongst the specimens exhibited you will find examples of Italian patchwork in velvets and silks, so used as to produce alternations in colour of the same pattern. A similar effect of alternation is to be seen in the cut brass and tortoiseshell work associated with the name of André Boule.

Another section in the class of cut work is to be seen in what is known as applied or *appliqué* work. In illustration of this, I have a diagram taken from part of an altar hanging belonging to Sir William Drake. It is of Italian origin, and dates from the 16th century, somewhat later than the period which Vasari assigns to the production by Sandro Botticelli of designs for cut work. Vasari speaks of the work as *di commesso*. It is not clear, however, that this expression should specially indicate either patch or *appliqué* work. It may apply to both. In any case an interest is aroused by the association of Botticelli with decorative needlework. *Appliqué* work differs from patchwork, since the details of the pattern to be worked by the *appliqué* method are cut out of a stuff and then stitched down to a ground of material, which latter plays a visible part on the ornamental effect of the finished work. As a rule, the cut pieces thus applied are edged all round with stitches or with a cord or thread; also applied and stitched down. Finished and clear definition is thus given to the different shapes. This stitching down is virtually identical with tent stitching. It is the principal stitch used in other variations of applied work, of which a few have become specialised, as in the case of gold thread enrichments or embroideries. As illustrating the method of stitching down, I have a diagram of Indians at work doing applied embroidery with gold threads.

The sumptuous heavy golden trappings and saddle-cloths, canopies or howdahs, are frequently worked with gold threads "couched" or stiched upon a padded foundation or over stout threads. The essence of "couching," so far as needlework is concerned, is the up and down stitching. But it is not merely a question of holding the gold threads upon a surface, by means of such stitches; for "couching" involves display of skill in so taking the stitches (the threads of which show themselves upon the glittering gold threads lying close together) that patterns and diapering effects are pro-

duced by them upon the face of the gold threads. This group of Indians is at work upon a material stretched in a frame. The use of the frame for embroidery purposes is a matter which should, perhaps, have been mentioned sooner. The frame shown here is large ; very much smaller ones are used by the domestic embroiderer. All embroidery is done upon material stretched in a frame, or held loosely in the hand. Frames are almost always used for *appliqué* work in its various classes, others of which we shall shortly notice. Returning, for the present, to gold thread "couching," we find specimens of such work intermixed with coloured silk embroidery, dating in Europe from the 12th century. Before then, gold threads were used more often for weaving than for embroidery. There are occasional exceptions to such a general statement, but, as a rule, the use of gold threads in embroidery is later than their use as wefts in weaving.

The specimen of gold "couching" of which I have a diagram, is taken from a funeral pall belonging to the Fishmongers' Company. This pall is supposed to have been used at the funeral of Sir William Walworth, in the reign of Richard II. But the character of some of the ornamental details in it gives it a later date, probably by some fifty years at least. A Pope in the act of blessing is seated upon his throne ; on each side of him is an angel swinging a censer. Gold couching, done over layers of threads so as to increase the effect of low-relief, is used for the background and Pope's seat, the censers, and bands upon upon the robes of the figures. The other portions are, for the most, worked in long and short stitches with silk. Another specimen of similar work is to be seen in this portion of a Y-shaped orphrey for the back of a cope. The composition of the crucifixion is almost entirely worked with coloured silks in long and short stitches. Gold thread, to occasionally heighten the outlines of certain details is used. The bordering and the architectural canopy over the saint bearing a chalice are of gold thread couching. This specimen is considered to be Italian or Flemish in origin, and of the early 16th century.

Previously to this class of sumptuous enrichment of ecclesiastical vestments, came that which has been connected with the modern idea of the *opus anglicum*. The peculiarity of this work is thought to have been the use of a chain stitch or split stitch. The diagram now before us is of the celebrated Syon cope, preserved in the South Kensington Museum. The figures are worked in the chain or split stitch. It has been described by the late Canon Rock with very high antiquarian skill When attributing it to a distinctively English nationality, I do not find, however, that he mentions that similar embroideries as I previously said are to be seen elsewhere, and are traditionally of other nationality in workmanship. Here, for instance, is a smaller specimen, but equally finished, in skill of chain or split stitch

work. This is certainly later than the Syon cope. It is probably of early 15th century Italian work. The Syon cope is unquestionably of the 13th century, so, too, were vestments of the Popes, some of which are preserved at Anagni. The specimen (Fig. 21) before us is taken from a panel about 16 inches long by 11½ inches high, in which a female saint is represented at her prayers. A crowd of men are standing behind her near a belfry, and a few of the figures in the group are here shown on a large scale so that the

FIG. 21.

Part of Panel, Embroidered in Gold Threads and Coloured Silks. The draperies and faces worked in chain stitch. Italian; 16th century.

character of the stitchery may be noted. The saint was found by Canon Rock to be Santa Francesea Romana, of whom he recounts saintly and devotional acts. But the present and particular interest of the diagram before us lies in its expounding a skilful use of a supposed typical stitch of the *opus anglicum*. In Persian embroideries, representing hunting scenes, the same sort of stitch occurs, used much in the same way as in this specimen. In Abyssinian robes chain stitch is largely used.

The Indians and Chinese have often produced chain stitch work.

For figure subjects this chain stitch in European ecclesiastical embroideries was preceded and succeeded by long and short stitch, the surface of which presented a more painting-like and less granulated effect. This smoother lying stitch was used especially for faces and hands, and we find such treatments in conjunction with draperies, which were rendered by means of fine coloured silken threads whipped around gold threads. A rich golden glow or shimmer pervades such embroideries. Here, for instance, is a specimen of this kind of work, done from a design by Raffaellino del Garbo, in the 16th century. The shading of the drapery is done with blue, red, and green silks, whipped round the gold threads. A golden orphrey is exhibited, as well as a few coloured photographs of some remarkable specimens of this sort of work done perhaps in Spain or Flanders. From the raised "couched" gold thread work we pass to other sorts of "couching," in which the threads to be "couched" are laid flatly upon the under material, no padding being employed. Such work is also frequently done with floss silks, as shown here (Fig. 22). The details are outlined with a thick cord, about the flat couchings of floss silk. This is part of an extensive set of furniture trimmings and hangings, made possibly in Italy or Germany in the 17th century.

The use of cords stitched down to a material, and producing ornamental effect, is exemplified in this jacket of English 16th century. Of a different sort of work, in which long, short, and chain stitches are used, is this jacket, also of English work of the 16th century. The pattern consists, as we see, of an orderly distribution of pomegranates and roses, with slender twisting stems. It is wrought with black silk. This black silk embroidery on white linen, in certain cases, is supposed to be "Spanish stitch," the origin and special intention of which is not known. They furnish matter for antiquarian research.

To return, however, to the flat laying of threads and cord, we may look at a specimen of modern Japanese embroidery. The Japanese appear to excel in skilfully doing the flat gold and silken thread work. The clouds and sky in this specimen are done with gold threads, stitched down to the ground of black. Other portions of the panel are done by means of stuffs and silk cords, and stitched down in portions to padding interposed between them and the black velvet, as, for instance, in these two figures and the trunk of the tree, beneath whose spreading branches the man and woman are watching the approach of message-bearing storks.

We noted the use of padding in its connection with the gold thread relief "couching," and now these figures and the tree may introduce us to a class of English work which was done in the 17th century, in which curious modelling effects were attempted by the em-

broiderer. Intermingled with the relief were portions worked in long and short stitches flatly. Then there were details worked out in needle-point lace stitch. Silks, gold and silver threads, silken and metallic gimps were used. Here is a diagram of such work. Actual specimens may be examined in the room. This sort of work frequently decorated boxes and mirror frames. It was an ingenious, strange, and entirely *malapropos* class of embroidery. Its influence is to be seen in such insignia of state as a Lord Chancellor's bag. The different padded details were, as a rule, worked separately, and then applied to

FIG. 22.

Embroidery on Linen, with floss silks laid or "couched;" between outlines of black silk cord stitched down to the linen ground.

the place assigned to them in forming grotesque compositions upon a ground of silk or satin.

I think there is but one other distinctive group of stitchery which I have not yet named, and that is quilting. In this, again, the essential features are the up and down stitching, and the employment of two bits of stuff through which the stitches are taken. Sometimes, to obtain stronger accentuation of forms, especially in quilted work done with stuff and thread of the same colour, a cord or padding is inserted between the two bits of material to be quilted. The stitches are then

E

taken on each side of the cord or padding, and an effect of low relief is obtained.

But some of the more notable quilting is such as Indians have done with yellow silk on white cotton. This sort of work, usually embellished with sprawling flowers in rich red and gaudy green silks, gold threads "couched," flat, or in relief, was highly prized in the late 17th and during the 18th centuries, by Western Europeans.

More sober in effect, though not, I think, less surprising in workmanship, are the minutely quilted coverlets, or *portières*, made in the 16th century at Goa, and largely imported by Portuguese, Dutch, and Spaniards. Here is a small portion of a large quilt of this kind. Hunters, musicians, heraldic bearings, and fleets of vessels are depicted in thousands of minute up and down stitches, with red and yellow silks. The actual quilt is also exhibited.

I had hoped to have been able to have touched more fully than I have upon the use of embroidery in connection with costume. The limits of my lecture, however, prevent me from doing so. Neither can I enlarge upon those fanciful long and short stitch pictures in medallions, frequently done after compositions by Cipriani and Angelica Kauffman. Indeed, the representation of figure compositions by means of embroidery is a subject of itself almost—not, however, from the point of view of stitches that we should find that their production involved any special stitches not already referred to, or that on the whole any form of embroidery is well adapted to making representations of the human form.

The study of embroidery, even if we restrict it in the first instance as, perhaps, it should be, to examining stitches and the designs they appropriately or inappropriately depict, is wide in scope. It is, of course, essential to those who practice the art from natural inclination or from choice. It becomes simplified, I think, if one takes one thing at a time—as for instance a classification of stitches. The number of typical stitches does not exceed half a dozen, unless it be determined that the smallest variation in length, direction, or arrangement shall be held to constitute

a new type—and then of course one may become quite bewildered with hundreds of new names. It is, however, easy, I think, to detect, in the apparently most elaborated of specimens, which of the dozen type stitches have been used, and to form some idea of how they have been used. It is also easy to separate off into another class of operations those methods of using various materials, such as withdrawing threads, cutting out forms, using paddings for effects of relief, couching, &c. Of course, they are all connected with embroidery, but the employment of them, while involving the use of one or other of the few typical stitches, does not create new ones. Having thus assured one's self that there is no cause to become confused by novel applications of well-established methods, one may take up the study of designs in embroidery. Here, I am free to confess that the field is altogether wider, for to intelligently appreciate designs in embroidery, it is necessary to equally appreciate them as wrought in other processes and materials. Moreover, the designer is generally distinct from the embroiderer. Many skilful needleworkers imagine that they are qualified to make patterns; this, however, does not at all follow. For us amateurs, after analysing and classifying stitches, and obtaining an insight into the composition of patterns, no doubt we may feel inclined to consider the historical side of embroidery and the possible meaning of odd old terms; and this is perhaps the more attractive to those who are neither practical embroiderers nor designers. In this respect, I speak for myself; at the same time, I cannot but feel that it is more interesting to try and understand the technicalities of the art, and the constructive meaning of patterns.

I must apologise for the incompleteness of my remarks this evening. I hope, however, that I may have suggested a few topics worthy of your consideration, and whether I have done so or not, I gratefully acknowledge the encouragement in my efforts which your attention throughout these lectures has given me.

[These lectures were illustrated by a series of diagrams thrown upon the screen by means of the electric light.]

LONDON : PRINTED BY W. TROUNCE, 10, GOUGH SQUARE, FLEET STREET, E.C.

SOCIETY FOR THE ENCOURAGEMENT OF ARTS, MANUFACTURES,

AND COMMERCE.

CANTOR LECTURES

ON

MEANS FOR VERIFYING ANCIENT EMBROIDERIES AND LACES.

BY

ALAN S. COLE.

Delivered February 18, 25, and March 5, 1895.

LONDON:
PRINTED BY WILLIAM TROUNCE, 10, GOUGH SQUARE, FLEET STREET, E.C.
1895.

SYLLABUS.

LECTURE I.

Sources from which may be taken indications of ornament in textiles ascribed to Egyptians, Assyrians, and other kindred Oriental people—Actual embroideries from 1000 B.C.—Distinction between embroideries and weavings—Three broad classes of embroidery, and the antiquity of them—Climate as affecting the use of materials—Linen and wool chiefly used by Egyptians, Assyrians, and Greeks—The darning or inweaving method of embroidery predominant with them—Its development later as a weaving process—Gold thread employed with coloured threads in the darning embroideries—Examples of ornamented textiles from early Egyptian paintings—Patchwork a notable method with Egyptians and Assyrians—Examples of Assyrian and Persian embroideries.

LECTURE II.

Types of Assyrian and Greek textile ornaments compared—Homer's references to ornamental textiles—Grecian women and embroidery—Lighter kinds of embroidery produced by Greeks than by Egyptians, Assyrians, and Persians—Examples of textile ornaments taken from Greek vases of 6th century B.C. ornament—Varieties of embroideries taken from Græco-Scythic tombs of 3rd and 4th centuries B.C.—Fresh varieties of ornament displayed in actual specimens of Egypto-Greek and Roman-Saracenic work—Saracenic and Byzantine specimens (about 8th or 9th century A.D.) of silk and linen work—Early Christian emblems in embroideries.

LECTURE III.

Lace—Its development from twisting, plaiting, and looping threads together into ornament—Early instances of simple nets for useful purposes only (Assyrian and Egypto-Roman)—Absence of suggestions of lace until about 16th century A.D.—Ornament in white linen embroideries—on net-drawn and cut-linen work—Gradual changes in the texture and dimensions of laces—Lace in connection with linen—Geometric and wiry lace—Fuller patterned and "tapey" textured laces—Laces with bars holding the details of patterns together—Laces with mesh grounds between the details of the patterns—Relief patterned laces—Specimens of the different sorts compared—The different sorts of lace identified with the indications of them in portraits from 16th to 18th century.

383

MEANS FOR VERIFYING ANCIENT EMBROIDERIES AND LACES.

By ALAN S. COLE.

LECTURE I.—DELIVERED FEBRUARY 11, 1895.

Allow me to say, as a preface to these lectures upon " Means for Verifying Ancient Embroideries and Laces," that having no original discoveries to place before you, I can offer you only a few suggestions which have occurred to me, after looking at various things, comparing them together, and dipping into different books. My researches have not been as thorough as I could wish, and the compilation of the lectures has, I am afraid, been too hasty.

The ancient embroideries—or rather, in the first place, those indications of them which we will consider—are to be ascribed chiefly to Egyptians and Assyrians, Babylonians, and other kindred Oriental people, who, according to history, were brought into frequent intercourse with one another during the two or three thousand years B.C. Later on, their descendants and successors, inheriting ancient traditions in the pursuit of ornamental arts, were similarly brought into contact with the earlier historic nations of Europe, such as the Greeks and the Romans. Various epochs of the embroidery art being thus linked together, a sort of general review of its ups and downs, its developments and modifications may be attempted. And such a review I am going to attempt in the first and second of this course of lectures. The third, and last lecture, I reserve for laces. These do not involve so extensive a survey as embroideries. For laces are virtually European in their origin; and the epochs of their growth in many varieties fall within a comparatively recent and short period, say from the 16th to 18th century. The 19th century, with a preponderance of machine-made laces (reproductions, to some extent, of the older and much more elaborate hand-made laces) is a period that I shall not be able to

deal with in the present course of Cantor lectures.

The means for verifying or identifying the materials and methods used in the making of ancient embroideries from, say 3,000 to 1,000 B.C, are not very precise. Many suggestions that various methods of textile ornamentation were then in use may be easily gleaned from the folio volumes of Champollion and Lepsius which contain admirable illustrations of Egyptian sculpture and painting. For corresponding indications of Assyrian textile ornamentation there are the splendid Assyrian sculptures in the British Museum, as well as illustrations in the folio publications of the late Sir Henry Layard and Monsieur Place to turn to. From such sources we see that ornamental textiles for costume, for other articles like cushion covers, hangings, horse trappings, and the like were extensively used. Many of them were woven : on some the ornament was dyed or stamped, on to others it was stitched and embroidered, whilst into others (and these, possibly, by far the more numerous), it was darned or in-worked with a needle. No actual remains of these very early things have been handed down to us. The references to them in records or writings give us very small clue to the peculiar technical ways in which they were produced ; we can at best only guess and conjecture what these were ; but in this respect we have within the last few years become possessed of collateral evidence, which helps us to guess rather more correctly, I think, than formerly.

Now, from about 1,000 B.C., as concerns Egypt, and from about 400 to 350 B.C., as regards Greece, we have, in public collections, specimens of actual embroideries made about the times, of Shishak, king of Egypt, who took all the towns of Judah, and pillaged the temple

2

of Jerusalem: and of Alexander the Great, whose exploits and conquests were of much greater proportion and extent. Neither Athens nor Rome existed at the earlier of these two dates; at the later of them, Rome was just commencing to make herself felt, and Athens was close on to the period of her gradual decline. From about 100 B.C., and up to 700 or 800 A.D., we have a vast number of pieces of actual textile ornamentation from many disused cemeteries in Egypt, and these show us phases of such work as was done towards the end of the Ptolemaic or Greek domination in Egypt, the best period of imperial Roman times, the succeeding centuries of the later Roman empire, and of the Byzantine court, and the first century or two of the Mohammedan invasion. Roughly speaking, then, from 1,000 B.C. onwards, we have to-hand a series of specimens, from the consideration of which we make deductions as to the probable technical character of works indicated in more ancient sculptures and paintings of textile ornamentation. Within the period of the 8th and 9th century after Christ I propose to fix the limit to my remarks. Embroideries made from after the time of Charlemagne, during the Crusades, the so-called Middle Ages, the Renaissance, and subsequently, we must look upon as relatively modern and outside the scope of our present consideration.

Style or character of the forms of ornament on textiles, which are indicated in paintings and sculptures, is, I think, important, as somewhat of a guide to the probable manner in which such ornament may have been either woven, stamped in colours, or worked with a needle. But before developing suggestions on these lines, I must briefly indicate what are usually held to be embroideries.

Embroideries are distinct from weavings with a shuttle in a loom. Weaving produces a stuff, and ornamental effect is not an essential element in the production of a weaving. Embroidery, however, adorns a woven stuff, and cannot be dissociated from ornamental effect. Some stuff or material is therefore a first necessity to an embroiderer. There are many ways by which he may do his work. He may darn or run stitches into a stuff without much changing its flexible quality or the general flatness of its surface. By other stitches, such as long or short stitches, chain and satin stitches, laying and couching threads, he may load one surface only of a stuff, and to that extent alter its flatness. Again, he may cut out forms from other stuffs and sew them on

to the foundation stuff, and thus affect the flexibility and flatness of it. But besides these ways of embroidering a stuff, there are other needlework methods often classified with embroidery. And the principal one of these is patching, or sewing together pieces cut out from different stuffs to fit one another. Patchwork when well made should have a flat surface and be uniform in its texture. Other branches of embroidery known as drawn thread and cut work bring us closely to needle-made laces, but of these I shall speak later. For the present let us keep ourselves to darning or passing threads into stuffs, to stitching threads on to stuffs and to patching bits of stuff together. Here then are three distinctive sorts of embroidery, two of which (the first and third) do not greatly affect either flexibility or flatness of its surface: whilst the second, of the three, results, by comparison, in inequalities upon the surface, thereby loading or stiffening the foundation material.

The antiquity of these three sorts of embroidery is unquestionable, since traces of their use are abundant amongst people whose primitive culture is presumably analogous to that of the ancestors of ancient Egyptians, Assyrians, Babylonians, Persians, and Greeks. With the means at their disposal, these latter historic and civilised people did certain kinds of embroidery in a way far in advance of anything nearly corresponding to them that modern embroiderers in civilised countries attempt. Certainly the regard or respect for the suitable use of materials seems to have been more intuitively felt and observed by earlier than it is by modern embroiderers; and this strengthens a supposition that methods of producing textile ornamentation by needlework, which would not greatly change the texture of a stuff to which it was applied, were for some time subject to little variation. Just as the few needlework methods seem to have endured for long periods, so, too, do style and character of highly conventionalised ornamental designs.

Now, besides the respect for material, and the prolonged adherence to similar conventional ornaments, climate, I think, had some influence in assisting lengthened survivals of methods of work and use of certain sorts of materials by ancient historical embroiderers. In very warm climates one would not expect to find stout textile materials loaded with heavy embroideries. In cooler climates one would not look for indigenous art in the embroidery of delicate textiles like muslins, which would not be suited for use under such conditions. Again, elaborated work, necessitating the use of delicate threads and fine needles would not be looked for amongst nations who, according to historical evidence, possessed neither the one nor the other. Whatever may have been taking place in the far East, as in China, in the use of fine silky threads and delicate implements 2,000 or 3,000 years B.C., it is fairly certain that silk and fine needles were practically unknown to Egyptians of such a time. Neither were silks and fine needles known to the Assyrians, of whose gorgeous textile ornaments we have so many suggestions in the sculptures at the British Museum, dating from the 9th to the 7th centuries B.C. Let us therefore dismiss from our mind's eye any pictures we may have formed of glistening and delicate silken embroideries having been made by ancient Egyptians, Assyrians, and even Greeks. If we agree to do this, we shall, I think, simplify the aspect of the matter we are considering.

By excluding silk, which is so freely used in later embroideries, we restrict ourselves to stouter textiles, made of flax, hemp, wool, and cotton. In Leviticus (about 1490 B.C.) reference is frequent to garments of linen and wool, and I think reflects the use of linen and wool, in Egypt, on the one hand, and in the Mesopotamian country on the other. Now, as regards cotton, its employment in Egypt dates from a later time than that we are first going to deal with. Pliny certainly speaks of cotton being grown in his day in Egypt, and alludes to its employment by priests and by the Government for the use of temples. But Pliny is comparatively modern. He tells us that the invention of cotton-weaving in Assyria is attributed to that legendary queen, Semiramis, which is not very valuable as evidence. Herodotus, fully five centuries earlier than Pliny, refers to something which some translators have accepted as cotton; but other specialists have more closely examined this technical point, and have shown that, whatever Herodotus was referring to, it was not the cotton fibre capable of being spun and woven, as was the Indian cotton.

In Yates's "Textrinum Antiquorum," a most valuable work, which apparently sums up almost all the ancient knowledge or information available in regard to textiles, a map is given, showing the natural distribution of raw textile materials in the ancient world. A copy of this map is now thrown on the screen. First, let me remark that the gradual use for manufacture by people of raw materials not grown in or

common to their particular countries, arose, no doubt, when, through trading operations, foreign raw materials came to be largely dealt with. Extensive trading in raw textiles was not, I imagine, carried on by the Egyptians and Assyrians at the time we propose to talk of them. The map before us should be tinted with colours ; if it were, we should see that a yellow tint in the far right indicates the silk-growing region—or rather the outskirts of the vast region unknown to the ancients—the inhabitants of which clothed themselves in silk. The tint (red) which stretches across the width of the map and includes Assyria and a great part of Southern and Central Europe, indicates countries in which sheeps', camels', and goats' wool and hair formed the staple textile material. The tint (green) indicates where flax was cultivated in lowlands bordering on rivers. The tint (brown) indicates the cultivation of coarser textile material such as hemp, which however, has been commonly used chiefly for sails and coarse cloths. The tint (blue) indicates cotton-growing districts. From this map then it appears that in Egypt, Assyria, and Greece the prevailing textiles were woollen and linen ones. Egypt's pre-eminence as a manufacturing country of fine linens is practically co-incident with the earliest known periods of her history. The late Sir Henry Layard was of opinion that the Assyrians made their costumes of linens and wools. Gold threads were also employed by the Assyrians and other Orientals for purely ornamental purposes.

Now I think it is interesting to find, as we certainly do, that the most ancient ornamental textiles in existence are made of linen and wool. Some of them preserved in the Hermitage at St. Petersburg are from Græco-Scythic settlements along the north-west coast of the Black Sea, and date from the 4th or 5th century B.C. or from 2,000 to 200 years subsequently to the dates of those indications of Egyptian and Assyrian embroideries we are to examine.

Notwithstanding this interval in time, we may perhaps regard the use of linen and wool in the make of the Græco-Scythic pieces, as reflecting earlier and similar use by other wool and flax-growing people, who were in frequent contact and communication with each other, such as were Egyptians, Assyrians, Persians, and Greeks, successively. Identical in make to the Græco-Scythic embroideries, and so displaying these materials and the particular process in using them at a later date, are a large number

4

of Egypto-Greek and Roman specimens of the 1st century B.C. to about the 9th century A.D. And the predominant method of embroidery in these latter specimens is a darning or in-working of coloured woollen threads into portions of linen garments and cloths. This darning or in-working was done with a bone or wooden needle, and is quite different from shuttle weaving.

In my Cantor lectures upon Egyptian tapestry, I endeavoured to explain how this darning or in-weaving method of needlework, so well suited to the adornment of costumes and small textile articles, came by degrees to be developed into a process involving the use of large frames containing only a web of warp threads for the production of great tapestries. It thus lost its character as an embroidery or needlework method, and became a weaving process. I need not go over the ground again. I will merely repeat, here, that ordinary shuttle weaving, such as the ancients practised, is a process which was universal and of all known time. The most intricate ornaments woven with shuttles were in the nature of stripes, checks, and other straight line patterns, and spots dotted at regular intervals throughout a stuff. All these may be wrought by simple changes in the grouping of coloured warp threads, and throwing in be-

FIG. 1.

EGYPTIAN KING IN STRIPED DRESS OF COLOURED SHUTTLE WEAVING.
From a wall-painting in the Ramesseum. About 1400 B.C.

tween and across them shuttle threads of other colours. Here, for instance, is an illustration of Egyptian weavers, at least 2,000 years B.C., engaged in making such work. In this case the ornament of the textile in the weaving loom is a check or chess-board pattern. Another slide displays a well-known type of an Egyptian king overcoming his enemies. His dress, and the cloth on his horse, are striped (Fig. 1). The dress stripes are blue and yellow, those on the horse-cloth are blue, yellow, red, and green. I take it that these textiles were of ordinary shuttle weaving. The original painting from which this diagram is taken is on a wall in the Ramesseum, and dates from at least 1400 B.C.

When, however, people first sought to infuse ornaments having curved forms into stuffs which had been produced by shuttle weaving, they either stamped or embroidered them. Such ornament was not woven with a shuttle, for the mechanical contrivances for intricate pattern weaving in a shuttle loom are, apparently, of comparatively modern invention, even amongst such renowned weavers as the Chinese, Persians, and Indians. By comparatively modern I mean not earlier than 200 or 300 years B.C. Apart from stamping, what then was the process which was the more likely to have been used much earlier for intricate ornament? It was, I think, the darning, or inwrought needle process.

Here is part of a linen tunic, possibly of the 4th or 5th century A.D., made by some Egypto-Roman (Fig. 2). The darker devices were darned, or inwrought, with a needle and coloured worsteds, into openings purposely left in the linen as it was manufactured in the shuttle loom. Some of the worsted threads have disappeared, but the under linen threads over which they were darned still remain. It will be noticed that the darning-in of the wools completes the entire fabric, and does not substantially change the flexibility and flatness of its texture. It may be readily gathered that any sorts of ornament could be darned in this way, which, therefore, I suggest, exemplifies a

FIG. 2.

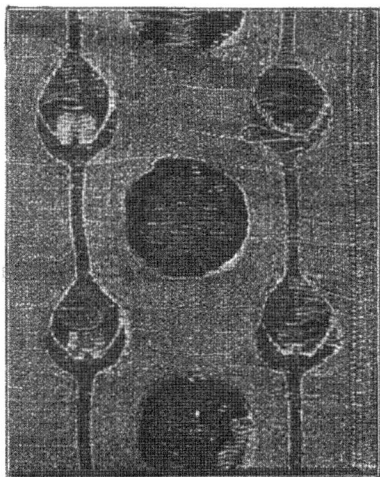

LINEN, WITH COLOURED WORSTEDS DARNED OR INWROUGHT WITH A NEEDLE.
Egypto-Roman. About 4th or 5th century A.D.

better regard or respect for materials than would be the case had the ornamentation been stitched, and thus loaded, on to the linen. The next diagram is from a similarly-darned and inwrought fabric. The pattern consists of repeated birds—ducks (Fig. 3). This piece is of Græco-Scythic work, of the 4th or 5th century B.C., so that it is some 800 years earlier than the previous piece, and is therefore an evidence of the prevalence at that time of the same method of ornamented needlework. It is most probable that Egyptian specimens of embroidery —described with much minuteness by Herodotus in the 5th century B.C., but produced some 150 years before he lived—were made according to

this darning method. These specimens—and Herodotus evidently saw and examined them— were corselets, sent as presents to the Greeks by Amasis, king of the Egyptians. Of one, Herodotus writes that it was of linen, with " many figures of animals inwrought, and adorned with gold and tree wool." The character of these corselets is considered by various authorities, Birch and Rawlinson, to be indicated in such corselets or breast coverings as are seen in the paintings of the wall of the tomb of one of the Rameses at Thebes Here is a photograph of a series of such corselets overlapping each other; the outer one exhibits the ornamentation—a pair of winged animals—above two lions. How much or which of the parts were adorned with gold cannot now be defined. The painting itself dates from 1,500 B.C.; and accepting the statement that it represents such corselets as were described by Herodotus 1,000 years later, we then have some ground for holding that the darning or in-wrought needlework with coloured threads into linen was practised 1,500 years B.C.

And here allow me to make a slight digression with regard to the use of golden threads in early embroideries. From the book of Exodus (chapter xxviii.) we learn that the ephod, the girdle, and breast plate (a sort of corselet), provided for Aaron, were made in needlework of blue, purple, scarlet, and gold threads. And in chapter xxxix. we find that the people charged to carry out the needlework " did beat gold into thin plates and cut it into wires (strips, probably) to work it into the blue and the purple and in the scarlet, and in the fine linen with cunning work." We can almost see the glisten of the gold wires or strips enhancing the effect of the deader looking coloured worsted work. This record of embroidery, and of gold in embroidery, dates from about 1490 B.C. and after the Israelites had been in Egypt. Their method of work probably resembled that of the Egyptians, and if so, then it is likely that it was of the darning, inwrought character. With the descriptions of Herodotus at one end, and those from Exodus at the other, of a period from 500 to 1500 B.C., it is not, perhaps, too bold an assumption to hold that the intermediate Assyrians, intimately associated with Egyptians and Hebrews, and renowned for ornamental splendour in their robes of State, were producers of technically similar darning and inwrought work of linen, coloured wools, and gold. It is rather remarkable, however, that amongst the Græco-Scythic fragments, contemporary with Herodotus, we should find no inwrought gold thread work. The only thing approaching the use of gold in the Græco-Scythic textiles are pieces of head-dresses, or sorts of diadems, of which I have a photograph. The leaves here shown are of thin plates of gold stitched on to the woollen material or foundation of the head-dress. That gold, however, was otherwise also used by the Greeks is evident, for in both the Iliad and the Odyssey there are descriptions of needlework with gold. Greek writers

from the time of Alexander (4th century B.C.), as well as Roman, well on into the Imperial Roman period, give innumerable references to the use of "cloths of gold." Of Asiatic historic nations "none," according to Yates, "was more remarkable than the early Persians for the display of textures of gold."

I now pass on to the series of diagrams illustrating indications of ornament on textiles to be found in Egyptian paintings, &c., and with the help of the preliminary remarks I have made I hope to be able to offer some reason-

FIG. 3.

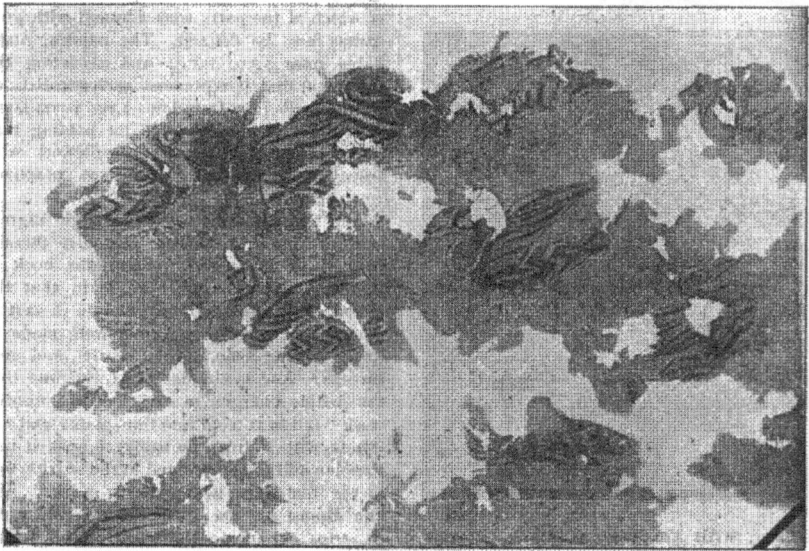

FRAGMENT OF LINEN, WITH DUCKS IN COLOURED WORSTEDS DARNED OR INWROUGHT WITH A NEEDLE.
Græco-Sythic. About 4th or 5th century B.C.

able suggestions upon the different ways in which such ornament was wrought on actual stuffs.

In the diagram on the screen we have four figures said to represent an Asiatic family brought into Egypt. To some extent this group might be regarded as similar to what might have been depicted had it been a question say of Joseph's brethren coming down into Egypt to buy corn. This is from a painting at Beni Hassan and dates from about 2100 B.C. The dress of the second figure to the right is powdered with spots—a sort of simple ornamentation not unlikely to have been produced in ordinary shuttle weav-

ing. The ornament on the other dresses was probably either stamped on to the linen, or else it was darned or inwrought with a needle.

From the same series of paintings is this figure with an ibex (Fig. 4). And although straight line ornament is shown on the dress and might therefore be said to have been of shuttle weaving, its disposition or arrangement is somewhat irregular, and leads me to think it more likely to have been of darning or inwrought needlework.

The next diagram on the screen is from a painting about 1540 B.C. on the wall of a tomb at Thebes. The personage in the ornamental dress is an attendant upon an Ethiopian Prince Hui, who paid tribute to a king of Egypt. There are two kinds of powdered spot ornament on the attendant's dress. On the white portions of the dress are red and blue spots, or rosettes, the darker portions of the drapery are blue, with red rosettes. As before noticed, whilst quite simple spots could be woven with a shuttle into a dress, it is doubtful whether these slightly more intricate rosettes devices would have been so produced. The commoner way of rendering them would, I think, have been by darning or inwrought needlework. On the other hand, they may have been stamped in colours. This, in regard to the red rosettes on the blue stuff, would have implied the employment of mordants as well as dyes, with both of which, however, the Egyptians appear to have been acquainted from early times.

FIG 4.

FIGURE WEARING A DRESS, PROBABLY OF LINEN, WITH PATTERN IN COLOURED WORSTEDS DARNED OR INWROUGHT WITH A NEEDLE.
From a wall-painting at Beni Hassan. About 2100 B.C.

The two figures next displayed on the screen are Syrians clad in loose dresses, somewhat rudely ornamented. They occur in the paintings on a wall in the temple of Seti I., about 1400 B.C. On the dress of the left-hand figure, the odd-shaped devices, derived apparently from the markings of a leopard skin, were probably stamped in colours. The simple outline ornament of the other figure's costume might suggest simple stitches on to it, were it not that the inner side of the dress is seen to be the same as the other,

whence one might conclude that the stuff was one of those of divers " colours of needlework on both sides" mentioned in the Bible, in which the needlework would have been probably of darning, though a satin stitch might have been used, and have been equally effective " on both sides."

The figure now shown is that of an Egyptian princess about 1500 B.C. She holds a sistrum with lotus flowers, and an ivy garland hanging from it. Her dress is decorated with simple and dainty ornament, such as could have been done on to it with short stitches.

Hathor and King Meneptha I. appear in this next diagram on the screen, the original of which dates from 1325 B.C. Hathor's dress is covered with ornament, consisting, first, of a diaper of hexagons, scarcely perceptible : for within the hexagons are repetitions of symbols producing the effect of horizontal arrangements across the dress. These may have been either stamped or inwrought by the darning method. If the subsidiary hexagonal pattern stood alone by itself, then it might have been of shuttle weaving ; the other devices, however, would not have been so produced.

Dating from 700 B.C., and taken from an Ethiopian temple at Naga, in Upper Nubia, is this figure robed in a costume covered with small crosses. The arrangement of these is not very regular, hence I conclude that they were not of shuttle weaving. They are more likely to have been darned in short stitches in to the dress. From the temple at Kalabsheh, in Nubia, and about 110 B.C., I have taken this figure of Osiris. His cloak is covered with a trellis or diaper pattern, which was, most probably, of darning or inwrought needlework, and this conjecture is supported by the fact that specimens, rather later in date, of kindred ornament wrought by this method have been found in Egypto-Greek cemeteries.

Of ornamented textiles for cushion covers, I have an illustration from a painting at Thebes dating about 1250 B.C. Those on the two upper chairs are white with powderings of red blossoms—those on the two lower ones are respectively of red and blue grounds with yellow discs. All of them may have had the ornament stamped on them—but if not stamped then the two upper chair covers would have been of inwrought needlework, and the two lower ones probably of shuttle weaving.

My next slide gives a specimen of the thread and bead work so often found upon mummies. It is not however a needlework in the sense of embroidery on a textile—although the little flattened beads were possibly passed on to the threads by means of a needle of some sort : on the other hand they may have been quite easily slipped on the threads without a needle. In the pieces before us we see the well-known Egyptian beetle or scarabæus.

The foregoing series fairly illustrates prevailing types of ornamentation, wrought by different methods on and into the surfaces of textiles, during a period B.C. of over 2,000 years, in Egypt. That the materials used were almost entirely linen and wool, I have little doubt. It seems doubtful whether the earlier Egyptians made much use of gold thread. Yates gives no instance of their having done so. The only ones that occur to me are the corselets already mentioned, and quoted from Herodotus. These, however, are of a com-

paratively late period for Egypt, namely, a century or two before the commencement of the Ptolemaic dynasty. Egypt had then been continuously, and, I think, strongly influenced by Assyrians, with whom, as with other Orientals, the use of gold thread was familiar. Hence the inwrought gold threads of the corselets, and, indeed, some of the character of the design for the ornament on the corselets, may be held to indicate, in some degree, Assyrian usage and feeling. Certainly the designs of animal forms on the corselet present a difference in style from much of the Egyptian needlework ornament just reviewed.

Such difference is still more marked when we look at indications of ornament on Assyrian stuffs. The first of these, in point of date, is that of the fine robes worn by King Asshurnazirpal and his attendants, sculptured upon great

FIG. 5.

KING ASSHURNAZIRPAL AND ATTENDANTS IN EMBROIDERED ROBES.
From the Nimroud Bas-reliefs. 884 B.C.

slabs taken from the palace of Nimroud, and dating from about 884 B.C (Fig. 5). Both robes are fringed, and the ornament on each is largely composed of human and superhuman beings, of elaborate sacred tree emblems, and of radiating palm devices, from which it is usually thought that the Greeks modified their long famed honeysuckle ornament, or anthemion. The borders only to the dress of the king's attendant are decorated with similar figures and emblems. The style of this elaborate ornamentation will be better seen in the enlarged diagram of the shoulder and upper part of the king's dress (Fig. 6). By no shuttle and loom weaving, so far as we know of it at that date, could this ornamentation, involving complex curves and intricate forms, have been produced. It was no doubt rich in colour, and in the glisten of gold threads. Sir Henry

Layard suggested that it may have been like the " prey of divers colours of needlework on both sides, meet for the neck of them that take the spoil," for such a potentate, indeed, as was Asshurnazirpal. Needlework on both sides could not have been an embroidery of long and short feather stitches, nor of chain stitches, nor of *appliqué* work, each of which makes a display on one side only of the material so worked upon. It could hardly have been of patchwork, which may make an equally effective display on both sides, for the details are too elaborate for such work. We shall presently see very beautiful patchwork which was made in Egypt a century earlier than Asshurnazirpal, but with different materials from the linen, coloured wools, and gold thread, which I think must have been used in this Assyrian embroidery.

9

The only method of using these materials to make an effect on both sides must, I think, have been a darning method. Let me again say that, with the ancients, the ornamental possibilities of materials were strictly observed. It is only in much later phases of art that the craving for effect supervenes and breaks through the apparent restraint of well developed early art. With this to weigh with us, as well as the apparent prevalence of the darning or inwrought method, together with the notion of the embroidery on both sides, I conclude that that method is the more likely and suitable one, by which the Babylonian embroiderers at the court

of King Asshurnazirpal wrought his robe of State. Babylonians, as is well known, were for centuries notable for their cunning embroidery, and supplied all parts of the ancient world with it down to the times of the Romans. Achan, in the 15th century B.C. confesses to Joshua that he coveted and took from amongst the spoils of his Syrian foes "a goodly Babylonish garment"—a well embroidered one no doubt, and Ezekiel 900 years later tells us of the "blue cloths and broidered work" in which the merchants of Tyre traded with those of Asshur or Assyria.

Before dealing with the remainder of my

FIG. 6.

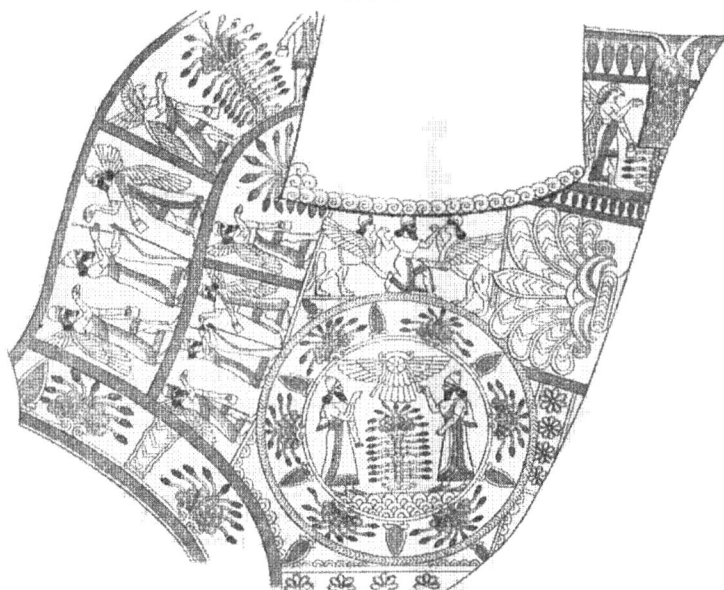

ENLARGEMENT OF EMBROIDERY UPON THE BODY OF KING ASSHURNAZIRPAL'S ROBE.

Assyrian diagrams, I wish to refer to the patchwork method as practised in Egypt about 1000 years B.C., somewhere about the reputed time of Homer. An actual specimen of such work has been fully described by Mr. Villiers Stuart, and from his work I have ventured to borrow the two illustrations of this specimen on the screen. The first one displays an Egyptian boat conveying a canopied bier, which contains the remains of a defunct Egyptian queen. The size of the canopy and the proportions of its ornamentation may be inferred from its relation to the size

of the persons on the boat. The lower side—which we see before us—of the canopy is of a large check pattern. Above it is a border of squares, containing different emblems.

We get, on a larger scale, the top and other border of the canopy in the next slide (Fig. 7). Half of the main part of the top is powdered with blossoms; the other half has a series of oblong spaces filled in with vultures. The upper border has repeated scarab cartouches, with inscriptions, and discs and serpents. The lower border, which was also figured on the boat scene, contains a central radiating lotus device, a goat on each side of it, pairs of conventionalised ducks, and scarabs. All this ornamental needlework, now in the Museum at Cairo, is of gazelle hide, cut out into the different forms described, and patched together with coloured threads. The colours of the several pieces of hide are bright pink, deep golden yellow, pale primrose, bluish green, and pale blue. Possibly of similar material and workmanship was the border to the pedestal upon which this figure from the great temple at Philæ is seated. This, however, is considerably later than the funeral canopy, as it dates from about 200 B.C. The winged creatures are white, outlined in red, and the ground of their panels is alternately blue and green. The seat is covered with a scale

FIG. 7.

EGYPTIAN COLOURED KID PATCHWORK.
About 950 B.C.

pattern of green and blue and white, each scale outlined in red. The same sort of ornament appears upon the body of the figure, and may have been of patchwork, though probably in coloured textiles. I think we may assume that patchwork was a method of decorative needlework, well-known and pursued with artistic finish at least from about 1,000 years B.C. in Egypt; and if there, then also to some extent in countries like Assyria, which were in touch with Egypt.

And now, returning to Assyria, we may derive suggestions of patchwork from the character of the simple ornament upon such a figure as this of Sargon the King (Fig. 8). The original is of coloured enamelled brickwork from Khorsabad. It is some 160 years later than

the Nimroud sculptures of Asshurnazirpal. The ornament consists of what I take to be feather-shape devices arranged along the borders of the king's dress. The colour of the dress is blue, but the feather devices are yellow. These, I think, were probably patched into the blue ground.

FIG. 8.

KING SARGON. THE ORNAMENT ON THE DRESS IS POSSIBLY OF PATCHWORK.
From coloured enamelled brickwork of Khorsabad. Assyrian. 719 B.C.

The same may be said of the costume of this winged figure, also from Khorsabad. This winged figure, in the original enamelled brickwork, precedes King Sargon. Behind him, and at some distance from him, comes his Vizir. His dress consists of a robe, striped upon the upper part of it, and bordered with deep check pattern; both of these seem to me to have been of shuttle weaving, rather than of any sort of embroidery.

There are, amongst the Assyrian sculptures, one or two instances of patterns generally considered to represent ornamental stuffs, which were used as rugs. Here, on the screen, is one of them. It was taken from the ruins of the palace at Kouyunjik (705 B.C.). The border is composed, first, of a series of lotus flowers and buds, then of a series of daisy blossoms, next of a series of radiating palm devices, and then of a series of daisy blossoms. The ornament of the main portion, or field of the rug, is of intermingling six-limbed stars, formed by the intersections of repeated circles. This ornamentation may, perhaps, have been made in patchwork; but it is complex and difficult for reproduction in that method. It was not of shuttle weaving, therefore it must have been of some sort of embroidery on to or into a foundation stuff. That it was a rug or a floor-covering suggests a textile with a cut-pile surface perhaps. But this special kind of manufacture is, I am led to conclude, of much later date than the times of either the Assyrians or the early Persian dynasty. The history of cut-pile carpet and rug making, having such a quantity of intricate ornamentation as that of this diagram, is involved with that of velvets and plushes, the existence of which, I fancy, is not to be traced until Byzantine times. Certainly the period of finest cut-pile Persian and Mohammedan carpets is that of the 16th century, A.D. If, then, the surface of this Assyrian rug were flat in texture, with no sort of pile, the ornament would have been made by the inwrought darning method, just as are many Eastern rugs of the present day even. If, however, it had some sort of raised or shaggy surface, then I think it would have been a linen or hempen stuff worked with loops or tufts of wool; and the oldest known examples of such tufted-surface needlework are to be found amongst Egypto-Roman textiles dating from about the second century A.D. Here is a photograph of such work. All the ornament we see is of bold needlework of thick worsteds. These are darned into the foundation material, and the threads of each stitch are regulated to form close-lying loops or tufts, so that the whole of the outer surface of the needlework is soft and yielding. I think that there is no great improbability in the notion that this looped-needlework method was known some centuries earlier than 100 A.D., and to the Assyrians, amongst other people.

There is little connection between it and the fringed borders which were so commonly used for Assyrian costumes and cloths. And with the question of fringes I shall not venture to trouble you now beyond showing a diagram of costumes with fringes worn by humbler persons than the kings and ministers whose fringed embroideries must be accepted as evidence of the highest class to which the art of the Assyrian needle-worker then attained. The individuals here represented are bearing tribute from Jehu to Shalmanazar (880 B.C.), and are from the sculptured pedestal of that date in the British Museum.

It will have struck you that the simple ornamentation of the robes from Khorsabad, in which I suggested the use of patchwork, was different in style from that of the Nimroud sculptures. The Khorsabad enamelled bricks date from 719 B.C. and the Nimroud sculptures from 884 B.C. From this circumstance alone

FIG. 9.

COLOURED ENAMELLED BRICKWORK, WITH ARCHERS IN RELIEF. THE ORNAMENT ON THEIR LINEN DRESSES IS POSSIBLY OF COLOURED WORSTEDS DARNED OR INWROUGHT INTO THE LINEN.

From Palace of Darius at Susa. About 520 B.C.

we might imagine that as time went on Assyrian ornamentation became simpler. This however was not the case. For the Assyrian sculptures of 668 B.C., from Kouyunjik, supply instances of the return to, or perpetuation of, a style of ornament in textiles similar to that of over two centuries previously. Here on the

12

screen is King Asshurbanipal out lion hunting. His dress is powdered over with the traditional daisy blossom embroidered in the inwrought darning method. It is fringed, and his saddle cloth is edged with pointed tassels. The harness is embroidered or enriched with daisies perhaps of thin beaten gold.

We are now getting near the time when the Assyrian monarchy was overthrown by the Persians. According to Sir Henry Layard, "the Persians were probably a rude people, possessing neither a literature nor arts of their own, but deriving what they had from their civilised neighbours." They employed the handicraftsmen and artists of the conquered Assyrians and Babylonians; and what can be called Persian art of the period, say of Darius I. (about 520 B.C.), is a direct descendant of Assyrian and Babylonian art. I have been unable to find many traces of early Persian embroidery. The best specimen is from the enamelled brickwork discovered by Monsieur and Madame Dieulafoy, and identified as part of the palace of Darius at Susa. The original brickwork is now at the Louvre at Paris, but an excellent *facsimile* of it has been acquired by the South Kensington Museum, and from that, the two figures now shown have been taken (Fig. 9). They are, as you see, soldiers armed with bows, carrying big quivers on their backs. The shape of the costume of each is the same, but the ornamentation differs slightly. In both dresses it consists of an orderly repetition or powdering of similar details. On one of the dresses these details are circular blossoms, with white, green, and blue petals, a reminiscence, but not a precise copy of the Assyrian daisy device; in the other dress, the details consist of small brown squares, each containing a triple tower fortress, picked out in white, yellow, and green. The narrower borders to the sleeves and dresses have repeated discs

and alternations of the lotus flower and its bud, picked out in whites and greens, &c. On the brown, large arrow quivers, fastened to the backs of the archers, are scattered in regular series, dark and light grey green, bean-shaped devices. I think that the embroidery of the dresses was of inwrought darning, and the materials probably were woollen. The colours of the original enamelled brickwork are fresh. The whole of the surface, from which the moulded figures stand in relief, is of turquoise blue. The dress of the first archer with the squares of embroidery is white, with yellow sleeves, whilst that of his fellow with the circular embroideries is yellow, with dark brown sleeves. Both have brown complexions, their tightly curled hair and beards are black, and the bindings round their heads are green.

I have thus endeavoured to present to you some ideas of the ways in which Egyptian and Assyrian embroideries may have been wrought, suggesting that the more frequently used methods were those of in-wrought or darning needlework and of patchwork. The materials were linens and wools, enriched sometimes with gold threads. The difference between the styles of Egyptian and Assyrian ornament in its relation to textiles has also been touched upon.

Next Monday I propose to treat the indications of Greek embroideries in a similar manner, deducing, from the new ornamental features we shall find in them, additional methods of needlework. From these we shall pass on to Roman, Byzantine, and Saracenic specimens, from which we shall obtain a further insight into the use of all the methods previously noticed, as well as evidences of variations of ornament due to the influence of lingering traditions and remains of earlier and more formal ornament, upon later and mixed races of people.

LECTURE II.—DELIVERED FEBRUARY 18, 1895.

You will, I think, remember that in my first lecture I endeavoured to explain how it was that the methods employed by early Egyptians and Assyrians for their ornamental

needlework seemed to consist, in the main, of two: namely, an inwrought, or darning method, and a patchwork method. I tried to show further, by instances of ornamental designs on ancient textiles, that these two methods were peculiarly adapted for the rendering of divers compositions in which curved forms predominated ; whilst straight line forms, stripes, checks, trellis patterns, and powderings of spots which grew, almost naturally, through the crossing of different coloured wefts and warps, were more readily produced by shuttle-weaving than by embroidery, and were therefore woven, and not embroidered. By needlework, it was practically possible to render any kind of ornament in textile materials, but by weaving, the kind of design or pattern was limited. In both cases, however, through the regard for the nature of the materials used, and through other causes, such as symbolism and meaning in ornament, the range or style of ornament fluctuated but little. Certain conventionalities were adhered to for very long periods, so far as concerned the composition of, and details in, ornament produced by early Egyptians and Assyrians ; and this fixity of fashion in ornament no doubt helped in conserving the two principal methods of embroidery I have alluded to. Now this conservativeness is in striking contrast to what would be seen, were we to review a series of examples of European embroideries produced during the last 400 years. We should find that their styles of ornament and methods of needlework abounded in changes and modifications almost innumerable. This changeful and vivacious European period is, therefore, in antithesis to the sedate and conservative Egyptian and Assyrian periods.

Now something of the same changing character seems to mark what, for present purposes, I will call the Grecian period of embroidery ; and whilst we shall detect the use of the darning and patchwork methods in Grecian embroideries, we shall find a free use of other methods, well suited to new varieties of ornament, invented and developed from earlier sources by the Greeks. To broadly illustrate this change of style in textile ornament, as between Assyrians and Greeks, I have made a few sketches of typical ornaments ordinarily employed by these two nations respectively in their textiles.

According to this diagram (Fig. 10), Assyrian ornaments (for a period from 880 to 550 B.C.) for textiles consisted principally of simple devices, to be arranged along bands and borders, or in orderly powderings. As I have previously pointed out, fringes were generally worn on the edges of skirts in Assyria. They are

rarely met with in Egyptian, Grecian, and Roman costumes. The devices in the first two borders of Fig. 10 are simple loop forms, set out singly. The third border has an upper set of these single loop forms repeated above recurrent oblongs, in the centre of each of which is a daisy. Such daisies or rosettes—

FIG. 10.

BORDERS AND OTHER PATTERNS ON ASSYRIAN COSTUME OF THE 9ᵗʰ TO 7ᵗʰ CENTURY B.C.

as we have seen—were also powdered over stuffs. All these curved devices were probably inwrought or darned into the stuffs. The series of squares represents a frequent and simple textile ornamentation, which, as we saw it with Egyptians of 2,000 B.C., and later, was probably the outcome of shuttle-weaving. The vertical band of and chevron forms, also, was probably of shuttle-weaving ; but the border to the right of it, with radiating palm device and daisy blossom repeated in alternations, was embroidered with darning or inwrought needlework. Far more intricate ornament, reserved, apparently, for the robes of kings and dignitaries, included sedately-conventionalised winged and other figures, sacred tree devices, and so forth. So much, briefly, for Assyrian ornament and its comparative limitations.

From a fewer number of sources than those I consulted for the foregoing Assyrian ornaments, I have selected these Grecian examples. (Fig. 11.) The familiar varieties of the rectilineal key-patterns, or squared continuous scrolls, are purposely omitted. Curved line devices are for the most part, here given, and some were probably embroidered on to the stuffs in long and short and chain stitches.* I mention these stitches, because they will be found in specimens of Grecian needlework, which I will presently show. In the first of the two upper borders we have single curves, much lighter in effect than any of the Assyrian ornaments. The second border has a waved line, suggestive of continuity in ornamental line, a quality almost absent from either Egyptian or Assyrian ornament. This waved line was apparently of simple stitch embroidery on to stuffs. The pointed tooth-shape border is usually indicated in the designs on Grecian vases as being darker or lighter in colour than that of the stuff it adorned. Such a border would be suitably

FIG. 11.

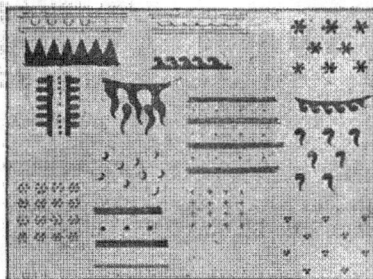

TYPES OF GRECIAN TEXTILE ORNAMENTS.

6th and 5th centuries B.C.

rendered in patchwork; I am doubtful if it would have been of *appliqué* work, and whether that kind of work was ever in vogue with Greeks; I hardly think it would have been, as it would have tended to load and thicken textiles in a manner opposed to the apparently prevalent sense of appropriately using materials. Next to the dentated or tooth-shape border is a familiar Grecian ornament, the continuous wave device. This again is generally different in colour from the stuff it adorns. It too might have been of patchwork, but its curving character makes it more likely to have been darned or inwrought, as were the flame and tear forms near it. The various spots and bands with spots be-

* Since writing these lectures, I have, through the kindness of Mr. A. Higgins, seen a good many photographs of the coloured Grecian sculptures (dating from before the Persian invasion of Athens, early in the 5th century B.C.), now in the Museum of the Acropolis, at Athens. The patterns (picked out in colours) on the dresses of many figures are various, and their appearance leaves little room for doubting that they were of the darning or inwrought needlework, done with coloured worsteds into linens. They are valuable links in the history of textile ornamentation.

tween them may have been of shuttle weaving, whilst the other curved devices used as ornaments scattered, irregularly and regularly, over stuffs were, I think, darned or inwrought.

We may, therefore, fairly conclude that Grecian ornamentation for textiles gave occasion for the use of methods of embroidery more numerous than those chiefly in vogue with Egyptians and Assyrians. Not only were inwrought-darning and patchwork methods applied to the rendering of new ornamentation that sprang from the lively genius of Grecian designers, frequently influenced by earlier designers, but stitching on to stuffs became more common than it had been with Egyptians and Assyrians. A new phase in embroidery thus seems to have arisen. Whereas ornament in the inwrought-darning was an integral part of the fabric it adorned, and whereas by patchwork an entire and ornamental fabric was made, embroidery on to stuffs was an addition to an already completed stuff, and was merely an embellishment.

I fancy that little is known of the intimate history of Egyptian and Assyrian embroiderers. Of the Grecian, however, we certainly know more at present, and one of the noticeable facts is the indication of the widely spread employment of women in connection with the textile art, both in its ornamental and utilitarian aspects. To this fact is due much of the variety in methods of Grecian embroidery. One naturally turns to the Odyssey or Iliad as the earliest sources of information in this respect, and there we find a good many references to Grecian weaving and embroidery and the employment of women in those arts. But in making use of such references we have to remember that in countries near and practically adjoining to Greece there was a wide-spread practice of the arts long before Homer was in existence—further, that the version of the Homeric poems to which we are accustomed dates from the 6th century B.C., when Pisistratus, tyrant of Athens, caused the poems of Homer, previously in a state of confusion, to be brought together and written in the form now known. The domestic incidents in them are, therefore, probably flavoured with views of life in the 6th century B.C. In addition to this we should remember that Homer, who is reputed to have lived about 1000 B.C., is generally considered to have been an Asiatic Greek. Consequently, it is likely that Asiatic or Oriental influences have entered into the descriptions of ornaments of all sorts, as well as of methods of work given in the Homeric poems. Penelope throughout the day "weaved an ample web, but in the night, by torchlight, unravelled it." Her weaving, according to a design on a 6th century Grecian vase was of the nature of inwrought ornamental work on hanging warps, rather than of plain shuttle weaving on stretched warps. So also was that of Circe, who "sang with syren voice, whilst weaving fabric large, fine, splendid, beautiful." Ulysses wanders in the palace of Alcinous and comes upon female domestics "a few whereof did grind the yellow corn, in hand mills; others sitting wove the web" . . . . "like, as Phœacian men excel all else to guide ships o'er the sea; their women do in weaving webs; the Goddess Pallas hath gifted these with most ingenious minds to form fine works most beautiful in art." Again, how suggestive of ornamental skill in textiles, is Ulysses' description of his "fleecy purple cloak" . . . . "with double cape; and button of wrought gold; which had two loops. Its front had cunning work: a dog in forefeet held a spotted fawn, gazing upon it gasping—wonderful, though being of gold. He gazed upon the fawn, while strangling it; and, eager to escape, the other struggled, quivering with his feet." I know that some translators have decided that this hound and fawn incident was wrought upon the gold button or clasp of Ulysses' mantle, and not upon the mantle itself; but there are as many other translators who determine in favour of the hound and fawn having been embroidered in gold and coloured threads into the mantle. Pope and Chapman are among the latter; and Wakefield's notes to Pope's translation seem conclusive in favour of the embroidery. Of recent translators, Butcher and Lang incline to the ornamentation of the gold button. Certain it is, however, that amongst some of the earliest embroideries extant, this incident of one animal springing or preying upon another is given. Many references by Grecian writers to ornamental inwoven needlework, as well as to women's part in carrying on the art, might be quoted; enough perhaps has been given to indicate that at an early date Grecian women were peculiarly skilled in ornamenting stuffs. In the 5th century, and earlier, the women's rooms in the houses of the Greeks were called gynecia, and the mistress of the house superintended the women at work. She, like Pallas with the Phœacian women, instigated her work women to produce divers ornaments of cunning work

in textiles. Up to the times of the Roman emperors this domestic interest, in embroideries and such like, continued. But Roman matrons were not as faithful to it as their Grecian predecessors had been. The use of the name gynecia was kept up, but almost entirely in respect of public or tradesmen's workshops, which during the 3rd and 4th centuries A.D. became subject to Governmental regulations. In these the *gyneciarii* were those who wove imperial robes with golden and silken threads—for by the 3rd and 4th centuries A.D. silk had come into use for the making of costly costumes in Rome; though not until after Justinian, that is in the 6th century, was it more freely employed.

Let me, however, return to the 6th century B.C. with its linen, worsted and golden threads, and show a diagram from Miss Harrison's new work on Grecian vases (Fig. 12). It represents part only of the design in black and red, painted and scratched upon the inside of a flattened bowl. The centre is occupied with the design of a hero (Hercules probably) struggling with a marine monster (Nereus). The border consists of a string of dancing women hand-in-hand capering after each other. There are varieties of simple patterns on their dresses. Those which are powdered or scattered, and diapered, are more likely to have been of shuttle weaving. Dresses of a light colour have borders along the skirts, and these borders have ornament which was probably of the darning inwrought needlework. The ornament on the dress of one of the figures to the right is a diapering of scale forms, which were rather of chain-stitch needlework than of shuttle weaving.

The next illustration, also from a vase given in Miss Harrison's book, represents Danaë upon a couch with the golden shower falling on her. Her many folded costume has a dark-coloured bordering, another variety of which may be noticed on the veil or head-dress hanging just beyond the end of her couch. These borders were probably of the darning inwrought needlework. The covering of the couch has a pattern of trellis and crosses, and this was possibly of shuttle weaving. The vase upon which all this is depicted is of the 5th century B.C.

From another Grecian vase, in the Hermitage at St. Petersburg and of a slightly later period, perhaps early 4th century B.C., I have taken this group of gods and goddesses. The ornamentation of their robes (rather faintly reproduced) is a good deal richer than that previously seen. The continuous wave scroll is

B

16

used a good deal here as an edging to bands containing spots or tear shapes. These would be, I think, of darning inwrought needlework.

Of about the same period of Grecian art—4th century B.C.—as that of the group we have just looked at, are the fragments of Græco-Scythic embroidered stuffs which I mentioned in my

FIG. 12.

DESIGN ON A GRECIAN BOWL OF THE 6TH CENTURY B.C., SHOWING DIFFERENT TEXTILE ORNAMENTS IN THE DRESSES OF THE DANCING FIGURES.

first lecture. The first of them is a bit of red woollen material, with two bands of repeated bell blossom or calyx forms. These are of the darning inwrought needlework, done with red, green, and yellowish woollen threads. The type of ornament differs a little from what has been previously seen; but much of this difference is due to the effect of such designs when worked, as here, in actual materials, and not merely sketched in outline upon a vase.

Very probably of similar needlework and materials were the ornamental features of the skirt, and shoulder covering, of this figure of Hercules. (Fig. 13.) In these we find diversity of motives. The cloak on which he sits is bordered with the vandyked shapes which we found in Grecian ornament of two centuries earlier. Upon the skirt of his tunic we see a snake ornamentally treated; below it, is a bordering of repeated leaves. His cape is rich with its band of honeysuckle, or radiating ornaments, alternating with spreading lotus flowers. Blossoms, with four petals, are scattered over the stuff of his sleeves and body. All these I take to have been of coloured thread darning,

and probably gold may have been introduced to

FIG. 13.

HERCULES SEATED: PORTIONS OF OTHER FIGURES ON EITHER SIDE OF HIM.
From a Grecian Vase. About late 5th or early 4th century B.C.

heighten the effect. To the right is part of a

figure of Minerva, with the gorgon mask on the upper portion of the dress, which is powdered with crosses and edged with vandykes. Vandykes occur upon the dress of the third figure —the one on the left, towards whom Hercules is looking. This, perhaps, is Mercury. His cloak, like Minerva's robe, is powdered with crosses, and edged with vandykes, whilst to the upper semicircular piece, there was an outer edging of the familiar continuous wave scroll, of which a portion only remains in the diagram.

Here are two more of the Græco-Scythic fragments. (Fig. 14.) It is somewhat difficult to

FIG. 14.

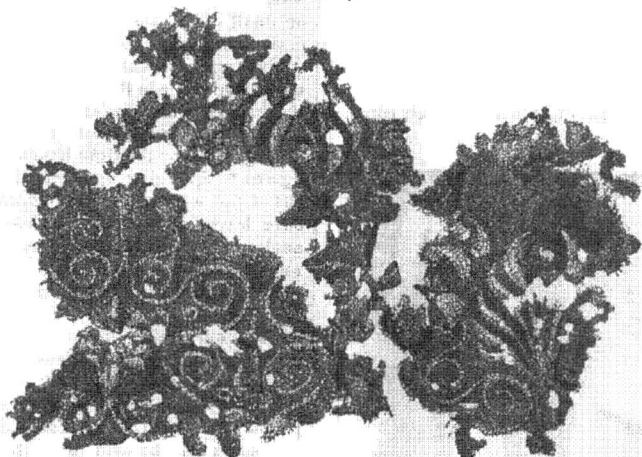

GRÆCO-SCYTHIC CHAIN STITCH EMBROIDERY ON A STUFF.
About 5th or 4th century B.C.

perceive at first what the ornament on them is. But the eye, growing accustomed to the fragmentary effect, soon realises the beauty of the ornament and the general effect of such work as it appeared originally. The embroidery is of chain stitch, with threads of yellow linen, I think, and the ornament is of radiating honeysuckle devices and convoluting stems, lighter in effect than more solid ornament usually done in darning inwrought needlework.

The dainty ornament on the tunic worn by this figure of Paris, with his Phrygian cap, seems to me to have been so embroidered with chain stitch, and probably with goldenlooking threads of linen or worsted. His close-fitting sleeves and leggings, or pantaloons, were, I think, of shuttle-woven material, whilst his cloak, with tear shapes and vandyke edge, was probably of inwrought needlework. The draperies of Helen and her attendant are without embroidery. This group is from a Grecian vase of the 3rd or 4th century B.C., preserved at St. Petersburg.

I am afraid that it is something of a task to attempt to grasp the interesting and technical information conveyed by this photograph, taken from the last of the Græco-Scythic fragments. However, I will briefly describe it. The stuff, upon which there are rather obscure indications of embroidery, is a thinnish shuttle woven stuff of rather dull red colour. It is bordered on the lower part with fragmentary darning and inwrought needlework of worsted, thus proving that this method of needlework was used with other and different embroidery on the same fabric. On the specimen before us the indications of such other embroidery are found to be of long, short, chain, and cross-stitches. When the embroidery was in tact, it represented a man on horseback. He wore a short tunic, with an ornamental border. His left hand held the reins, and his right was uplifted behind him ; his horse was apparently prancing.

And now let me point out the actual indications of what I have described. Here, first of all, is the horse's head ; here the indications of his legs ; here is the man's head ; here his left arm and shoulder, fairly complete ; here are his feet, and here the border to his tunic ;

above are the remnants of his right arm and hand. In this tattered rag we have evidence of how human figures and animals were sometimes embroidered by Greeks in the 4th century. As an ornamental device, the horseman is distinctly Scythic or Persian; it survived for many centuries subsequently, in later Grecian and Roman designs strongly influenced by Oriental traditions.

Less Oriental in feeling, and more strictly Grecian of the 4th century B.C., are the ornaments on these fragments of sculptured drapery recently discovered at Lycosoura, in Arcadia, and described in a pamphlet, entitled

Fig. 15.

SCULPTURED ORNAMENTED DRAPERY.
From Lycosoura. 4th century B.C.

" Fouilles de Lycosoura," published at Athens in 1893, from which I have ventured to take this illustration. (Fig. 15.) The forms are in low relief, but I do not suppose that this relief corresponded with, or was intended to convey an impression of heavy raised embroidery. The earliest raised or padded embroidery I know, dates from many centuries later—the 14th or 15th century A.D. at earliest. There is great diversity of ornament in this 4th century B.C. sculpture of Grecian embroidery, and judging from what we have seen I should say that much of it was (originally, in the real stuff) of chain, long and short stitches. The upper

portions are decorated with bands of ornament, free in style, and not of such formal arrangement and severity as were noticeable in the suggestions of 5th and 6th century embroidery. In the bands are birds, sprays of olive leaves, mythological female figures mounted upon sea horses and fish-tailed personages; both of the upper portions are edged with a graceful little ornament of heart shapes or small discs, and little pendant or tassel devices hanging down from them. This edging was probably of darning inwrought needlework. Upon the larger, lower spaces of the drapery we find Grecian female figures bearing pedestals surmounted with vertical ornament grasped by the right hands of the female figures.* Springing up vertically in front of one of the women will be noticed a spray of olive leaves and berries, which is at right angles to a corresponding spray running horizontally. Beneath this comes a band of small grotesque figures, and below this, finishing the edge of the drapery, is the continuous wave scroll, which latter would be appropriately of inwrought needlework.

And now I come to a break of two or three centuries in my series of illustrations. The period of the richly ornamented drapery from Lycosoura may be said to be that preceding the time of Alexander the Great, i.e., the later portion of the 4th century B.C. One result of his conquests and settlements in Asia Minor, Syria, Egypt, Babylon, Persepolis, Bactria, Cashmere, and the Punjab, was the infusion, into Grecian ornament at least, if not also into Grecian methods of work, of a mixed Oriental feeling, as well also as the diffusion of Grecian spirit in certain sections of Oriental art, and instances of these could be readily quoted. I must however restrict myself to embroideries, and in these the readiest to hand are samples of Egypto-Grecian ornament produced in the pervading method of inwrought darning needlework.

The first of these is the inwrought ornament to a neck trimming, perhaps of the 1st century B.C. or A.D. It comes off an Egypto-Grecian tunic, and the prominent ornamental feature in it is a series of Grecian honeysuckle or radiating devices. It was found at the disused cemetery at Akhmîm, near the Nile in Upper Egypt. Akhmîm is the modern name of the old Grecian town Panopolis or Chemmis, which was well-known to Strabo and Herodotus.

The next piece (from the same place) is a

* These are barely traceable in the illustration, though they were well seen in the lantern slide.

fragment from a Grecian or Roman tunic of shaggy linen material, of which latter Pliny gives a description. The circular panel rested upon the shoulder of the wearer—the two bands below it run along the extremity of a short sleeve. The little dancing figure (not unlike some of the grotesque figures in the Lycosoura sculpture) perhaps represents Mercury. Around the panel in which he appears is a series of pointed bud shapes. The playfulness of the design is Grecian, and might suggest as early a date as the 1st or 2nd century B.C. for the origin of the piece. But the waved stem and leaf ornament along the sleeve is of a heavier character, and seems to imply a later influence, consequently the whole of the piece belongs to a later date—possibly the 2nd or 3rd century A.D.

Another style of decoration is shown in this diagram on the screen—a photograph from an inwrought worsted panel, with a portrait in it. This, again, is also probably of the 2nd or 3rd century A.D., and of Egypto-Grecian or Roman work ; but it might very fairly be accepted as a specimen of the tapestry heads or portraits described as having adorned the hangings in the Palace of Ptolemy Philadelphus in 3rd century B.C.

The very great skill exhibited in the Egypto-Grecian and Roman inwrought or darning needlework is, more remarkably, displayed in specimens of later date, and of altogether different style of ornament. This piece is probably of the 7th or 8th century A.D., and is a mixture of late Roman and Mohammedan styles. The dainty workmanship of the fine white-lined geometric patterns is far beyond anything comparable with it in modern needlework. The whole of the specimen is actually not much more than two feet square. The elaboration of the ornament in it is well worth close examination. Take one of the corner portions : first comes a plain narrow bordering to a band, barely an inch wide, filled with double-lined interlacing angular stems ; between each of the interlacings is a small outlined cross. A plain bordering comes next, and then a broader band with double-waved stems interlacing one another and worked into it. In each interlacement is a ten-petalled blossom. A delicate cable pattern is picked out in white threads upon the interlacing stems, and so on. The darker portions of this piece of wool, and the bright lines are of linen thread.

The next specimen is of similar darning needlework, and is even of finer texture, due

not only to the great skill of workmanship, but also to the employment of silk threads, far smaller than the linen ones of the previous specimen. The ornamental shapes are of a poor degraded style ; but this defect is compensated for by the beautiful contrast of the colours, chiefly red, yellow, blue, and black. This is a piece of Saracenic needlework, belonging to the period of the Khalif Al-Mustansir billah, who was living in 1047 A.D. A number of such inwrought needle darnings with silks on linen threads have been brought to light recently. Into some are worked Kufic inscriptions, such as, "In the name of God the Merciful, the Gracious ; " "There is no God but God ; " "Mahommed is the Apostle of God ; " "Ali is the favourite friend of God ; " "Al Mustansir billah, Prince of the Faithful, the blessings of God be upon him, upon his fathers, the pure Imams, and upon his sons." Apart from the delicate texture of these later specimens of inwrought darning needlework, let it be noted that the employment of this particular method of needlework has now been practically demonstrated to have existed for fifteen hundred years, from the Græco-Scythic specimens up to those of the date of Khalif Al Mustansir billah ; whilst, for at least as long a period previously to the 3rd or 4th century, B.C., the embroiderers of Canaan, of Babylon, and of Egypt had apparently also pursued it, although with different materials, and in rendering very different sorts of ornament, into all of which, however intricate, curved forms entered

The remaining illustrations of this lecture are of embroideries recently obtained from Pagan-Roman and Christian burial places at several places in Egypt. To do full justice to them would require considerably more time than is allowable ; they call up many associations which, if properly treated, would form an epitome of events in respect of Roman rule in Egypt, the early Christian church, and its numerous sects, the Arab conquest, and the decay of the Byzantine or Eastern Roman Empire.

Amongst these embroideries there are hundreds of the inwrought darning work. In addition, however, there are several pieces of other work in which the embroidery is stitched on and into woven stuffs. Few of these other embroideries differ, technically, from those noticed as gradually developing through the ingenuity and taste of the Greeks ; and the preponderance of the Pagan, Christian, and Saracenic specimens is of coloured wools and linens, just as was the case with the needle-work of ancient Egyptians, Assyrians, and Babylonians. Those worked with silks belong to the later of the times that I cannot touch upon. Here, now (Fig. 16), is a little specimen of

FIG. 16.

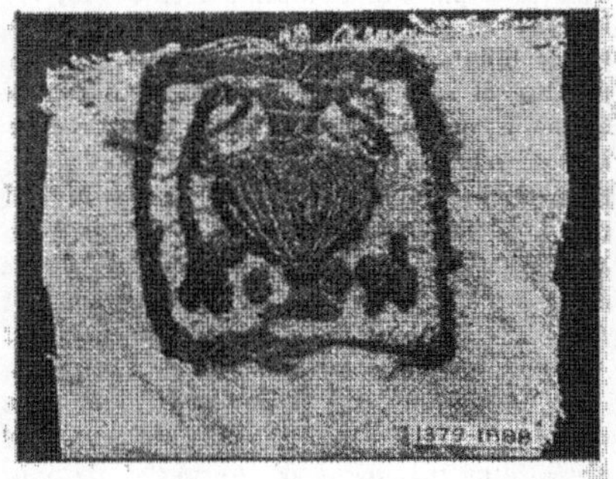

SMALL VASE AND LEAF ORNAMENT OF LONG AND SHORT STITCHES, WITH WOOL ON LINEN.
Egypto-Roman. About 2nd or 3rd centuries A.D.

Egypto-Roman embroidery with brown wool, in long and short stitches worked on to linen. The design is of a Roman double-handed vase, the handles terminating in leaves. This small panel was one of a set of four that ornamented the skirt of a child's tunic.

My next example presents another kind of needlework. I referred to it in my first lecture, and connected it with Assyrian or Babylonian rugs. Here, however, this class of needlework is used for another purpose, namely, for a loose linen cloth which may have been worn or else thrown over a seat. The woollen embroidery consists of longish loops left projecting upon the surface of the linen into which they are sewn, and forming a raised ornamentation. In this piece the ornament is composed of a number of single heart shapes or rose-blossom petals, variously coloured, pink, red, and green, and placed at regular intervals from one another. The same petal device, repeated in a close order, runs along the border.

This is a comparatively simple ornamenta-tion ; a more elaborate one is seen in this next illustration on the screen, which represents two cupids in a boat, surrounded by a border of over-lapping leaves, with a man's head or mask in its corner. The original, in the British Museum, is of the looped worsted embroidery, and its date may be placed as early as the 3rd cen-tury A.D., if not earlier. The design, espe-cially of the border in connection with a figure composition, recalls that of the work done in the embroidery or weaving competition between Minerva and Arachne, the incidents of which are told with consider-able detail by Ovid.

The earliest Christian embroidery, that is to say, ornamental needlework presenting em-blems of Christian significance (similarly with other branches of Christian art) directly re-flects methods of work and schemes of orna-ment prevalent with the various non-Christian people amongst whom the Christian faith gradually had taken root and grow, blossoming variously according to the cults of local sects, or different schools of thought. In a piece like this, of inwrought needlework, we find a Romanesque style of design—a square about a circle—each of the corners filled with a sort of acanthus calyx device, and the centre filled with a large cross and four birds between the limbs of the cross. Of the same period—about 4th century A.D.—is this next specimen. (Fig. 17.) This, however, is of rather close needlework

FIG. 17.

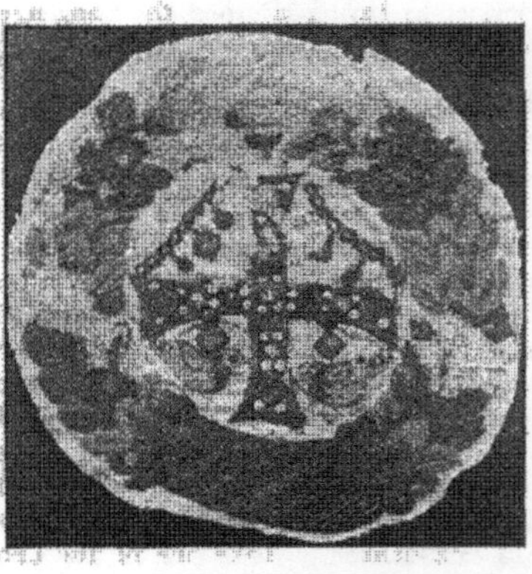

LONG, SHORT, AND CHAIN STITCH EMBROIDERY IN COLOURED WORSTED AND LINEN.
Egypto-Roman, 4th or 5th century A.D.

upon linen, for which bright red, green, and yellow wools have been used. The stitches are long, short, and chain. A wreath encircles a jewelled cross, with chain and pendent jewels ; on either side of the lower limb of the cross is a dove. The style of the design belongs to the time of Constantine the Great, probably ; but it was a style that lasted for some centuries later, and the gold and jewelled visi-Gothic votive crown of King Recesvinthus of the 7th century, is an important evidence of the survival of this style, though in other materials. The specimen here, however, is worthy of notice as a sample of 4th or 5th century embroidery, loaded, as it were, on to a stuff and for ornamental effect solely.

From the point of view of Christian symbolism, the next three pieces of Egypto-Roman, or Coptic, inwrought needlework are very interesting. The first of them has a series of the debased renderings of the Egyptian symbols of life and fertility—the crux ansata or Ankh. Now, when the Temple of Serapis, at Alexandria, was destroyed in the 4th century A.D., Christian writers of a hundred years later recorded that many of such venerated and Pagan symbols were found there, and, although known as such, fervent Christians did not disdain to imagine that these symbols might equally typify, prophetically, the redemption of the world. In consequence of this, a Christian meaning was imported into the Egyptian symbol ; and, according to Sozomen (5th century), many Pagans were duly impressed with what they were told concerning the new meaning given to their old symbol, and were thereby converted to Christianity. Besides giving a new meaning to the old symbol, its representation was subjected to changes, as we see here by the introduction into the loop, upon the tau cross, of Christian crosses and of stars, &c.

In the second piece we find the old Egyptian symbol again, but with a face inserted in the loop of the ankh. Two Romanesque vases stand below the horizontal limbs of the cross, and a smaller vase is placed on each side, above the loop. The continuous wave stem and leaf bordering is, of course, but a poor survival of the more graceful Grecian device of the same construction or design.

The third of these Christian inwrought needleworks is probably of the 5th century A.D., the scheme of the pattern is Roman. (Fig. 18.) In the centre is a red-legged bird, perhaps a partridge, which is said to be connected with a legend concerning St. John. In each of the corners is a fish-tailed creature, each with a different head. One is a bull's head, the emblem of St. Luke ; the lion's head for St. Mark ; the eagle head for St. John ; and the last one, apparently a dog, stands evidently for St. Matthew. It is interesting to note here that certain of the emblems of Ptolemaic Serapis, *i.e.*, the chief god invented by Ptolemaic Greeks to take the place of the venerable Osiris of Egypt, were akin to these fish-tail and animal-headed creatures ; and it is certain

that the Christian emblems we are now looking at were made not so very long after the extinguishing of Serapis worship at Alexandria. From the mere ornament point of view, these Christian emblems seem to owe something to the Pagan emblems of Serapis. In later emblems of the evangelists, St. Matthew is represented by a man's head, according to St. Jerome, but elsewhere an angel typifies St. Matthew. St. Augustine held that the lion symbolised St. Matthew, and that the man's head, or angel, stood for St. Mark. However this may be, the inwrought needlework before us is of great interest to Christian iconography, and may be worth elucidation by some authority upon the influences that may have been brought to bear upon designers

FIG. 18.

of symbolical ornament by such varied Christian sects at Alexandria, as the Monophysites, the Nestorians, the Jacobites, &c.

It looks like bathos to descend from such engaging topics to simple needlework again ; but it is desirable for me to refer to a few examples of Saracenic embroideries which help to develop the general story of the growth of embroidery. Kindred to the inwrought darning process is such work as this, in which the pattern is simply darned into the linen, and does not help to complete the fabric itself. This work possibly dates from the 7th century, A.D., and of course is like much that is made now-a-days.

Of the same class of embroidery, but more ornamental, is this linen cloth with small squares, forming a subordinate trellis pattern to the blossom shapes placed at the centre of one of which is each lozenge space (Fig. 19.)

SARACENIC OR EGYPTIAN ORNAMENTAL DARNING OF COLOURED WORSTEDS ON TO LINEN.

About 7th century A.D.

The colours of the worsteds are light blues, greens, and browns. This, too, is needlework of the 7th century, found in Egypt. This class of ornamentation was also worked in the in-wrought darning method, as in this next piece. Here we find a subordinate trellis pattern, or general framing, within which are different devices, some suggestive of blossoms, some of trees and leaves; others, again, are circular panels, with star forms in them; and some of these star forms are Saracenic in style. Within the border to this cloth are a number of small forms, which appear to be derived from the peacock feather, with its dark central spot or eye. You will notice, too, from the parts from which the coloured wools have disappeared, that the darning, or inwrought work, was limited to those spaces which had been left uncrossed by weft threads, as the entire linen was woven in the shuttle loom. As I have already remarked, in respect of previous pieces of the same class of needlework, the inwrought wools completed the entire fabric, and were not darned into a completed stuff. The two different methods of darning were concurrently used at the same time we are now dealing with; but I think it has been shown that one has an older origin than the other.

Further examples of stitching on to and into a finished woven stuff are given in this next slide. The upper band is embroidered with black wool, in short and satin stitches. It is Saracenic work of the 7th or 8th centuries A.D., and came from Erment, in Upper Egypt. The next band below is embroidered with blue, green, and brown silks, in short and long stitches. This is of the same date, is Saracenic, and comes from Mataieh, in Upper Egypt. The third bit is of darning embroidery, whilst the fourth is of short or tent stitches, giving an outline effect, a much lighter one than that of the fuller work in the third piece.

The next slide gives us a part of a linen dress or cloth, embroidered with coloured silks in long and short and chain stitches, with two horizontal bands of crosses and geometrical ornament, one of which is bordered on each side with a row of palm trees with a pair of birds at the base of each alternate tree. Between and beyond these trees are scattered numerous small forms, such as pairs of crowned figures seated, peacocks, other smaller birds, lions, crosses, leaves, and triangular emblems. Towards the lower part are three roundels, with borders of illegible Kufic characters. This is, perhaps, of Coptic work of about the 10th century A.D., and comes from Meshaieh, near Girgeh in Upper Egypt. The use of silk in it gives it special interest.

Of close, long, short, and chain stitch embroidery is this portion of what was once a roundel (Fig. 20), some 9 inches in diameter, filled with figures of personages, wrought in silks of brilliant crimson, yellow, green, &c., the forms of the figures being outlined in black silk. Such style of ornamental figure composition doubtless belongs to a later period of the Byzantine empire, say the 7th or 8th century. But it had been in vogue for a century or two previously. Rich persons adopted sacred subjects to be embroidered on their costumes; one senator boasted of having at least six hundred figures upon his robes of office. And in the 5th century, Asterius, Bishop of Amasea in Pontus, preached at the vain-glorious " who wore the Gospels on their backs instead of in their hearts. Every one," he said, "is eager to clothe himself, his wife, and his children with stuffs ornamented with flowers and numberless figures, and to such an extent is this done, that when the wealthy classes show them-

selves in public, little children gather round
them in crowds and point their fingers at them,
making merry at their expense. The more
religious of the wealthy classes require artists

FIG. 20.

PART OF AN EMBROIDERED ROUNDEL TO A DRESS.
Probably 7th or 8th century A.D. and Byzantine in style.

to supply them with subjects taken at their
suggestion from the New Testament, of Jesus
Christ and his Disciples, or else from his
many miracles."

I conclude my series of illustrations with the
well known group of the Empress Theodora and
her suite, taken from the famous 6th century

mosaics at Ravenna. The ornamentation of
the dresses will be seen to be plentiful, though
not so extravagant as that seems to have been
which Bishop Asterius denounced. Figures
of the Magi bearing offerings appear along the
border of the Empress' cloak; on the skirts
of her attendants we see trees or else birds
profusely scattered in regular series, reminding us of that bit of Græco-Scythic inwrought
stuff figured with ducks, which we saw in the
first lecture. The cloaks are dotted over with
small blossoms or crosses, or else covered with
a pattern of repeating circles and such like.
The dentated or vandyke bordering, such as
we saw in Grecian costume of some 1200 years
earlier, is to be found amongst the ornamentation, so, too, is a trellis pattern not unlike that
on the cloak of the figure of Egyptian Osiris
shown in the first lecture. Much of this variety
in ornament was done according to the long
surviving inwrought darning into a stuff,
whilst some was of later long and short stitch
embroidery on to a stuff; other of the ornament
was, perhaps, of simple shuttle weaving. The
whole illustration, however, is, I think, a suitable one with which to conclude my diagrams
this afternoon.

I feel that my suggestions upon means
for verifying ancient embroideries have been
of a slight character; still, I hope that at least
they are not misleading, as far as they go. I
think you will agree with me that the subject
generally is one that has very many and far-
reaching ramifications. It is certainly one that
I should like to pursue very much further.

Means for verifying laces will be the subject of my next lecture, and I think that we
shall find that lace is a not altogether remote
offspring of weaving and embroidery, although
so different in appearance from both.

LECTURE III.—DELIVERED FEBRUARY 25, 1895.

In a lecture upon means for verifying ancient
hand-made laces, and one for which I find it
necessary to have a considerable number of
illustrations, it will be advisable at the outset
to give a definition of lace. In the first place,
it is a fabric of itself, as a loom-woven stuff is,
though in texture and appearance lace is quite
different from a loom weaving. Lace is not an

embroidery on to a stuff, though very often it is
a needlework, but wrought independently of a
foundation stuff. It is distinctively an ornamentation, and is not what is termed an article
of necessity. It grew from a desire to produce
ornamental effects by adapting methods in
using loose threads to such a particular purpose—methods, however, which for long periods

had been used, and, indeed, are still also used for useful as distinct from ornamental purposes. When lace began to grow, its growth under the hands of women was comparatively rapid. We may look for signs of it amongst such lovers of ornamental textile fabrics as the Assyrians; but the nearest approximations to it are tasselled fringes, of which I now show an example or two. The tasselled fringes were formed sometimes by binding groups of loose threads together, and sometimes by twisting and plaiting them together, as in cords, braids, or boot-laces. Knotting was also sometimes resorted to. Twisting, plaiting, and knotting

threads together are methods which are used in making some laces. But it is obvious that the Assyrian fringes cannot be called laces.

Again, to turn to other thread fabrics for making which other methods were used, let us take such nets as we see in this sculpture of Assyrian hunters. The nets here shown were made by looping and knotting a continuous thread. Looping a continuous thread is also a feature in some lace-making.

I can find no evidence that Greeks of classical times made laces. They had nets, and nets of different kinds, thereby evincing some desire for variety of ornamental effect,

FIG. 21.

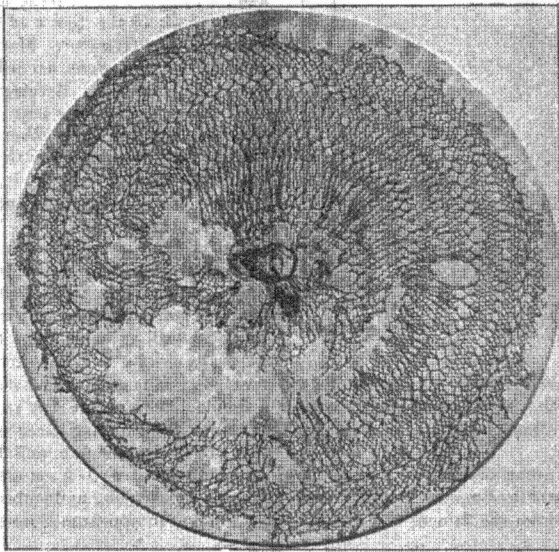

NET—PROBABLY A HAIR-NET.
2nd or 3rd Century A.D. Egypto-Grecian.

in net. Suggestive of such varied nettings are specimens of Egypto-Grecian nets made, probably, about the 2nd or 3rd century A.D. Here, now, is a fragment of an oblong net. What its particular use was I cannot say; but there is ample indication of variety in the arrangement of the loopings and knottings. The next specimen (Fig. 21) of similar varied net work is circular, and was used, possibly, as a hair net. This, too, is Egypto-Grecian work of the 2nd or 3rd century A.D.

I believe that no further light, from times before the 15th or 16th centuries, can be

thrown upon the origin of lace-making. From the mere process point of view it may be said that the progenitors of one sort of lace work were fringes, and those of another sort were nets. When, as in fringes, a number of of threads twisted, plaited, and interwoven amongst themselves are to be detected in a lace, then it is a pillow or bobbin lace; and here are a pillow with bobbins arranged for making lace. The pillow is of an ordinary type; but the size and shapes of pillows and bobbins have altered from time to time, and according to the different kinds of lace made at various

COVERLET OF WHITE LINEN, WITH BORDERING AND INSERTIONS, OF DRAWN AND WHIPPED THREAD WORK.
Italian. 16th Century.

places. The lace being made on such a pillow as this would be of a very simple character.

For making nets, I said that a continuous thread was looped and knotted. When in a lace we follow a continuous thread through a succession of loopings, then such lace is either needle or machine made. But with machine-made laces I cannot now deal. Laces made by hand are to occupy your attention. As regards the characteristic of looping in needle-made laces I show this diagram on the screen. In the upper strip you may just see the pattern drawn in outline upon a bit of paper or parchment. Below it you see part of this pattern with an outline of thread stitched on to it; adjoining it is part of the lace fully worked out in thread upon the pattern; and if we could look into this worked portion we should see that the whole of it was made by a series of looped stitches cast by the needle, first upon the original thread outline, and then amongst themselves and drawn together into compact

textures. The lowest strip is of the lace made from the design above, after it has been detached from its paper or parchment drawing. The relation of needlepoint lace to net is only in respect of the looping of a continuous thread, which operation is common to both. Needlepoint lace-making is, therefore, as high a development from net-making, as pillow or bobbin lace-making is of fringes. Thus it is only as regards methods that these several articles have a common parentage. When ornament, which, as I said, is a paramount element or feature in lace, comes into question, then the genealogical trunk of lace spreads off into distinct branches.

The sources of ornament for lace, as first made, are to be found, for the most part, in the embroidery of white linens, canvases, and square-mesh nets. This class of embroidery arose under the influence of an extending use, and confection, of white linens in the 15th and 16th centuries, when fancy and taste dictated a demand for the ornamentation of such fabrics. Splendour in weaving silks and velvets and cloths of gold had been reached for centuries, but ornamented white linens were practically unknown; and the attractiveness of white thread-work to enrich white linens had not been experienced to any great extent Time allows me to show a few specimens only of this class of work, and those must be of a matured style, such as had been acquired by the commencement of the 16th century. In one branch of this ornamentation of white linens, threads would be pulled or drawn out to form interstices about ornamental forms left in the plain linen. And here is an example of drawn thread-work. (Fig. 22.) It is Italian, of the 16th century. As threads were pulled out, so those remaining

would be whipped round, or prevented from fraying by buttonhole, or, in this case, whipped stitches. Here, on the screen, is another example of drawn thread-work with whipped stitches; this is Persian, and possibly of the late 15th or early 16th century. Its ornamentation is comparatively simple, and perhaps hardly commensurate with the amount of careful work put into it. It is more than probable that from such Eastern work, as well as from somewhat similar work done in the Grecian Archipelago, the Italian and other European art of drawing out threads and stitching over them was derived.

The next specimen of pulled or drawn thread-work is an Italian linen cloth of the 16th century. (Fig. 23.) The ornament of the insertion in this piece is more varied than that

FIG. 23.

CLOTH, WITH DRAWN-THREAD AND BUTTON-HOLE STITCH WORK.
Italian. 16th Century.

of the Persian cloth, and is strictly of a geometric style. The plan of the ornament is a repetition of open squares filled in with devices arranged along and about the diagonals of the squares. To make the open squares, a great number of threads have been pulled out from the linen. Those which remain are overcast with looped or button-hole stitches, and thus converted into the thick vertical and horizontal sides of the squares; they may be tracked from the outer margin of plain linen on one side to the centre of linen within the open ornament work. The work between the sides of the several squares is of closely compacted looped stitches. The whole

insertion of open ornamental work is practically identical with the earliest needle-point lace. The difference being that the thread-work in this case starts with the linen, whilst in needle-point lace you would draw a pattern on a bit of paper, and fasten tracing threads on to it, and then sew over and between them, and thus make a fabric independently of any foundation of linen.

The inevitable tendency of the drawn thread-work was to give a geometrical style to its ornament, and for a short time this style prevailed with lace - makers. Many books of patterns, published in the 16th century, contain instances of this geometric style. Here is a page of the repeated squares with varying star, rosette, and diagonal devices within them. These are for bands or insertions of geometric lace, which would be produced independently of linen, and only added to it afterwards as taste might direct. Here is another page from the same old pattern-book, and on this we have a series of tooth shapes or vandykes to be worked in lace as borders to the edges of cloths, or they might be, as they frequently were, joined on to the edge of a lace border or band, and thus convert it into a deeper piece of lace.

I have here a specimen or two of the deeper vandyked laces, two of large proportions and one of much smaller proportions. (Fig. 24.) The rather stiff and wiry character of this geometric pattern lace should be noticed, as I shall have to return to it shortly in connection with portraits, which are the means by which the dates, when this sort of lace was first made and used, may be verified.

Before I show these portraits I must mention one or two other kinds of embroidery, those done on square mesh nets—there were no circular mesh nets in the 16th century—from which we gain suggestions of more elaborate ornament than that of the geometric style of squares and rosettes and vandykes. Here, then, is the end of a fine linen cloth

having insertions of square mesh net, into which ornament has been darned. Besides the darning into the net, we note in the

FIG. 24.

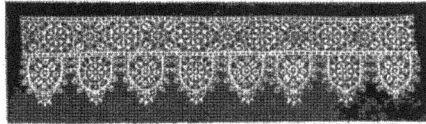

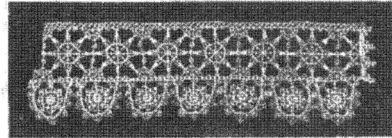

VANDYKED BORDERS OF GEOMETRIC-PATTERNED NEEDLE-POINT LACE.
End of 16th Century.

intervening linen that some circles have been cut out of it, and into them are introduced little open wheel and star devices of needle-point lace. Along the edge of the

FIG. 25.

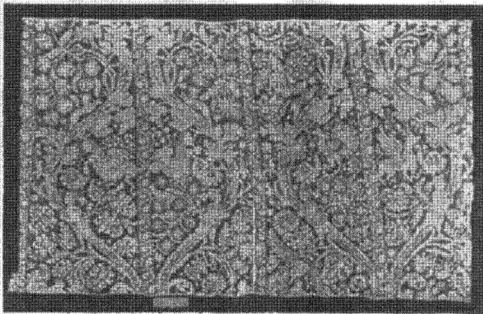

EMBROIDERY (OTHER THAN DARNING) ON TO NET.
Early 17th century.

piece is a simple bordering of vandykes, wrought by plaiting and twisting threads. This last is early bobbin or pillow lace.

A different kind of embroidery on net is shown in this next diagram. (Fig. 25.) Here, the needlework is not simple darning, other stitches are used; and the adoption of them

enabled the worker to reproduce the flowing curves and intricate forms, flowers, birds, and fantastic figures of men and animals, &c., with more freedom than darning strictly according to the square meshes of the net would permit.

Such varieties of ornamentation in white

linen and net embroideries not only preceded laces, but were also subsequently made when laces were in their incipient stage only; but, having reached that stage, they were not likely to stop there; and, as they became popular and fashionable, the ingenious makers of them competed amongst themselves, as well as with the linen embroiderers, to develop successive phases of increased ornamental effects, which, whilst reflecting those secured by other means, became specialised in the laces. A new industry was thus started, growing simultaneously in Italy and Flanders. This simultaneous growth is no curious coincidence, but a natural result of close artistic and commercial relations between the two countries. The industry as quickly gave signs of life in France and England; and, looking back over the circumstances, it may be said that an international community of lace-makers rapidly came into existence. The same general styles of ornament were observed successively by the sections of this community; and sub-varieties of such styles came to be associated with localities, whence, as time went on, there were the laces peculiar to Venice, Milan, Genoa, Bruges, Brussels, Mechlin, Valenciennes, Paris, Alençon, Honiton, and the Midlands of England. By far the greater quantity of these laces were of white thread; some were made with gold and silver threads; and some with black and white silks; all, however, were made according to either the pillow and bobbin or the needle-point method. Wiry, geometric laces, as we have seen, came first; then the ornament was less severe, and more flowing, and the forms, instead of looking wiry, had much more the character of narrow braid or tape; and the texture of such lace was rather more pliant and lissom. Then there was a phase of heavy, close-textured lace, with bold scrolls, in which parts were of raised work and most elaborately wrought with the needle. In contrast, as it were, to these, the pillow-lace makers made laces in which the braid and tape-like scrolls, were opened out, and set-off by intricate mesh groundings. The needle-lace makers responded to this by making lace also of similar ornament, but with much finer mesh grounds, or grounds composed of endless hexagons, and wheels and stars, &c., for which a bewildering complexity of looping and button-hole stitches was resorted to. Very large pieces of such laces were produced for use as flounces, fichus, ample cuffs,

and bed curtains even. And finally, when ornamentalism had, as it were, run riot with all the quips and cranks of restless fancy, there was a speedy decline into the simplicity of lace-net grounds, spotted over with little bunches of flowers, sprays, single blossoms and spots. Hence it is, that with all these varieties of ornamentation and different textures, we see at the present day all of them counterfeited, with varying success, in the cottony machine fabrics, so that one day ladies wear things that somewhat resemble the vandyke geometric laces, the next something like the stately heavy-raised laces of Colbert's time, and the next clouds of nets, akin to the spotted fichus of Marie Antoinette.

And now, by means of my illustrations, I hope to give you some visible indication of what I have briefly described.

This is a portrait of Catherine de Medici, at about the age of 20. (Fig. 26). It was painted by

FIG. 26.

PORTRAIT, CATHERINE DE MEDICI WEARING A HIGH STANDING LINEN COLLAR, WITH CUT AND DRAWN-WORKED ORNAMENTS IN IT.
About 1539.

Jean Clouet in 1539. In her high-standing stiff linen collar we see insertions of drawn thread-work. Along its edge are little pointed ornaments, probably of button-hole stitch work.

Here on the screen is a portrait of Mary Queen of Scots, painted about 1587. About the edge of her cap and along the edge of her long veil are similar small pointed ornaments of thread work, probably of plaited and twisted threads, or very simple bobbin lace.

This portrait of Charles of Savoy, chief of the leaguers who defended Paris against Henry of Navarre, is dated 1582. His ruff is bordered with a narrow band of squares filled in with circles and lines of needle-point work, whilst the tiny ornamental edging to it is of dainty devices, which may have been either of needle-point or of plaited and twisted thread-work.

To give you a clearer idea of this lace work,

I show an enlarged specimen of it. Parts of the square framings and the ornaments within them are wrought with the needle, but the vandykes are of twisted and plaited threads.

The foregoing portraits displayed lace work in conjunction with linen, but here (Fig. 27) in this painting, by Paul Moreelze, of Amelie, Countess of Hainault, we have a ruff made entirely of lace, of which material her dress is also trimmed. In this lady's lace you will recognise the style of those needle-point van-

FIG. 27.

PORTRAIT OF AMELIE, COUNTESS OF HAINAULT, WEARING A HIGH-STANDING VANDYKED RUFF OF GEOMETRIC PATTERNED NEEDLE POINT LACE.
About 1600.

dyke borders shown a short time back. The painting dates from about 1600.

A few years later is the portrait—painted by Vandyke, when a young man—of François de Bassompierre, Marshal of France. He wears a wide horizontal linen collar, trimmed with a deep border of dentated lace. The ornament of it consists of repetitions of squares, containing star forms, &c., as well as fleurs de lys. But these forms are fuller look-

ing than the corresponding ones in the earlier lace of this geometric style, and they have more of a "tapey" appearance about them.

This fuller and "tapey" quality is more noticeable in the next portrait of Count Oxenstern, Minister to Charles the IXth of Sweden, an early 17th century Bismarck. The photograph is taken from an engraving of a painting by Mirevelt, of 1630. The collar here is turned down, and is of linen, trimmed with bobbin or pillow lace. The ornamentation indicates a change of style; it is not divided into a band and an edging of tooth shapes or scallops; it is designed to fill the entire width of the lace. Again, the " tapey " forms in it are well defined, by their being opened out, and merely held together by little bars or tyres, which cross the small spaces between the separate details.

Corresponding with this character of lace ornament is that in this specimen of actual lace which is of needle - point work, and has a " tapey " appearance. We may consequently say that this piece of lace dates from about 1630, or a little earlier.

How the gradual development of the "tapey" and pliant qualities in lace was accompanied by the adoption of forms constitutting further departures in ornamental designs for lace may be inferred from such a specimen as this

deep triple scalloped bit. (Fig. 28.) In each scallop is a sort of carnation or corn-flower blossom on a rather clumsy stalk. This sort

FIG. 28.

TRIPLE SCALLOPED CUFF OF PILLOW-MADE
" TAPEY " LACE.
About 1630.

of lace was in fashion in 1630, and in proof of this I refer you to the next slide. In this (Fig. 29) the "tapey" and pliant qualities of

FIG. 29.

PORTRAIT, BY VANDYKE (1634), OF PRINCE OF SAVOY, CARIGNAN, WEARING
DEEP COLLAR AND CUFFS OF PILLOW-MADE "TAPEY" LACE.

the lace are apparent, as well as the ornamental features, such as radiating blossoms in the scallops. The portrait, by Vandyke in 1634, is of a Prince of Savoy, Carignan. His collar consists of one entire piece of lace, and is not like earlier collars of linen trimmed with lace.

It is, therefore, an indication of the assertion of lace as a fabric by itself, and independent of linen altogether.

But for some time ornamental linen work continued in its race for public favour with lace. And here is an effective painting by an artist of the school of Rubens, dated about 1639. There is a lingering suggestion of the earlier and formal scallops or points in the

open work of the fichu or scarf which this lady wears. I think that this open work is not lace, but is of cut linen work. And in support

FIG. 30.

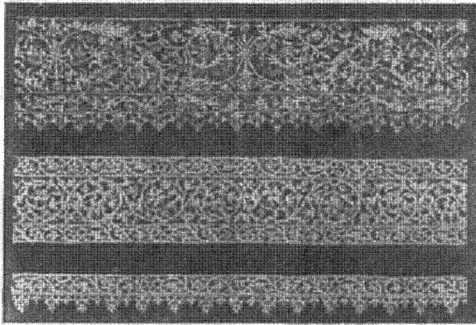

BORDERS OF CUT LINEN (TO IMITATE " TAPEY " LACE), AND EMBROIDERED WITH GOLD THREAD AND COLOURED SILKS. About 1639.

of this supposition I have here some borders of cut linen work, much of which has been enriched with coloured silk and gold thread embroidery. (Fig. 30.) The ornament is composed of many well curved and continuous scrolls and floral devices, and the facility with which they could be cut out of linen, as they are, very much assisted the accurate rendering of the design. Corresponding scroll ornamentation, when adapted in lace at this period, is not quite so freely rendered, as we may judge from such a specimen as this, which is an important piece, namely, 1640 or so.

A group of Charles Ist's children, painted by Vandyke in 1639, gives an example of vandyked collars and trimmings made of "tapey" lace, and worn independently of linen. The size and varied shapes of the vandykes at this period mark a gradual change (which was taking place), in passing from pointed tooth-shape borderings to rounded scallops. And an early instance of such rounded scallops in "tapey" close-patterned lace—probably pillow lace—occurs in Rembrandt's painting, dated 1640, of a lady. The original is in the Royal Gallery at Windsor. The masterly ease with which the lace is painted in this portrait is all the more apparent when we come to compare the lace with a sample of corresponding real lace, such as we see in this next slide.

Three specimens of pillow laces are shown in Fig. 31. The first shows us the tendency to change from tooth shapes to more rounded and

varied forms; the second gives us the rounded scallops, just as we saw in Rembrandt's

FIG. 31.

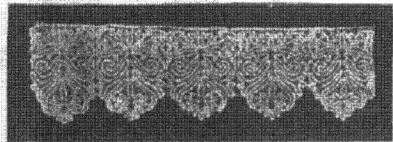

(1)

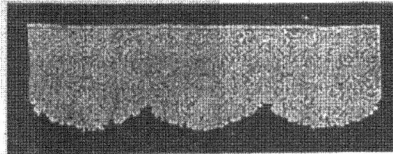

(2)

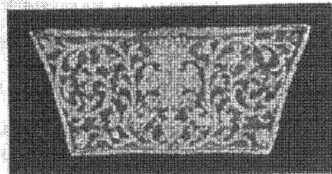

(3)

THREE SPECIMENS OF PILLOW-MADE LACES. (1) About 1640. (2) About 1630 to 1640. (3) About 1650.

painting; the third piece belongs to a few years later, twenty years at least. This third

o

bit is of pillow lace. The pattern of a crowned double-headed eagle in the centre, and scrolling devices supporting it on each side, has a well-marked "tapey" effect, which makes a good contrast with the grounding of meshes in between it. This kind of lace is soft and lissom to the touch, and, as we shall see, was made in much larger pieces.

For instance, here are two bits of the same kind, and one of them—the larger one—is at least a foot in width. The narrow piece has a ground of crossed lines, or barrings, not meshes, and this is an indication of the way in which the lace-makers began to vary the grounds to their well-marked "tapey" patterns. The mesh-grounds are usually called *réseaux*; the ground with lines sometimes placed regularly, as here, and often, later on, irregularly, and merely to tie or link the portions of the pattern together are called *brides*. This is worth remembering in classifying laces; some are laces with *réseaux* or mesh grounds, and

FIG. 32.

PORTRAIT OF FRAULEIN VERBIEST (BY GONZALES COQUES, 1644), WEARING PILLOW-MADE LACE À RESEAUX.

some are laces with *brides* or bars; and these two divisions will be found from about 1640 forwards, so that the older geometric laces, and the close "tapey" laces are gradually being left behind.

This portrait of Esprit Flechier, a Bishop of Nismes in the middle of the 17th century, gives a cuff only of such lace, *à brides*, as we saw in the smaller of the last two specimens.

And in the next portrait of Francis de Montmorenci, Duke of Luxembourg, we see, indistinctly, that he wears a large lace cravat of lace *à réseau*, similar to the larger of the two specimens.

The bold "tapey" lace with the *réseau* ground was generally called "Point d'Angleterre," because such great quantities of it were made for the English market, especially in the 17th century. For years after, this name—"Point d'Angleterre" was retained for trading pur-

33

poses, in respect of very differently patterned laces. It was, however, made in Flanders, where pillow-lace making flourished more than needle-made lace. The "tapey" lace, à *brides*, also of pillow make, was produced in Flanders too ; but being apparently more to the taste of the Flemish, it was commonly called "Point de Flandres."

Here is a big cravat of pillow-made Point de Flandres, or "tapey" lace à *brides*.

The very considerable variety in the patterns or designs for lace which date from the middle of the 17th century is almost perplexing ; and in so short a time as that at our disposal, it is impossible to do more than glance at a few specimens which tell us of this great variety.

This, now, is a portrait of a French noble, painted by Lefebure in 1666. The diagram is from an engraving of the painting. The pattern of the lace cravat is of flowers, closely arranged together, but well defined by the spaces between them, across which we can see little tyes, bars, or *brides* holding the stems and blossoms together. This is evidently a needlepoint lace, more stiff looking than the soft and lissom pillow lace.

Although the pattern is not identically the same, the likeness in style is quite marked in this piece of floral-patterned needlepoint lace, à *brides* ; so that we may feel pretty certain that it is of the same date as the portrait, namely, about 1666.

Here again we seem to meet with the same class of lace, à *brides*. This is a portrait of a certain Herr Verbiest, painted in 1664 by Gonzales Coques, of Antwerp. The flowery pattern is more open than in the previous piece.

By the same artist is this portrait of Fraulein Verbiest (Fig. 32). But her lace trimming is softer looking, and is, therefore, probably of pillow lace. But the flowery style of "tapey" pattern with a *réseau* ground is still maintained. I cannot pause to enter into an argument in favour of this lace having been made at Valenciennes in preference to Mechlin, or Bruges, or Antwerp, or Brussels. At all these places the industry was flourishing. So, too, was it at Venice, and Milan, and Genoa ; so, too, was it beginning to flourish in a most marked manner in France ; for a great lace-making company, under the very special patronage of the Grande Monarque, Louis XIV., had been floated by his Minister, Colbert. Laces had, according to a humorous poem of the time, got into a revolt, and all sorts were jostling each other for public favour. Alençon

was vying with Venice, Havre with Ragusa, Flanders with Spain, and so on. But we must always bear in mind that it was entirely due to Colbert's diplomacy, in importing some fifteen to twenty Venetian lace workmen into France, that lace, identical in style and make to the splendid Venetian laces, was produced in that country, although, through the more playful fancy of the French designers and workers, it came to be metamorphosed into the famous Points of Alençon and Argentan. Of the great Venetian laces of the middle and end of the 17th century, I can but show a sample or two.

Here is part of large border (probably for an altar cloth or a priest's robe) which is

FIG. 33.

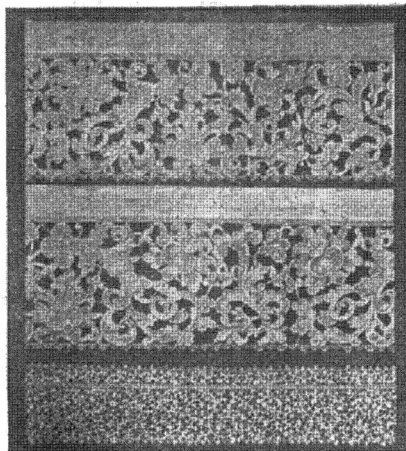

SPECIMENS OF RAISED, RELIEF OR "ROSE POINT" VENETIAN NEEDLEPOINT LACE.
About 1660-1680.

typical of the stately and elaborate raised Venetian lace. The whole of it is of needlepoint work, reducible however to the one stitch, the buttonhole stitch, that we found the simplest patterned early needlepoint laces commenced with.

Three more specimens of the same kind of work and style of design are shown in Fig. 33. The lower smaller piece is a marvel of stitchery. There must be hundreds of thousands of stitches in it. Spotted about the slender graceful scrolls are little blossoms with clusters of small loopings upon them. Some particularly fine examples of these raised Venetian laces are to be seen in the collection at the South Kensington Museum, from which, indeed, most of the pieces photographed in my lantern slides have been taken.

In the portrait by Pierre Mignard, of a young princess of France, we have the front of a dress made entirely of needlepoint lace, much in the style of the Venetian scroll-raised laces. But here the scrolls and floral devices are more opened out, and in between them is a ground work of large hexagons. This sort of ground work, but on a small scale, is usually considered to be one of the principal characteristic of the Point d'Argentan, which, in a way, competed very closely with the equally famous Point d'Alençon.

Towards the end of the 17th century, lace was worn in great profusion by men as well as women ; and in illustration of this I show a photograph of a portrait, painted in 1700 by Trinquesse, of the High Admiral of France, Louis Alexandre de Bourbon, son of Louis XIV., and his mistress, Madame de Montespan. The lace itself is not of any considerable distinction, as regards the ornamentation in it, though no doubt the High Admiral's cravat and shirt, which can not be well seen, were more elaborate in design than the trimmings to his coat.

Intricately patterned laces were much worn by men, especially by church dignitaries; and in this connection I may now show a photograph of part of the lace worn on his alb by Fenelon, Archbishop of Cambray. This fine piece of Flemish pillow lace, of the end of the 17th century, was presented to his Grace by Madame de Maintenon, the Veuve Scarron, whose fascinations so greatly swayed Louis XIV. The design for such a piece as this was probably made by ornamentists of such standing as Le Brun or Berain, and the lace made perhaps at Bruges or Brussels. Kindred in make and design, is such a flounce with *réseau* ground as this. (Fig. 34.)

The fanciful conceits of designers of ornament for lace at this time are most remarkable, and, for the most part, have little æsthetical relation to the materials in which they took shape ultimately. At the same time, they were arranged in such a manner as to produce, when seriously regarded, well - balanced fritterings of incongruous objects or details, suited to the sort of frivolity, in most things, which delighted the fashionables of the day. For instance, let us quickly examine the details in this portion of a lace cravat. They are all carefully arranged to secure balance of pattern. In the centre is a sort of canopy, beneath

which is a dancing lady. To her right and left, and below her, is a pair of corresponding little beings, also tripping. At the lower corners of the piece are palm trees, and by the side of each is either a seated lady, possibly playing some musical instrument, or a gentleman in high peruque certainly playing a violoncello or a viol da gamba. Heaps of other devices are scattered about, and all are connected together by small tyes or *brides*. The entire design is almost like a transformation scene at

FIG. 34.

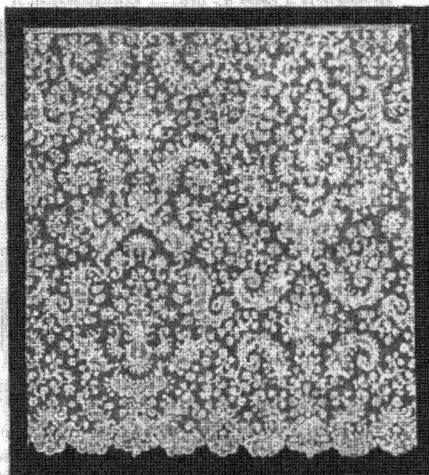

DEEP FLOUNCE OR TRIMMING FOR A PRIEST'S ALB.
Pillow-made lace from Bruges or Brussels.
About 1680-90.

pantomime or ballet. From the costume of the figures we could fix a period, if we could not, as we can, from the style of this frolicsome ornamentation, as well as well as from its use in a cravat. The make of the lace with its *brides*, and the enrichment of the larger forms, fillings in of fanciful ornaments, *modes* as they are termed, tell us its date, and we therefore know it to be of the early 18th century.

In corroboration of this let us look at a portrait of the comic poet, Destouches, painted by Dubuisson about 1720. His cravat is of such lace as we have been looking at—only it is in folds—and if we could but undo it and flatten it out we should be almost sure to find in it many such fantastic figures and details as we saw in the last slide.

Rather more stately, but still very busy with

35

its curls and twirls of imaginative leaves and flowers intermingled with stoutly constructed rococo framework, is the design of this fine flounce with its formal ground of small hexa-gonal meshes. (Fig. 35.) All this is of needlepoint lace—and is probably a grand specimen of Point d'Argentan. Such big pieces were sometimes called Point de France

FIG. 35.

NEEDLEPOINT LACE FLOUNCE OF THE EARLY PART OF THE 18TH CENTURY.
Probably of French design and make.

—the glorification of the Country in such a case superseding that of the little Norman town.

Charles de Vintimille, Duke of St. Cloud and Archbishop of Paris, in 1730, is evidently wearing such a flounce as the trimming to his alb, which falls over his lap. But the styles of ornamental design were becoming exhausted. The fanciful designing, of which we have seen a specimen or two, was succeeded by a style in which a realistic imitation of flowers played the principal part.

And here is a wide Brussels pillow-lace flounce, in which, I think, you will see a number of blossoms and leaves which are closer imitations of natural forms than the previous conventionalised and imaginative details could pretend to be. (Fig. 36.) I think it may be accepted, as a rule, that close imitations of things as they look, cannot be successfully used for ornament. Ornament implies the observance of conditions in designing. Realistic imitation implies the endeavour to accurately counterfeit what is seen. It is, therefore, not an arbitrary arrangement of lines and forms, made specially with a view to ornament. This, however, is a subject which is much too extensive to be discussed now. Suffice it to say that when one sees a marked tendency to give flowers and leaves and sprays,

FIG. 36.

FLOUNCE OF BRUSSELS PILLOW-MADE LACE, OF FLORAL DESIGN.
About 1730-50.

&c., a natural look, in lace, such lace is sure to be of a comparatively late period, that is to say, of a period about from 1730 to 1780.

We shall note this tendency in these three lace lappets, in all of which flowers and leaves or sprays are the essential decorative features. The first lappet is of Brussels pillow lace, and the chief means by which we know it is Brussels, is the fine groundwork of meshes. For a similar reason we know that the third lappet is of Mechlin make; and if we had a magnifying glass to examine the peculiar twisting and plaiting of the threads forming the meshes of these two lappets, we should perceive the difference between them. Again, you would find in the Mechlin lappet a fine thread line running round all the details, and that in conjurction with the special make of the meshes is a sure mark of Mechlin lace. If the outline were omitted, then we might be led to think that the lace was from Valenciennes. But if it were from Valenciennes, then the meshes would be differently plaited and twisted. The design might remain the same, whence we may conclude, and rightly, that designs were interchanged between different places. The interchanging and imitation of designs were most frequent, especially between Valenciennes and Mechlin, between Brussels and Alençon and Argentan, between Honiton and Brussels, and elsewhere. So that although design may be the means for fixing the date of lace, it is not a safe guide for discovering the place where the lace was made. The centre lappet is of needlepoint lace, and was made either at Alençon or Argentan. A distinctive feature of both these makes of lace is the pronounced and slightly raised outline to the various details of the designs in them. Another feature is the insertion of little enrichments or *modes*; and another feature, one generally thought to

FIG. 37.

BRUSSELS PILLOW-MADE LACE.
About 1780 to 1790.

be special to Argentan, and one I have already mentioned, is the ground of honeycomb meshes, each of which is worked with close-lying button-hole stitches. How later lace patterns became altogether less elaborate and lighter in effect may be judged from the next two slides.

This (Fig. 37) is a piece of Brussels lace of the end of the 18th century, and you will notice that the same details are repeated several times. They are much less intricate, and much less important in shape and construction, than those of twenty or thirty years earlier. Still the specimen is typical of the more involved styles of designs that were being used for laces at the end of the 18th century.

The then prevalent fashion in laces did not exact such ornamental elaboration or size of laces as had distinguished the immediately preceding period. Such pieces as these two specimens of Mechlin lace trimming would be used for sleeves and narrow flouncings. The design of the sprays and blossoms in them does not rise to any height in imagination on the part of the designer, whilst the general ornamental effect depends upon the orderly repetition and arrangement of the same details over and over again.

How such modest filmy laces were worn, as a softening contrast to stiffer glistening silk and satin, may be seen in this portrait of Queen Christina, of Bohemia, produced about 1780.

Ample scarves and fully trimmed cloaks and doublets were no longer worn by men; and in illustration of the diminishing use of lace by them, I show a portrait by Drouais of Turgot, one of the many successive ministers of Louis XVI., 1778. His lace is but a small ruffle or edging to his shirt-front, and its ornament is of very simple character. Turgot held office for twenty months, and lost it by proposing to replenish the Treasury by a tax on the clergy, the nobility, and Parliament—a proposal, as Carlyle writes, that caused " one shriek of indignation and astonishment to reverberate through all the Chateau Galleries." The French Revolution almost extinguished lacemaking in France. Other countries, like Belgium and England, continued to produce hand-made laces ; but the artistic genius which had so largely nourished the industry in France, and had been widely reflected through Europe, was practically extinct.

It is not for me to now refer to the subsequent revival of hand-made laces. I have attempted to indicate means for verifying the more marked types of hand-made lace, from its birth in the 16th to its decline in the 18th century. That period has clearly provided us with a rich legacy of beautiful and various work, together with a knowledge of how cultured taste and demand exercised their influence upon lace-making. If women of the present day make complete use of this legacy, much can be done towards releasing the industry of lace-making by hand from the depressing conditions with which it has undoubtedly struggled for a considerable part of this century.

In conclusion, I thank you cordially for the interest and attention with which you have so kindly listened to my lectures upon " Means for Verifying Ancient Embroideries and Laces."